A PRAIRIE GIRL

Living in Baghdad

The story of Sarah Powell

Keating

ISBN: 9798676964719

This book is a historical, non-fiction novel inspired by a true story. In some cases, dialogue or emotions expressed are created by the author based upon facts or situations in history that could have led to such conversations.

Front Cover Image provided by Mary E. "Betsy" (Powell) Polglase and designed by Jan Keating and graphic artist, Tara Keating-Jaap.

Printed by Amazon

First Printing Edition 2020

Other published books by this author:

A Normal Boy: Living in an Asylum – Published January 2020 (available on Amazon in many countries in paperback or Kindle)

Published by:

J. L. Keating
Box 63
Kenosee Lake, SK S0C 2S0, Canada

For my family, my hometown of Weyburn, Saskatchewan and for Sarah and the Powell-Jamali family.

)

Acknowledgements

I have listed the people below in the order in which they came into contact with me in regard to writing this book. There is no significance as to the importance of one above the other. They all were significant and important and appreciated.

Jim Keating, my husband - Thank you for your patience and many hours of proofreading. Your love, support, honest critiquing and countless hours of discussion have been invaluable to me.

Tara Keating-Jaap, my daughter - Thank you for sharing your thoughts as a fellow writer and for proofreading. Your keen eye and years of experience as an editor proved invaluable.

Trenna Keating, my daughter and twice award-winning playwright - Thank you for your support and encouragement as well as your patience with proofreading once again for me.

Stewart McKendrick, my cousin in Scotland - Thank you for helping me to connect with Dr. Monica Spooner which, in turn, led me to Usameh and Abbas Jamali (Sarah's sons).

Dr. Monica Spooner, MB, BS, AKC - Thank you for responding to my request for attaining Sarah Powell Jamali's book, *The Story of Laith and his life after encephalitis* and for putting me in touch with other members of Sarah's family.

Usameh Jamali, second son of Sarah Powell and Dr. Mohammed Fadhel al Jamali - Thank you for your invaluable contributions from sharing contacts to sharing your memories that helped to breathe life into the story of your enchanting parents. Your patience and willingness to answer all my questions was so helpful and much appreciated.

Abbas Jamali, third son of Sarah Powell and Dr. Mohammed Fadhel al Jamali - Thank you for your contributions and for the video conference call that brought us together in a pleasant way to share. Your ability to recall and share information was most appreciated.

Mary Elizabeth "Betsy" Powell Polglase, daughter of Louis Harvey Powell and Virginia Wetherbee (Sarah Powell's niece) - Thank you for countless emails, sharing photographs and family history, for proofreading the manuscript and for writing the Foreword for the book. I enjoyed our correspondence and your genealogy records were invaluable.

Fatima Jamali, MSc. PhD, Head of Neuroscience Research, University of Jordan, and daughter of Abbas Jamali (son of Sarah Powell and Fadhel Jamali) - Thank you for your contributions as a family member and for organizing our video chat with family members.

Jeannine Kater, present owner of the historical Powell house in Weyburn - Thank you for your cooperation and sharing of materials and information about the house.

Thank you to all the Powell and Jamali extended family members who took the time to reach out to me and to share your family memories. Perhaps one of the nicest things that came from this project was the reuniting of some of the family members who have either never known one another or have been out of touch for many years. We had a mailing list of family members and the information shared was shared to the whole group. I was so appreciative to be included in the group and given access to so much information.

Table of Contents

Foreword

I read this book with great interest, as my father, Dr. Louis Harvey Powell, grew up in Weyburn, Saskatchewan, Canada. I was both charmed and delighted with the massive amount of research that went into this book and found it engaging and informative to read from beginning to end. I hope to hear more of Jan Keating's interesting writings, and was honored to help with some of the genealogical and family information.

My Father was brother to Sarah Hayden Powell, about whom this book was mainly written. I began working in earnest on genealogy back in the 1970's, after attending the University of Minnesota as a classical voice major with a dual minor in German and English, and have continued actively working on my own and others' genealogies to the present day.

Mary Elizabeth "Betsy" (Powell) Polglase

August 23, 2020

Preface

My interest in the Powell family began in June of 2010 when an artist friend, Janis Eaglesham, and I collaborated on an art show held at the Allie Griffin Art Gallery in Weyburn. One of the paintings that Janis submitted was her painting of the Powell House in Weyburn. At that time, I was not aware of the significance of this historical home and after a brief explanation from Janis, I began to seek more information.

The Powell House, located at 815 Fourth Street Southeast, is one of several century homes on South Hill, just down the street from two well-known landmarks, the Moffat House and Eaglesham Manor (Janis's family residence). [1]It is the only one of these houses on the Crocus Tour, which was inspired by Weyburn native W. O. Mitchell's "Jake and the Kid" series.

Mr. and Mrs. Powell had six children: Knox Archibald (1894 – 1962), Oliver Stanley (1896-1963), Lyman Bearcroft (1902 – 1983), Louis Harvey, (1904-1957), Lydia Elmira (1905 – 1982) and Sarah Hayden (1908 – 2000). The youngest child, Sarah, was the only one of the Powell children born in Weyburn. My interest and focus for the book is with Sarah and, yet, one cannot write a book about Sarah without including all the wonderful family members with whom she was connected.

---

[1] Weyburn This Week, October 29, 2010

The reason I wanted to write about Sarah is because I was very intrigued by a young prairie woman who had the courage to move far from home and family to Iraq for the sake of love. A move such as this in the early 1930s was significant. Not only would Sarah be leaving her family and country but she would be entering a whole new world where the language, culture, religion, climate and environment would be so totally different to anything she had ever known. I was moved by the strength of this woman from her early years through to her final days. She endured many hardships along the way and, yet, she managed to keep going. She never gave up on people she loved. I like to think that her early life in our home town of Weyburn had a little to do with her grit and guts to carry forth when things got tough. I wanted the people in Weyburn to have an opportunity to learn about Sarah's life. I regret not knowing of her before she died. But I hope I've written something that will pay tribute to her and her family. I hope my book will raise awareness of one of Weyburn's historical characters.

When I decided to write about Sarah, I thought I would be writing a book that was, for the most part, a fictional story based on some true facts. However, very early on, I was fortunate enough to make contact with two of Sarah's sons (Usameh and Abbas Jamali) and one of her nieces (Betsy Powell-Polglase). With their gracious acceptance of my interest in Sarah and her family, their cooperation and sharing of their personal stories, I soon realized that the book was now more non-fictional. I did take the liberty of creating dialogue between characters based upon the facts of what was happening in their lives. I wanted to breathe life into the characters rather than just write a biographical account of names, dates and facts. I kept as true to the realism of the story as possible. I could not have done this without the added information from Sarah's family.

The Powell House is a beautiful house and well deserving of its place on the Crocus Tour as a historical house; however, the house is just a house until you know the story of the family that lived in it.

Chapter 1

As pioneers began moving across the vast stretches of Canadian soil, Weyburn was nicely getting started. By 1905, it had attained town status since becoming a village in 1900. The curious name, Weyburn, came from the Scottish term "wee burn", meaning small stream. This is most positively because Weyburn is located on the Souris River, nestled in the southeast corner of the province of Saskatchewan, near the United States border, just north of North Dakota.

Many a sod house still dotted the prairie landscape as farmers staked their claims to land. The Canadian government had advertised: "Free land for the taking, Ten Dollars down, six months occupation and ten acres per year broken. Every man has the same chance. Hurry before the best is claimed," etc. The word was spread throughout Europe, the British Isles, eastern Canada as well as the United States. And so they came to the Promised Land.

[2]The Canadian Pacific Railway (CPR) reached the future site of Weyburn from Brandon, Manitoba in 1892 and the Soo Line from North Portal on the US border in 1893. A post office opened in 1895 and a land office in

---

[2] Wikipedia – Weyburn History

1

1899 in anticipation of the land rush which soon ensued. In 1899, Knox Presbyterian Church was founded with its building constructed in 1906 in the high-pitched gable roof and arches, standing as a testimony to the faith and optimism in the Weyburn area.

[3]The Weyburn Security Company began operations in 1902. It was a partnership formed by Alex Simpson, O.H. Hellekson, F.K. Murphy, Joseph Mergens (all from Wheaton, Minnesota), S.E. Oscarson (White Rock, South Dakota) and John Erickson (Hancock, Minnesota). These men were the original investors in the Canadian Investment Co. Ltd. Before long, as the area developed, branches of the Weyburn Security Company were established in the towns of Yellowgrass, McTaggart, Halbrite, and Midale. Their business was so successful that they were approached by an already established bank that wanted to purchase their business. However, they decided not to sell but, instead, to expand their business and establish a private bank headquartered in Weyburn. It was at this time that the investors approached Harvey O. Powell to come to Weyburn and take over management. Its operations at that time not only included banking but real estate, general business and mortgage loans. In March of 1907, Harvey started his position at the bank. Shortly after Mr. Powell's arrival, a new building was constructed in 1910.

By 1911, the bank had advanced to the point where it obtained a Canadian bank charter. During its years of operation, the bank expanded to having assets of $6 million and serving 33 communities. It had 24

---

[3] Hey Seeds! pp132

branches and sub-branches, all in the province of Saskatchewan. Mr. Powell was considered one of the foremost financiers in the province. He was the first general manager of the Weyburn Security Bank; in fact, he was the only manager of that bank until, in May 1931, due to the onset of the great depression, the bank was purchased by the Imperial Bank of Canada. The Weyburn Security Bank building is a designated provincial heritage building.

The new building for the bank was designed by a Minneapolis architectural firm. The use of Classical Revival style is evident by the two-storey pilasters and decorative motifs on the face of the building. These design elements are more commonly seen on the financial institutional buildings in the mid-west United States and reflects the Weyburn Security Bank's desire to project a western image in its bank architecture.

H.O. Powell

[4]Harvey was born in River Falls, Wisconsin on April 24, 1868, a son of Oliver Samuel (1831 -1888) and Lydia Elmira (nee: Nichols) Powell. He pursued an interest in banking and was active in that connection in Wisconsin and South Dakota from 1885 to 1907. He also took up the study of law and this was useful to him in his banking business. He was admitted to the South Dakota bar in1899. He was a cashier at the First National Bank at White Rock, South Dakota.

---

[4] *The Story of Saskatchewan and It's People* by John Hawkes, 1924.

3

Harvey was a strikingly handsome fellow with a strong jaw line, brown eyes and dark hair. He was slender but muscular. He had a very pleasing personality and knew how to make and keep friends. It was most likely that this quality, combined with his good looks, made him attractive to his lovely wife, Elizabeth.

Elizabeth Fayerweather Knox

[5]Elizabeth Fayerweather Powell (nee: Knox) was born February 22, 1869, in Brewster, New York. She was a wholesome girl with a porcelain-like complexion and dark naturally-curly hair that she preferred to wear in a tidy up-do suitable for a young woman. Due to the strong influence of her maternal grandmother, Jane Wood Bearacroft, Elizabeth (affectionately referred to as 'Libbie') never wore make-up but with her dark eyes and eyelashes and pink, heart-shaped lips, she was pretty enough without anything more. She loved to dress in stylish clothing. When she was younger, her older sister, Jennie, was an expert dressmaker and kept her little sister and the whole family well dressed. Jennie would work nights cutting and sewing clothes. After she left home, another sister, Anna made all of Libbie's clothes. Libbie remembered that the colours Anna put together were often "ill-matched." Although Libbie was not as good at dressmaking, she did learn to make rugs and quilts and began this craft at age four. When she was older, she created her own designs and some of her work was later shown in art collections. She had a passion for collecting bugs and butterflies and

---

[5] Mary E. Powell-Polglase (Family Historian)

she formed them into mounted collections. She also loved to read.

In her youth she was very active. She ice skated, fished and joined her older brother, Gilbert in a "horse radish route." They would grow, dig, peel, grate and sell it around the neighbourhood. She learned to horseback ride. On her first ride, her horse bucked her off—perhaps because of her riding skirt. She slid off and managed to roll out of the horse's way. She was too frightened to get back on the horse that day but did soon thereafter. She and a girl companion once climbed Mount Utsayantha in the [6]Catskills (over 3000 feet). While teaching at the Seminary and Union Free School in Stamford, New York, she and other "young folks" would get up at four o'clock to play croquet on the fine, rolled court at the seminary. She was known to be a bit of a character and was quite popular. She enjoyed social activities such as maple-sugaring parties.

She became a teacher who taught all subjects, including vocal music. At one time she was the Vice Principal in Red Bank, New Jersey. Later she obtained a position as Vice Principal in River Falls, Wisconsin. Later, she studied law along with her husband and became the first woman to be accepted by the bar in South Dakota. This would certainly have made her outstanding in her day when most women did not pursue secondary education as readily as they do today. However, Elizabeth said she never got the chance to actually practice law because, "the children came tumbling down." As was typical in that time, when a woman

---

[6] The Catskill Mountains – scenic area located in southeast New York State, between Albany and New York City.

did marry, she very often stopped working outside the home. Elizabeth did give up her career with the birth of their first son, Knox Archibald (December 24, 1894 – January 27, 1962). She would come to realize that being a mother was a career in itself.

She was the mother of five children when they first arrived in Weyburn: Knox (13), Oliver (11), Lyman (5), Louis (3), and Lydia (2). Much had preceded the family's arrival in Canada.

1888 – 1906 White Rock, South Dakota

Disaster struck the family on September 26, 1888 when Harvey's father, Oliver Samuel Powell, was killed in a terrible accident while working in his [7]sorghum mill in River Falls, Wisconsin. His coat was caught in a piece of machinery, pulling him into the mechanism. Sadly, he suffered a terrible death.

Harvey, being the eldest son, quit his job as a bank cashier and returned home to try to save his father's farm and business interests. He bought out the inherited interests of his siblings: Newell, Lucy, Sarah and Amy. He made tub butter which he sold to high-class restaurants in the twin cities (St. Paul and Minneapolis) in Minnesota. Libbie also worked hard on the farm raising chickens. Harvey thought it was the thing for her to do now that she was a married woman living on a farm. He felt that being a career woman was no longer appropriate.

---

[7] Mill process of making molasses from sorghum cane; stripped of its leaves and then fed between rollers.

"A woman's place is really in the home. The truth of the matter is, Libbie—we are farmers now and farming is a business. There is science and business management as well as hard labour involved. We need both our shoulders to the harness if we are to succeed. I feel I must insist that you forget about a career outside our home." Harvey bestowed his superior male attitude on the matter.

Considering that Libbie was already doing the books for the farm, she was quite aware of the business aspect of the operation and she had noted that at one time that their outstanding debts totalled $2500 which was a huge sum at that time. Although Harvey worked hard and tried his best, he was not considered a great farmer.

"Well, Harvey, I don't think I need to be told where my place is; however, I fully agree that this farm needs all hands on deck. I can see that it is too much for you alone and the boys are too young to be of help yet. If I'm to be in charge of raising chickens, then step aside and let me at it! I'll have the best hens and roasting chickens in the district—you'll see!"

Libbie was true to her word. She had just enough resentment about being put in her place to do the job justice. Amazing how a little rub the wrong way could push one on to not only do the job but to shine at it as well. She and Harvey both worked their fingers to the bone. Farming was not for the weak or the lazy. They were up at the crack of dawn and Libbie kept her end of the bargain but she noticed that not only was it her job to work on the farm but it was also considered her job to do all the house cleaning, laundry, cooking and care of the children.

After struggling on the farm, Harvey and his brother, Newell, sought a chance at a new business venture in White Rock, South Dakota. They combined their finances and bought a bank and in September of 1896, Harvey and Libbie moved to White Rock. Since Newell had more money to invest, he became Bank President and Harvey was cashier. At this time, the nearest lawyer was about 12 miles away, with no telephone connections, so it seemed necessary that Harvey, as cashier, become more familiar with business law. This led him to study and become a lawyer to help in the banking business.

On January 4, 1899, Libbie's mother suddenly died from pneumonia in Brewster, New York at the age of 67. Libbie left Harvey at home in White Rock with sons, Knox and Oliver, and went to help her father settle her mother's estate. Libbie stayed away that whole year and while she was in Wheaton, Minnesota (June 15, 1899), Harvey wrote the following to her:

> "You certainly will be a new girl all
> except for the skin and bone that is about
> what is left to start building on."

It was perhaps just before she had left for New York that she had suffered at least one miscarriage. There were others that followed over the years between 1899 and 1902. The time Libbie spent with her father and family back East was a much needed time to not only be of assistance to her father but, also, to rest and rebuild her strength to return fit to continue raising her family. She and her father had a very close relationship. Some years after she had married and moved away, his house burned down and she never got over feeling that she should have

8

been there for him. She felt guilty for marrying and moving so far away from her parents.

Libbie returned home in 1900. It wasn't long after her return that she and Harvey were blessed with two more sons: Lyman Bearcroft, born July 20, 1902 and Louis Harvey, born March 26, 1904. Following close behind was their first daughter, Lydia Elmira, born September 30, 1905.

In June of 1906, Little Lydia, not quite two years old, had come down with pneumonia and was gravely ill. Harvey, in desperation, turned to his mother and drove Libbie and Lydia to River Falls. Harvey's mother (also named Lydia) took to nursing the sick child and giving Libbie support to get some much needed rest. Mrs. Powell Sr. called in a homeopathic physician, named Dr. Ashley, who pulled the child through her pneumonia.

Once again, Harvey was holding the fort back home with his sons, Knox, Oliver, Lyman and Louis. Nearly one month later, on July 15, 1906, Harvey wrote from White Rock, South Dakota to Libbie, in River Falls, Wisconsin:

> [8]"My Dear Libbie:
>
> One more Sunday gone—nearly. This will make three weeks tomorrow night since I started with you for River Falls. It seems like six months. How the time drags. I would go wild if it were not for the children. How I stood that winter alone

---

[8] Quoted from notes from Betsy Polglase's family records.

while you were East is more than I can see now. After the boys get to sleep, it seems as if I must shout or something. It is so lonesome. I am getting quite a little experience out of the deal. Can wash Louis' drawers when he has an accident, which has happened three times. He is a good little fellow. He said tonight when I put him to bed, 'You go on the train, bring Lydia home.' He kept repeating in his insistent way. Guess we all want to see both of you. Both letters will reach you at the same time, and if you read in as much love between each line as goes with the two letters, you will soon have a genuine love feast. You can give some to Mother and Birdie (*Harvey's sister, Sarah was fondly referred to as Birdie*), and don't forget the little tots. Lovingly, Harvey"

ℬℭℜ

On March 8, just seven days after Harvey signed the contract with the owners of Weyburn Security Company, Libbie's beloved father, Henry Knox, passed away. Once more Libbie left for New York and little Lydia was deposited at her grandmother Lydia Powell's to stay while Harvey was left with his sons for a third time. On March 26, 1907, Harvey's mother wrote to him:

[9]"I'm afraid I cannot keep Lydia until after you move, as Miss Hicks may not be able to stay to help me. I shall travel to White Rock mid-April. I shall be glad for all of you to get together."

However, even though Grandmother Lydia had planned to return little Lydia to her home by mid-April, she was still caring for the little girl in May of 1907. Libbie was still out East and Harvey was losing patience. He confided to his brother, Newell, and his wife, Cora, that he was considering taking his sons and moving to Weyburn, leaving Libbie and Lydia behind, permanently.

Who can judge a young couple with the many strains with which this family was dealing? Harvey was doing his best to work in a partnership with his brother while caring for his four sons. He wanted to be supportive to Libbie while she tended to her duties to her family back East; however, there would seem to be a timely limit and Libbie seemed, in his opinion, to have well extended that limit. Her reluctance to return home, when he so needed her assistance to prepare for the move to Canada, seemed like adding insult to injury.

Libbie, on the other hand, had feelings, too, and perhaps her years of working so hard to attain all that education just to suddenly stop short and become a wife and mother made her feel like she wasn't getting to use her mind and certainly not her education. After all—wasn't she a very experienced teacher, accomplished vocalist, knew Morris code and had studied the German

---

[9] Quoted from notes from Betsy Polglase's family records.

language? Hadn't she accomplished something very special by becoming a lawyer? Was there not to be more in life for her other than cooking, cleaning and raising chickens? Was she appreciated for her intelligence and accomplishments? She may have been feeling a loss of her independence and the life she had loved before marriage, children and farm life.

Also, she had not forgiven herself for moving so far from her parents. They were both gone now but she still had siblings and friends back East. She loved Harvey, for certain, but she suffered homesickness every time she returned to the rugged prairie life in South Dakota. And what about this move to Canada? It was just going to take her even further away from her family and her mother-in-law's help. The death of her parents, the miscarriages, the babies, the housework, the moves from New York to River Falls and to White Rock and now Canada . . . it may have felt like too much and she was likely suffering nervous exhaustion.

To their credit, things were ultimately worked out and Lydia and Libbie moved to Weyburn with Harvey and the boys that summer. Libbie had accepted the move by now and one thing she was enthused about was that she felt the two older boys, Knox and Oliver, would have better schooling. She felt that the education in Canada was superior to what was available in White Rock.

It was a special time for the family with settling into a new home, new community and new country. Another new baby was also part of this when Libbie gave birth to another little daughter, Sarah Hayden Powell on February 22, 1908. This daughter shared the same birth day as Libbie and what a gift from God on her birthday!

Chapter 2

Harvey fit easily into his new role as General Manager at the bank. He had every right to feel proud and yet, he was still humble. He knew his achievements had come from hard, honest work and he continued to set new goals for himself. He was happy that his children were settling well into Souris School and that Libbie seemed happier and was finding her way as well. Maybe getting away from farm life was better for both of them. Having a sense of peace between them allowed him to tend to his business affairs with a clear head. He thought Weyburn to be a prosperous new agricultural community with lots of promise.

Their first home in Weyburn was located at 20 Second Avenue, southeast. It was a wooden, story-and-a-half home with a lovely screened-in front veranda. There was no front yard to speak of but a small yard in the back was at least some space. There was an empty lot beside the house which gave the boys lots of room to run and play. The boys were delighted that there was always a wind strong enough to fly their kites. In fact, it seemed there was wind of some degree at some point in every day. Libbie looked on the bright side and commented that her clothes always dried quickly on the line. She did feel that Saskatchewan was a rather barren land but she was happy to see a few trees in the town and a lovely green park along the Souris River just a short walk from their house. With the soon expected birth of their sixth child, Harvey agreed with Libbie to hire a servant girl. Emilie Van Den Bossche, a young Belgian woman, aged 21 moved in with the family and although it was not ideal to have a servant sleeping in the room next to them, they managed. Libbie was delighted to have some help with the house and meals and she knew they would rely heavily on Emilie once the baby was born.

On February 22, 1908, little Sarah Hayden Powell was born in the first hospital built in Weyburn (1905). The wooden structure was a private institution built by Dr. Hugh Eaglesham. There were only eight hospital beds at the time of Sarah's birth. Water had to be hauled and other conveniences were few and far between. Dr. Hugh Eaglesham made up his own drugs from supplies he kept on hand. It ceased to be a hospital in 1913 after the Weyburn General Hospital opened. Libbie was pleased when this new hospital opened as it was located on the south hill near their home. [10] It was the first publicly run medical facility in the community and the only hospital from Portal (North Dakota, USA) to Regina, Saskatchewan at the time. It contained a nurses' training school from the beginning until 1936. It ceased as a hospital when the Weyburn Union Hospital opened in October 1952. It was sold to the Sisters of the Cross and was operated as Mount Saint Mary's nursing home until 1984. The building was later purchased by the City of Weyburn for an arts centre.

Libbie liked Dr. Eaglesham. She was delighted when they became neighbours four years later. Another

---

[10] Weyburn's First Hospital – City of Weyburn (Internet: https://weyburn.ca/weyburns-first-hospital/)

daughter! How wonderful it would be to have a little sister for Lydia. Four boys were quite enough. Libbie loved her sons but had secretly wanted one more little girl for Lydia's sake.

℘ℛ

The proud parents were anxious to introduce baby Sarah to her siblings. Of course, the children all loved her instantly; although, Lydia, who was just a toddler looked at her with mild curiosity and was rather annoyed when this newcomer took her darling mummy's attention. In fact, it was downright insulting to her and she let her feelings be known. Libbie was well experienced with how to handle her children by this point and would come up with many cute ideas to help little Lydia learn to accept her baby sister more readily.

"Come Lydia. Come over here where the baby can see you. Maybe she will smile if she can see you. Can you show her your favourite dolly? Maybe you can make her smile."

Of course, these techniques worked some of the time and other times, it was just evident that little Lydia had a mind of her own and if her feelings were hurt, she might just decide to plop down on the floor and have a good cry.

Sometimes, Libbie couldn't help but wish that she had had a daughter first rather than a son because, as wonderful as her sons were, they were less interested in helping with the baby than they were with other boyish interests. But what wonderful sons they were and she was so very proud of each one. They brought her joy and love as well as all the headaches that any mother could have. They were always running and climbing trees or jumping off of something they had no business being up on, like the garden shed. Their knees of their pants were always stained with grass or torn open. She was constantly mending their pants or darning the holes in their socks.

"Boys—quit running about the house! I've just got the baby to sleep. If you have all that energy, get your coats and scarves and mitts on and get outside to play. I'll bake you some cookies this morning but you need to go play and get some roses in your cheeks."

"Quit punching me, Oliver!" shouted Louis. Louis was four and Oliver was twelve.

"I didn't punch you, you little squirt! I only patted you on the top of your head. Come on now, I'll help you put your snow suit on and wrap your scarf for you. Honest, Mother, I didn't punch him. He's being a wimp this morning!"

"I'm not a wimp! What's a wimp? I don't think that is very nice, Ollie. You aren't supposed to call me names—and I'm not a squirt either!"

"Just stay in the yard boys. I don't want to have to be out calling for you later. It's too cold this morning so stay in the back yard. Make a snow man or something, please."

"Okay, Mummy! That's a champion idea! Can we take one of Father's hats out for our snowman?" Oliver squirmed into his snow suit.

"Oh, I'd rather you didn't dear. Take one of your old toques instead, please. And please quit shouting. Honestly, you boys are so loud sometimes." Libbie made her way into the kitchen to start her baking. She shook her head and thought to herself that February wasn't the best month to bring a new baby home; however, before long, it would be spring and she would look forward to taking Sarah out in the pram for walks. That would be lovely.

Saturdays were a little hectic in the Powell household with all six children at home all day. Everyone would be expected to pitch in and do some chores. Harvey would see to it. Knox, the oldest, would have to shovel the front walk and steps off today. He was a great son. She noticed he had already cleared the walk and was out this morning delivering newspapers for the Weyburn Review. Mr. Marshall had hired him as a favour to Harvey but she knew Knox would do a fine job. She hoped he wasn't feeling too cold. She'd have a hot bowl of homemade turkey soup ready for him and the boys for lunch and peanut butter cookies and milk for dessert.

"What are you rattling away with in the kitchen this morning, my dear?" Harvey entered wearing his favourite sweater from his senior class. No matter how Libbie tried to get rid of it, it somehow kept showing up! He loved to wear it around the house on the weekend. It was a change from his usual suits, buttoned vests, starched shirts and ties that he wore all week to the office.

"Well, those boys are an endless pit. I'm nearly out of baking on hand since coming home with Sarah. I had managed to put a good supply in the cookie tins and keep them in the cold room in the basement but those

17

little rascals have been in the tins and they're nearly empty!"

"I have a confession to make—it hasn't been just the 'little rascals', there's been a 'big rascal' into the cookies too! We just can't help ourselves when it comes to your tasty wares."

"I guess you are forgiven," she smiled as she hugged him and kissed him on the cheek.

"Where are those little rascals anyway?" Harvey poured himself a cup of coffee and sat at the kitchen table with the newspaper.

"I've sent Ollie and Louis out to play. I warned them to stay in the yard. They're making a snowman. I had to shoo them outdoors to run off some their endless energy.

"After lunch, dear, you try to have a little rest and I'll get them playing a board game or something. Maybe I'll read them a story to entertain them so you can have some peace and rest."

"You are a dear. I'll take a rest when Sarah has her afternoon nap. She's being such a good little baby. I'm so thankful that she isn't colicky.

"She'll have to be a strong survivor with all these older brothers to deal with. It's a good thing she has a sister for an ally. Where is that little monkey?"

"She fell asleep after she had her porridge this morning. Could you please go check on her? She is due to be up any time now."

"Well, my theory is to let sleeping dogs lie. . . Where is Lyman?"

"He was a bit feverish this morning so I have him resting on his bed with a pile of books. He might be getting a cold and I don't want him coughing and breathing on Sarah. He seemed content to be on his own with his books. Check on him please. Take him some more orange juice and get him to go to the bathroom. If he wants to come down to watch me bake, or sit with you that is fine."

"Okay, Mother. You're the boss and in control!" he pinched her cheek affectionately as he made his way to tend to her wishes. Harvey was a very happy man. He had a pleasant disposition most of the time. He believed that anger, or holding grudges were a complete waste of his energy and chose to be optimistic as much as possible. He had a wife he adored and six healthy children. To him, this in itself made him a wealthy man.

Harvey had come from a long line of men who had worked hard and accomplished much. [11] His grandfather, Nathaniel N. Powell (1827 – 1862) led the Powell migration to the Northwest from Augusta, Illinois, in 1849, to St. Anthony, Minnesota. In 1850, his brother, Oliver Samuel Powell (1832 – 1888) followed Nathaniel to St. Anthony. Later, the brothers moved to River Falls, Wisconsin, where they platted the town of Kinnickinnic (later named River Falls). They operated a general store; farmed; operated a threshing machine commercially;

---

[11] Minnesota Historical Society

19

erected saw, flour, syrup, and vinegar mills; and took an active part in community life.

In 1860, Oliver Samuel married Lydia Elmira Nichols, daughter of Joseph Nichols. Joseph and his wife, (Lydia Pratt Nichols) and family moved to River Falls from Dover, Illinois, in 1854 to live close to their daughter and their grandchildren. Oliver and Lydia had several children, one of whom was Harvey Oliver Powell. One of their sons, Lyman Theodore Powell (1873 – 1941) became a lawyer in West Superior, Wisconsin.

Having a background in his family's involvement in so many agricultural and business affairs, served as an education in life that helped immensely in Harvey's ability to discuss and understand the dealings with his farming and business clients. [12]As well as being Bank Manager, he was also manager of the Saskatchewan Life Insurance Company.

Harvey knew where he came from and tried to live up to his family name. He believed that knowing where you come from is what guides you as you move forward in life. He knew how to work and how to set goals that were achievable. He expected to set a good example for his sons and daughters, with God's grace.

Before they had made their move to Weyburn, Harvey had been given some very important advice by his mother who wrote to him suggesting that he get someone to help Libbie with the housework and the children. His mother was a very wise woman and, obviously, she had an understanding of what it is like to be a mother and how

---

[12] *The Story of Saskatchewan and It's People* by John Hawkes, 1924.

sometimes the weight needs to be lifted. His mother had paid Miss Hicks $106 to help her look after little Lydia all the time she had the child staying with her. She trusted that Harvey could consider paying someone to help his wife as a good investment and that his marriage would thank him.

1913 The Powell House

Harvey and Libbie purchased two lots on the south hill on Fourth Street. At the time, there were very few other homes in this area and they really felt as though they were living in the country. They often referred to their home as "the ranch" which seemed fitting enough as they had a couple of horses on that property. They set to getting plans drawn up for their new house and it was designed with great care to make it suitable for their growing family. The house was designed in the Georgian style architecture. The single-pitched roof, symmetrical composition, covered entranceway, grouping of the windows and Neo-Classical porch spoke to this Georgian style which was so popular.

Due to his mother's good advice, Harvey made sure to include plans to include rooms for servants on the third floor. There was a separate staircase for servants to use that connected to the family staircase on the second-floor landing. This was designed to let the servants do their work from one floor to the next without being a distraction to the family.

The parlour, or reception room (to the left upon entering) at the front of the house, had a fireplace, large windows and a chandelier hanging from the center of the high ceiling, This created a visual focal point and suggested a romantic, magical intimacy. There were oak crown moldings, baseboards, and flooring throughout the house as well as wooden, sliding, pocket doors separating this room from the adjoining dining room. The dining room (to the right upon entering) was light and airy by day with large windows and ambient by evening with another sparkling chandelier centered over the dining room table.

The second floor had four bedrooms and a spacious bathroom with a large cast-iron, claw-footed soaker bathtub. Many homes, at the time, did not have the luxury of indoor plumbing. The master bedroom had an adjoining nursery for Sarah. She was a toddler by the time they moved into the house but Libbie wanted to keep her close. The third floor had a bedroom, a sitting room and another bathroom.

Harvey had a private tennis court built and completely fenced with a very high wire fence. He and Libbie had both enjoyed the sport in younger days and they both agreed it would be an asset to have an outdoor summer activity that the whole family could enjoy without having to leave home. This was a very popular sport and other friends, both adults and children, spent many happy times playing tennis at the Powell's "ranch".

A house such as this was evidence of status. It would be expected of Harvey and Elizabeth to do some entertaining on occasion. They welcomed the idea of this and were looking forward to having a place for such pleasures.

80CR

Libbie had gained some of her old self confidence back and had decided that raising children did allow her to utilize her teaching skills. There were always homework projects that she could assist the boys with and she was determined to give them spiritual guidance as well. However, she had recognized that she had a need to find interests aside from being Harvey's wife and mother to her brood. The family began attending services at the Knox Presbyterian Church almost immediately. Libbie's parents had been Methodists and they had given up playing cards and dancing, even though her mother had once been very good at dancing. Libbie had played cards only a couple of times. She once attended a revival service at a Presbyterian church in Stamford, New York. She was so impressed that she joined the church and became a Presbyterian. Harvey was raised in the Presbyterian faith so the children were enrolled in Sunday school classes and Libbie wanted to help teach classes once Sarah was a little older.

She became actively involved in the Women's Christian Temperance Union and was President of the Knox Presbyterian Auxiliary Women's Foreign Missionary Society (1909 – 1910). The Temperance Union promoted the work ethic of sobriety, thrift, duty and family sanctity, and undertook community work such as reading rooms, homes for women and children, and prison reform. The members believed that alcohol was at the root of all evil and was the cause of unemployment, disease, sex work, poverty, violence against women and children, and immorality.

These worthy causes helped to fulfill her need to be using her skills and education. She considered it very important to pursue personal interests and she prided herself in trying to make a difference in helping to improve conditions both at home and in other countries. Women at this time were not yet allowed to vote. Libbie was a strong advocate for women's right to the vote along with many suffragettes of the day. These outside interests offered her an opportunity to have meaningful conversations with her husband. In spite of all this outside interest, Libbie never put anything before her home and the children. She felt with the help of Emilie, she was able to keep harmony in her home. Harvey's view was somewhat in difference to Libbie's view of her interests. He was aware how much Libbie enjoyed being active in the community, he warned her gently by saying, "I want you to have a good time, but you don't have any idea of your limits and you need a balance wheel!"

Chapter 3

The Canadian Parliament didn't choose to go to war in 1914. The country's foreign affairs were guided in London. So when Britain's ultimatum to Germany to withdraw its army from Belgium expired on August 4, 1914, the British Empire, including Canada, was at war, allied with Serbia, Russia, and France against the German and Austro-Hungarian empires. The South Saskatchewan Regiment (Weyburn unit) received their marching orders in the fall of 1914.

"Father did you see the headlines in the Review? The government is looking for volunteers to train at a new camp at Valcartier near Québec. Did you know the army is using tanks? Those things are amazing!" Knox was already reading the morning paper. He and Oliver had a keen interest in keeping up with the news of the allied troops, as did everyone.

"Yes, I did read it," replied Harvey as he poured himself a second cup of coffee. "Did you see the Sports section? There's a hockey game at the Arena Rink between our Weyburn Beavers and Estevan this weekend. We should go support the team and Oliver. He's scheduled to play in that game." Oliver was an excellent hockey player. All the boys played the sport but Oliver seemed to excel.

25

"It will be interesting to see who wins the Soo Line championship." Harvey seemed to be trying to change the subject.

"Ya—sure, but Father— back to this article about the war; I want to sign up." Knox felt he should be doing his part to help in the war effort. He had a deep sense of loyalty to the cause of the allied forces. He was an intellectual boy who looked the part. He was a tall, slender lad—the tallest of the Powell boys and even taller than his father at this point. He wore eye glasses for his near sightedness and this gave him a more studious look. He was a serious scholar who had a natural aptitude for mechanical work. In no way did his appearance mean that he was a weakling. He was wiry and strong and could move quickly when he wanted. He hoped that wearing eye glasses would not keep him from joining up and doing his heart-felt duty.

"Shush, Knox, don't let your Mother hear you talking about this again. We've been over it. You will get your education first." Harvey grabbed the newspaper and folded it up under his arm.

"Father, some guys are signing up now. I'm nearly 20 and I'm old enough."

"Knox, it is not up for more discussion at this point. You are still under our roof and care and you will not be signing up yet."

Then Harvey patted his son on the shoulder and softened, "Son, I know you mean well and I'm proud that you want to do the right thing. Once you are 21 will be soon enough—be patient. You are close to pursuing higher education and you'll need it when this war is over.

It is best to get it now rather than to try to go back to school after the war ends. Trust me. I know a thing or two."

"Good morning sir, I have your breakfast keeping warm in the oven." Allie Langhost was the new maid from Holland. She was 24 and seemed very pleasant. She was a tall, slender girl with lovely silken, blonde hair that she kept done up in a very neat bun. She was recommended to Libbie by one of her church lady friends. She was a quiet young woman who always smiled but said little. This could have been due to her English not being quite as good as she would have liked, Harvey thought. Libbie seemed to communicate with her well enough.

As the rest of the family began appearing for their breakfast, the discussion was tabled but Knox knew that he and Oliver would one day do their part to defend their homeland.

Sarah was not a baby any longer. She was now a little school girl, aged eight. She was only slightly aware of all this talk of war. The adults didn't like to discuss things in too much detail in front of her or Lydia for fear it would give them nightmares.

℘℧

As Harvey and Libbie had wished, the two oldest sons, Knox and Oliver left home to attend the University of Minnesota in 1915. Knox was in the Engineering class and Oliver was in the Academic class. Knox was active in the Cosmopolitan Club and he joined the Cadet Corps.

It had been two years since the headlines had read, "England Declares War on Germany." Even in Weyburn, as far away as it was from the war, there was suffering. Foods had to be rationed. Sugar, flour, butter, margarine and milk were all rationed so that everyone got what they needed. Each person had special ration cards. The 152nd Battalion was a unit of the Canadian Expeditionary Force. The Saskatchewan infantry were definitely involved. Mothers and families in Weyburn fretted and worried about their loved ones and prayed they would return home. Winter was coming and it just seemed to make mothers worry all the more.

Everyone was talking about the battle of Verdun in France. It was one of the longest, bloodiest, and most-ferocious battles of the war, lasting almost a year from February to December of 1916. Weyburn boys had fought in that battle and some became part of the statistics of men who were killed. Initially, Canadians were sent in to relieve the pressure from the besieged and hard-pressed French forces trying to defend themselves against the Germans. More than 24,000 Canadians were killed, wounded, or went missing. The Canadian units gained the reputation of a formidable assault force.

While the war raged on, life for the younger Powell children was as normal and pleasant as Harvey and Libbie could make it. Lydia and Sarah were both taking piano lessons from Mrs. Cathcart. Libbie had insisted on getting a second-hand piano when they moved into the house. She had plenty of room for it in the study. The girls loved their music and often made up little tunes for fun. Although they loved playing tunes, they were not so fond of the technical scales and theory. Libbie made sure they got their practicing in right after school so Harvey could retreat to his study in the evenings in peace. Libbie loved that time with him and she would sit quietly with him while he read and she would work on one of her rugs or quilts, sewing quietly. Often, they would have some of their best chats during this part of the evening after the children had all gone off to bed.

On some occasions, Harvey would get out his cello and join the girls as they played a duet on the piano. With a little coaxing, they could get Libbie to sing a few tunes. She still had a beautiful voice.

Lyman and Louis were kept active with winter and summer sports and they missed their older brothers. They looked up to Knox and Oliver and worked hard at their studies so they could follow their brothers one day. They talked of moving to Minnesota to go to university there like their brothers. It seemed that teaching by example was running in the family.

ℰℭ

Libbie kept the children well entertained and well fed. She planted a garden. She and Allie worked to put down jars of pickles and other preserves. The cellar was cool and Harvey had constructed shelves for jars of beans, carrots, applesauce, jams and jellies, beets and relish. With all the rationing, Libbie and many other women were making the best of what they could for their families. Having a garden would assure fresh vegetables in summer and a stock of preserves for the winter.

Sarah loved being outdoors and she and Lydia often helped their mother pull weeds in the garden. Although, it might be debatable as to how much help they really were. They were often side tracked by Nature or by anything that caught their attention. They loved the sound of the yellow-throated meadow larks. The girls would sing, "I was here a year ago," or, "I left my pretty sister at home," to imitate the sound of the bird. When they heard the meadow lark, it would stop them in their tracks every time.

"Girls, are you going to help with these weeds, or are you going to stand there listening to the meadowlarks all day?"

"Sorry Mother!" they chimed together and got back to their task.

"Can we have some raw peas and carrots when we are finished pulling weeds?" Sarah asked.

"It's 'may we', Dear not 'can we'—and, yes—you may have some raw vegetables. I know you won't eat as many vegetables once they are cooked so at least you will get the vitamins from them raw. But don't be little piggies. Have one carrot each and a few peas. I need a lot for tonight's supper. I'm going to pick some of this rhubarb and make us a rhubarb pie for dessert."

"Oh, I love rhubarb pie Mother! Will you put some strawberries in it for us too? I like it best that way," Lydia pleaded.

"Yes, if you stop eating peas and get busy and pick some strawberries, I'll add them to the pie," Libbie walked over to the huge rhubarb plant and started cutting stalks off and putting them in her basket.

"What are you going to be when you grow up Lydia?" Sarah pulled a weed and then jumped over a row of lettuce to grab a carrot.

"I think I want to be a doctor or maybe a teacher, I'm not sure. You liked teaching didn't you Mother?"

"Oh yes, I certainly did! You can be a teacher Lydia. You girls just have to keep doing well with your school work and you will be fine. Education is the key to success." Then, she couldn't help but envision herself years ago, teaching and living a life that seemed like only a dream now, here, kneeling in the dirt of her garden. Oh well, she continued thinking—she was exactly where God intended her to be and she was happy to be here.

"Well I might be a teacher or maybe I'll be a film star," Sarah was munching on the peas now.

"A film star—what on earth put that notion into your little head?" Libbie got up from her knees and took off her gardening gloves.

"I just love Mary Pickford and I think that I kind of look like her, actually," Sarah smiled and had a smudge of dirt on her chin from eating her carrot.

"I don't think so, silly! Not with that dirt on your face, you don't." chided Lydia.

"Alright you two—go inside the house and wash those hands and faces. Use the nail brush to get that garden dirt out from under your nails. Take your shoes off before you go in the house, please. And throw your pinafores in the laundry basket." Libbie knew she had to give specific directives or the girls might easily show up to the dinner table with dirt still under their nails.

31

The girls scurried off giggling and chattering.

"Film stars—what next?" Libbie shook her head.

გი○○

Libbie had to find a new servant when Allie suddenly announced she was getting married to a young air force fellow and they were going to move to Ontario. Well, after all, she was getting on in age. She must have been about 26 and most girls were married long before that. Libbie found a suitable replacement in a younger girl, named [13]Julia Hillslad, aged 20. Libbie hoped this girl would stay single for a few years at least. Julia had come from the United States but her homeland was Norway. Her English was much better than Allie's. She had the same lovely blonde coloured hair as Allie—only fairer. She was a very solid, healthy and strong young woman. Libbie was thankful for her boundless energy and her ability to climb a ladder or crawl under a bed if need be to reach something impossible. She could cook and bake very well and she loved to bake bread every Friday. She would always have cinnamon buns cooling in time for when the children came home from school.

Sarah loved the smell of the lemon oil that Julia rubbed on the wooden furniture. Lydia loved the smell of the paste wax Julia used to shine the wooden floors; the boys loved to slide around on the floors with woolen socks on their feet to help shine the floors after Julia had

---

[13] Names of the servant girls found in Canada census records from Betsy Polglase's records.

waxed them. Lyman would often spin the younger children around on an old woolen blanket until the squeals and laughter got the better of Libbie and she would put an end to the noisy frolics.

One autumn after Libbie had harvested much of her garden, she and Julia were about to do some canning, Libbie went to light the gas stove and it exploded and knocked her across the room in a ball of fire. Julia went into action and grabbed a quilt from the back of one of the kitchen chairs and wrapped it around Libbie. Unfortunately, Libbie was severely burnt on one side of her face, ear and neck. The scars would be with her for the remainder of her life. She suffered a painful and slow recovery and cried out in pain for many months after this terrifying event.

1918 Weyburn Post War

The First World War had finally ended. Knox and Oliver had both signed up. Knox had been a private in the USA Corp of Engineers and had served time in Marseille, France. He and Oliver both settled in Hennepin County, Minnesota and Knox was employed by Minneapolis Moline Farm Implement Co. He also joined the Free Masons and the Legion.

Shortly after Oliver had registered, the war ended. While attending the University of Minnesota, he had specialized in banking, accounting and foreign languages. He achieved his bachelor's degree in economics in 1917 and then spent six months working for the National Bank of New York in Petrograd (now St. Petersburg), Russia where he witnessed firsthand the chaos of the Russian

Revolution and was forced to escape the country through Siberia. In 1918, he joined the US Navy.

Libbie missed her sons and she fretted over Oliver while he was in Russia. Harvey assured her that Oliver would be fine. Secretly, he had his own concerns and didn't rest easy until Oliver was safely home in the United States.

&)Q

Times were changing for women. Styles had moved away from the Edwardian style of long skirts and high ankle boots. Hemlines grew a little shorter so instead of ankle-high boots, the women were wearing more feminine and dainty styled shoes. This was, of course partly for style but it also was a result of the war and the economy. Shorter skirt lengths meant less fabric required; less leather, less expense to manufacture, more margins for profit. Women had been forced to take up some of the jobs normally done by men during the war as men were sent overseas to fight the war. Women took factory jobs, office and banking jobs; they learned mechanics and even how to drive. Clothing had to be more comfortable; styles that draped loosely around the torso with big folds, drapes and gathers around the skirt sides became popular. Corsets were too restricting.

Libbie welcomed this new style of dress and had several daytime house dresses made up by a seamstress in small cotton percale stripes, solid chambray, and gingham checks. For visiting, attending meetings, or church, she had several dresses made up in rich fabrics of taffeta, velvet, silk, crepe, and corduroy. Large collars framed the shoulders and provided a place to add some decoration such as a brooch. She bought a new fall and winter coat made from a heavy tweed. It was much more masculine styled with tailored lines and this suited her busy lifestyle giving ease of comfort minus all the feathers and frills.

[14]Women were making changes in more than just how they dressed. A Scottish-born, Canadian writer, named, Nellie McClung, had been a leader in the fight for the right to vote for women in Canada. In 1916, thanks to McClung's campaign, the new Liberal government gave Manitoba women the right to vote in provincial elections. Alberta, British Columbia and Saskatchewan did the same soon afterwards and by 1918, women (except service women) gained the right to vote in federal elections.

The Neighbours

Summer was such a favourite time on the prairies for Sarah and her sister. They could run more freely without so many layers of petticoats and long stockings. They would braid one another's hair and run about outdoors playing with other children in the neighbourhood. There were many children in the neighbourhood from families by the names of Lowes, Bieschelle , Leroux, Moffet and Eaglesham

Frank Moffet Sr. was an Irishman who was involved in real estate and was appointed as secretary for the Weyburn Security Bank in 1902; so, he and Harvey

---

[14] How the Scots Invented Canada by Ken McGoogan

were not only neighbours but business associates as well. Frank had tried his luck in provincial politics, and ran for premier, but lost. Not to be deterred, he turned to civic issues and became the Mayor of Weyburn in 1918. He and his wife, Mabel, had built their home in 1910 (later to become a historical house) and had four children: Frank Jr., Margaret Grace, Edward Allen and Kathleen. Edward Allen, who was only three, was referred to by his middle name, Allen. The name Edward seemed too old a name somehow for this little cherub of a boy.

[15]Dr. Hugh Eaglesham and his wife, Mary, had five children: Jean, Hugh Jr., twins Margaret Doris and Douglas, and Fergus. Margaret Doris Eaglesham, referred to as Doris, was eight and the same age as Sarah. They were friends in school but became closer pals over the summer holidays.

Sarah's best friend on the street was another little eight-year old girl named Ruth Leroux. Ruth had a twin brother, John, and two other younger brothers, George, age 5 and Fred, age 3. Sarah thought it was most interesting to have two sets of twins on her street and they were all the same age as she. Sarah and Ruth loved playing games with the boys, but they especially loved playing with their dolls or doing some creative thing like playing "house" pretending to be baking while they made mud pies after a rain when the dirt was soft. They loved dressing their dolls and, in winter, they made sleighs for their dolls out of cardboard boxes by attaching strings to the boxes so they could pull the dolls over the soft snow. Then they

---

[15] Canada census records from Betsy Polglase's records provided me with information on names and ages of neighbourhood families.

would go to one of their homes and have a cup of hot chocolate to warm them up.

The Leroux, Moffet and Eaglesham families were Presbyterians as were the Powells so it seemed the children were together at church, school and in the neighbourhood. Frank Moffet Jr. was ten and in the same class as Lydia. Margaret Moffet was six. She was two years younger than Sarah but a much beloved friend. Margaret looked up to Sarah and Lydia and was just thrilled to be in their company.

Mrs. Moffet (Mabel) was always smiling, it seemed to Sarah. She trusted Sarah and Lydia to take good care of little Maggie and Allen if they were outside playing. The girls quite enjoyed mothering the little children. They would play house and pretend the little ones were their children. [16]In later years Sarah was contacted by Allen. He, in turn, submitted her letter in response to him to the local Weyburn Review, newspaper. In her letter, she told Allen how much she appreciated his mother for always being "so welcoming and accepting the troops of children who passed heedlessly through her kitchen. We liked her very much although we never said so. I'm glad to have this chance to tell you that she has been a blessing to us all."

With this gang of playmates, they were never at a loss for some outdoor fun together. They would often play a game of softball on the spare lot beside the Powell house. They would play Duck, Duck, Goose, Tag, Hide

---

[16] Hey Seeds! - from a reprinted article submitted to the Weyburn Review by Allen Moffet.

and Seek, Red Rover – Red Rover. When they tried playing Anti-I-Over, Libbie could hear the ball bouncing on the rooftop and she would come out and put an end to the game sending the neighbourhood children home. The girls loved to skip and the boys played marbles. Actually, Sarah and Lydia loved marbles too, but mostly, because they loved to collect and trade the pretty ones.

ಬಂಜ

"Mother—where are you?!" Sarah called as she came in from outdoors. She and Lydia had been running around with their friends and were hot and thirsty. School was out for the summer and it was one of those hot Saskatchewan summer days in July. Birds were chirping, the robins were splashing and having a wonderful time in the bird bath. The air was heavy with the perfume of Libbie's roses and lilacs. The lawn was so green and lush that Sarah had kicked off her shoes and was running around barefoot. She and Ruth Leroux had been running around catching butterflies. Sarah was fascinated by bugs because her mother had a beautiful collection of many different species of insects and Sarah wanted to start a collection like her mother. [17]Libbie had a collection of over 1000 mounted, preserved, botanical specimens which were later given to the University of South Dakota. Libbie also had a collection of shells which were donated to the University of Saskatchewan in later years.

---

[17] Notes from Betsy Powell-Polglase's family records.

The girls had set up a lemonade stand out on the front lawn close to the sidewalk, early that morning. Libbie had made several jugs of lemonade for them. She was happy to have them outdoors so she and the maid could tend to some housekeeping chores together. Business had seemed promising earlier that day as a few kids and even some adults had come to purchase a refreshing glass for five cents. But after lunch, things really slowed down. The girls eventually got bored and began playing tag with Doris and Douglas Eaglesham, and Ruth and John Leroux.

Sarah went inside to get more lemonade. She opened the refrigerator (a newly acquired appliance which replaced the old ice box) to pour a glass of lemonade and stood with the door open to cool off. Lydia was close behind.

"Where's Mother? Lydia got a glass from the cupboard and poured herself a drink.

"I don't know. I just called to her—maybe she's upstairs. I'll go see."

Libbie was upstairs doing housework. It was nearly impossible to hear someone calling from the main floor. Sarah was so hot and climbing the stairs just made her sweat all the more. She found Libbie and Julia in one of the bedrooms. They were flipping mattresses—a task that Libbie was insistent they do often to keep them from getting saggy or lumpy and to be ever alert for any sign of bed bugs. They had the windows open in all the rooms, trying to get a cross breeze which seemed rather useless in the heat of the day. However, you could usually count on some breeze if not a lot of wind at some point in Saskatchewan on any given day!

"Mother, can we go swimming? It is so hot and Jean and Margaret Eaglesham are going. They said we can go with them." Sarah brushed her hair away from her hot, moist face.

"It's 'may we go swimming', Sarah." Libbie would drill it into that child yet. "What about your brother?"

"Louis?"

"No, I was thinking Lyman. I feel better if he is with you girls. Louis can go too but only if Lyman will take you all."

"Did I hear my name mentioned?" Lyman poked his head into the bedroom. "Oh good, you are flipping my mattress! I love it when it is all freshened up like that!"

"Lyman, will you take Lydia and I, and maybe Louis, for a swim today? Some of the other kids are going and want us to come." Sarah ran over to her big brother and put her hands together in a prayerful pose as if to beg him.

"It's not will you take Lydia and 'I', Dear—it's will you take Lydia and me—remember, 'me' is the object of the verb!" Libbie, always the teacher drummed proper English into the children every chance she got.

"Oh yes, Mother, I forgot. Lyman, please, pretty please and thank you!" Sarah went on with her begging routine.

"Yes, alright—go get your bathing suits on. We'll ride our bikes. I think Jean Eaglesham is going too. I hope she is anyway."

"Ooh—Lyman's got a girlfriend, Lyman's going to marry Jean!" Sarah teased in a sing-song voice as she ran to her bedroom to get her bathing suit. Lydia was at the top of the stairs by now.

"No I don't! She's just a friend. Besides, she's a year older than me and doesn't even notice me."

"Lyman, please be careful and watch your sisters. Be careful not to peddle too fast for them and no stopping to play on the riverbank. You know the rules. Stay away from the river. There are strong currents in that water."

"I know Mother. Don't worry."

ℰᆰ

All the children learned to swim. The family motored out to Carlyle Lake on a couple of summer outings. Libbie packed a lunch and they joined the many folks that gathered on Hotel Beach. There were cars parked everywhere. It was a very exciting event to attend the annual boat regatta. There were boat races and all kinds of water competitions like swimming and diving. Jack Mitchell and his younger brother, Bill Mitchell (*later to become author W.O. Mitchell*) from Weyburn were young teens and both boys were strong diving competitors. They often won first prize. Jack was just a year older than Sarah so they knew one another from school and she enjoyed seeing him perform. The Mitchells went to Florida in the winter which gave them

41

the advantage of being able to swim for several months of the year. They could do all kinds of dives in the water. They really stole the show because they were so good at all of the water sports.

The Powell children enjoyed swimming, fishing, boating, hiking, berry picking and telling stories around a campfire. Harvey and Libbie rented a cottage one summer for a week so Harvey could get some fishing in with his sons. He and the boys often took in a ball game as well. Harvey was an avid fan of sports and was particularly impressed by one player who had become well-known in baseball circles throughout the south country. Waldo (aka: Wally) Shupe was an outstanding athlete and to Harvey's delight, Mr. Shupe eventually moved to Weyburn, became a successful business man. He and his four sons contributed much to Weyburn's sports and community endeavors.

There was no refrigeration at the lake so Libbie packed a lot of her preserves, fresh as well as dried fruit, baked goods and roasted cold chicken which she kept cool by wrapping everything in newspapers with jars of ice packed around it for the journey. They stopped at a farmer's road-side vegetable stand and picked up a dozen cobs of corn for their supper for their first night. No one was attending the vegetable stand. It was 'on your honour' system where you left the money in a tin can and if you needed change, you helped yourself. Limited supplies of groceries could be purchased from the store on Hotel Beach so Libbie wanted to have the staples for meals while they were at the lake. Tonight's meal would be cooked over an open fire. Libbie would boil up the corn and Harvey would help the children cut twigs from the chokecherry bushes to skewer their wieners to cook over the fire for hot dogs. There would be fresh strawberries with cream and sugar for dessert.

The children would sit wrapped in blankets around the fire late at night and would take delight in watching the fireflies flit around the bonfire and look like little green lanterns floating up to the dark and starry sky. They would smell of smoke but they would go to bed and sleep soundly waking early and ready to run off to the beach. They would take a towel and the bar of soap and jump into the cold lake to get the night's smoke washed out of their hair. The boys would splash the girls and there were lots of squeals and laughter. Harvey and Libbie would let them run, swim and explore for hours. As long as they showed up for meals, no one worried. Life was good at the lake!

Mischief

Summer days were the best with church picnics, playing sports and sometimes even getting into a little mischief. There were crabapple and garden raids that were great fun unless you got caught. One time the "gang" was caught sneaking into the Bieschells' back yard picking crabapples. It was a hot summer evening just after supper. Frank Moffet Jr., Hugh Eaglesham Jr., Louis, Sarah and Lydia were all caught when George Bieschell turned on the outdoor light and hollered at them. They all ran and the boys made it over the fence but Sarah caught her skirt on the fence and Lydia tried to free her. It was no use. Louis looked over his shoulder and realized both his sisters were in trouble so he walked back to take his punishment along with the girls.

George and Lillian Bieschell were both very kind and decent neighbours but they wanted the kids to learn a lesson so they told them that if they didn't tell their parents, then George would talk to the parents himself. Louis, Lydia and Sarah knew things would go worse for them if George had to talk to their parents. They had to tell their parents themselves. They walked home rather slowly trying to get their stories straight.

When Libbie heard the story she marched them back over to the Bieschells' and knocked on the door. When George answered, Libbie stood with her arms folded across her chest and said, "Evening George. These three have something to say to you."

"Evening, Libbie. I figured you would want to know." George smiled.

"Go ahead Louis," Libbie shoved him from behind to push him forward.

"Um, we're sorry Mr. Bieschell," Louis looked down at his feet.

"Yes, we're all sorry Mr. Bieschell," Sarah and Lydia said in unison. Sarah thought she might start to cry and hoped this would be over soon.

"Well, as long as you are sorry, I accept your apology. You know if you had knocked on my door and asked, I would have given you the apples."

"Well, saying sorry isn't quite enough. George, I want you to give these 'criminals' a chore to do. Is there something they can offer to do for you in your yard this weekend?" Libbie insisted.

"Let me think—since they like crabapples so much, maybe they could come over and pick me a few pails full. I think they can handle climbing up the ladder and into the tree much better than I can." George winked.

"I'll have them here on Saturday if that is alright. They can come over after breakfast."

"Great, I'll expect them then. Would you like some crabapples, Libbie?" George asked." Lillian can't keep up to them. She's made jelly already."

"I'd love some but only after you check with Lillian to see if she wants to do something more with them. I'd love to preserve some with cinnamon. I'll do some for you, if you like them. Thank you for your kindness and for your forgiveness for these little rascals."

"We were all kids once, Libbie. We've got kids too and I'm surprised that Freddy and Evelyn weren't running around with them. I guess if they had been with them, they'd have been in someone else's yard!" he chuckled. "No harm done. Glad they will learn a lesson from it though. Good for you Libbie for straightening them out on this."

After they got home, one of the children reminded their mother that they had not been totally alone. The other kids got away with it.

"The other kids are not my responsibility. You three are. I've told your father and we've decided you won't be playing outside after dark unless you promise to stay in your own yard. There are consequences for your actions and you might as well learn that right now! Now, go upstairs and get washed up and ready for bed. I'll be

45

up to hear your prayers and I think you will have some confessing to the Lord tonight!"

On Saturday, the Powell children were surprised to see Hugh Jr. and Frank Jr. in the Bieschell yard. Hugh was washing Mr. Bieschell's car and Frank was mowing the front lawn. It turned out that they thought better about running away and had gone back later to confess to George that they had been part of the criminal gang. George told them about what the Powell children were doing to make things up and so they offered their services in the hopes of restoring their respective families' good names. All was forgiven.

Chapter 4

1918 – 1920 the Spanish Flu

[18]With the end of WWI, troops were coming home. Many were infected by the flu virus while overseas and carried it home. By the end of 1918, nearly 4000 people in Saskatchewan had died of the disease. It was an international pandemic that struck Canada very hard killing approximately 55,000 young adults between ages 20 and 40. The virus came in multiple waves. The first wave hit in spring of 1918; then in the fall of 1918, a mutation of the influenza virus produced an extremely contagious, virulent and deadly form of the disease. Subsequent waves hit again in spring of 1919 and spring of 1920. The global deaths claimed the lives of between 50 and 100 million victims in the prime of their lives.

Maritime quarantines previously used in the 19th century to prevent the spread of the Russian flu did little good to prevent the spread of this flu because people were travelling from east to west by train to areas where no quarantine measures were in place. Municipal and provincial authorities tried to save lives by prohibiting public gatherings and by isolating the sick, but these provisions had little effect. As more and more people became infected, the number of healthy workers decreased causing serious economic decline.

---

[18] Library and Archives Canada

"I spoke with Doc Eaglesham today at the bank. We had an interesting conversation about the Spanish flu. He told me that alcohol is considered one of the best treatments and preventatives against the flu. He has actually prescribed it because he said the government has now permitted pharmacists to dispense it," Harvey announced one evening at the dinner table.

"Well, that is the only way they will get any alcohol in this country now that we have Prohibition, thanks be to God!" Libbie's mouth tightened as she straightened her linen napkin on her lap.

"Yes, indeed. Doc made the joke that some of his patients don't care if they have the flu as long as he can get them a prescription of alcohol." Harvey chuckled.

Libbie didn't crack a smile. She didn't see the humour in this but she couldn't argue that if it was for medicinal purposes, then it might be worth some level of acceptance. But not for her! No, she'd suffer it out if she was ever to get the flu. Surely she would manage with other home remedies. It just made her angry—wasn't that just the limit to think that after all her hard work with the Temperance women, that now the government would find some miraculous reason to bring back alcohol.

"He says they are looking for volunteers willing to come to the hospital to do any type of relief work possible. Apparently, it has come to the desperate point where there are so many workers sick with the flu that they are very short staffed."

"Yes, I had a chat with his wife, Mary, this afternoon. We had tea to discuss some items for the agenda for our Presbyterian Ladies meeting this week.

48

Mabel Moffet was with us as well. I feel as though I should be volunteering myself as I'm healthy and able bodied. Sarah, eat your Brussels sprouts, dear."

"I'm trying Mother, but of all the vegetables, this one is the one I like the least." Sarah pushed the vegetable around on her plate with her fork and an expression on her face of great disdain and revulsion.

"And that's exactly how we want you to stay, my dear," Harvey continued directing his conversation to Libbie, ignoring Sarah's comment about her vegetables and smiling from the head of the table to his wife as he buttered his dinner roll.

"I think it would be commendable, Mother. What sort of work could you volunteer to help with?" Louis spoke up, his voice breaking. He was now 14. Lyman was 19 and planned to be leaving home to join Knox and Oliver by fall.

"Well, I'm not sure but I am particularly well trained in the care of babies or small children, so. . ."

"You can't afford to become ill, Libbie," Harvey interrupted her. "You are needed here and your family is your first responsibility," his expression darkened slightly.

"I don't need to be reminded about my first responsibility, Dearest; however, that is certainly my concern and I take your point as I'm sure you meant it in the kindest way." Libbie smiled as she passed the gravy on to Sarah. Although her voice remained calm and polite, Harvey could read the body language as she sat rigid and erect. He knew he had touched a nerve.

"Mother, I don't want you to get the flu. I would be very upset to see you get ill. Please stay home and let someone else do the volunteer work this time," Lydia looked worried as she used the back of her hand very delicately to push her glasses up. She was sixteen now and was old enough to wear her hair up. Sarah admired Lydia and thought she was so very pretty. She wanted to look just like her but Mother wouldn't let her wear her hair up yet. She was only just thirteen after all. She loved to dress like Lydia and they often wore matching outfits. At first it was Libbie's choice to dress them alike but later they chose on their own to do so. Now, to add to Lydia's beauty, she wore glasses which Sarah thought only made her beautiful eyes look even bigger and more beautiful. So, Sarah got a set of similar styled glasses to look just as much like Lydia as possible.

"Well, let's not all get ourselves upset over this right now." Libbie tried to calm the rest of them down. "I'm only thinking about it and I'm sure there will be much discussion about it at our church meeting. Perhaps we'll get a lot of volunteers there. At least we can pray about it and—I assure you all—if I do go in to help, I'll take precautions. I'll wear a mask. I'm sure there are some things that can be done that will not put a person in direct contact with the patients. Perhaps I could offer to help in the kitchen or the laundry. I would only offer one day a week—that is, if I do volunteer. I'm not saying I will . . .yet."

Harvey just shook his head and finished his meal in silence. He knew his wife and he knew it was useless to try to dissuade her once she got an idea in her head.

Of course, Libbie did volunteer and she did take precautions. She helped with folding sheets and delivering clean linens to the wards from the laundry department. As usual, she saw a need and she pitched in to make things better but she kept herself healthy so she could be strong for her own family. Not only was she helping others but she was instilling a very important lesson to her children to give of themselves to those who are less fortunate. It was important to teach them that you don't look the other way when there is something you can do to take care of the sick or the needy.

It seemed whether by her intent or whether just by her sheer good heart, she was always the teacher. Through just living the way she saw best, going by what she thought the Lord would expect from her, she led the way for her children by example.

ℰℭ

Harvey was opening the mail and called to Libbie, "Libbie! Come here, there's a letter from Oliver."

"Oh please don't let it be bad news," Libbie hurried into the kitchen and came up beside Harvey to read the letter along with him.

"No, it's good news," Harvey read aloud, "He says here that he's back in the United States and he has work in a bank in Minneapolis."

Oliver had spent the last two years in the Navy working as a Supply Officer on troop transports and destroyers. He had joined the Federal Reserve Bank in

Minneapolis and would be working in the Business Research Division. Libbie wept tears of joy.

1926 Weyburn

After a three-day snow storm in December, the drifts of snow were sculpted by the wind into peaks and valleys smooth as porcelain and whipped up like the frosting on a cake. The peaks were sparkling like tiny diamonds and the valleys were deep mauve and blue tones. Sarah couldn't help but stop and just stare at the beauty of the frost covered trees sparkling and shimmering all around her as she walked home from school. It was magical! The snow was soft as a cloud, all fluffy and white under foot. She felt like she should lay down in it and make snow angels. Of course, she was far too grown up for childish games now. After all, she was eighteen and in her senior year. She would be graduating from Weyburn Collegiate Institute in June.

She breathed in the crisp fresh air as she crossed the bridge over the Souris River just as she had so many times on her walks to and from high school. She waved to some of the young children who were skating on the Souris River. They were children from the South Hill and they would get on the ice quickly after school as it was so close to where they lived. They were out tobogganing and skating on the river as soon as it was frozen thick enough. They played outdoor hockey by the hours, often coming home with frost-bitten toes or fingers.

It was a long walk, for certain, but today the sun was shining and she was dressed warm. Her mother always made sure that she had her pink, woolen bloomers on underneath her dress before heading out in the mornings. She hated those things but Libbie warned her she'd get a bladder infection if she didn't wear them. She would go downstairs to the basement of the school to the girls' washroom before class started and take them off and stuff them in her school bag. Otherwise they would cause her to get a heat rash and they were terribly scratchy. She wore a long tweed coat and woolen stockings to keep her legs warm. Her fur-lined winter boots kept her feet toasty warm. Although the distance was considerable, there was always someone to walk with so the time would pass with jolly good conversation.

"Helen, are you prepared for the Christmas Recital? I'm anxious to hear you perform your pieces." Sarah snuggled her face into her scarf as she walked up the hill.

"Oh, I'm as ready as I can be, I guess. I've been playing some of my favourite Christmas hymns at church every Sunday for the past three weeks; so, I've been getting a lot of practice it would seem—how about you?" Helen was a fellow pianist who took lessons from the same teacher, Mrs. Cathcart. Both students were taking their Grade 8 from the Royal Conservatory of Music and had been friendly competitors for many years by now. Both girls were accomplished pianists at this point. Helen's mother, Mrs. Campbell, often had tea with Libbie. They were not Presbyterians like the Powells, but were Baptists. Libbie found the Baptists to be quite acceptable company as they were known to abstain from drinking alcoholic spirits and dancing.

"I'm practicing an extra half hour every day to try to prepare the Christmas pieces I'll perform. I think I'm going to be alright but there's one piece that I still have some difficulty with so I'm concentrating on that one. Do you like playing at your church?"

"Well, yes, but it is a little exhausting trying to do the extra playing on top of all my homework and regular practicing but they give me a little present at Christmas. They can't afford to pay me and Mother and Father wouldn't allow me to accept payment anyway. I do enjoy it most times and I try to play the livelier hymns when I get the chance. I hate old stodgy hymns that drone on. It gives me extra experience at playing in front of people and I think that is of good value to me."

"I see. So, I know you Baptists don't drink or dance. Father has told me that. But what is different about your church from the Presbyterian Church?" Sarah hoped she wasn't sounding rude to ask such a question but she was curious.

"I think the only thing I can say is different from all other churches is that we Baptists go for full body submersion under the water to be baptized."

"What? Do tell!"

"It's nothing really to be horrified over."

"Oh, no, sorry Helen—I didn't mean to sound horrified. I'm just curious about it." Sarah patted Helen on the shoulder.

"Well, the church has a deep tank and we stand in water up to our chest. We wear a white gown over a bathing suit and the minister gets in the tank with us and says some prayers and then dunks us under the water."

"He dunks you?!"

"Well, I guess he doesn't really dunk us. He puts his hand behind our head and then we cross our hands over our chest—the way you would see a corpse in a coffin—and we sort of stiffen our body and just let ourselves fall backward and he supports us as he lays us back under the water."

"Fascinating! I'd like to see that one day."

"Mm-hmm, yes, well another thing about it is we don't baptize babies—the parents can 'dedicate' them to the church and they make an oath to bring them to church and they enroll them in Sunday school classes."

"So, when do they get baptized?"

"Only when they are old enough to attend classes, around age twelve, I'd say. The church believes each person should be able to make that commitment to God themselves rather than someone else making it for them."

"How very interesting. Thank you, Helen, for explaining that to me."

"You're welcome, any time I can enlighten you just ask!" Helen giggled and they both chuckled.

"I'm always interested in things about religion. Do you know that the Catholics have to eat fish every Friday?"

"Yes, I know it and we also eat fish on Fridays, but it has nothing to do with being a Baptist. It is because my mother says they bring fish in at the meat market fresh every week for the Catholics. She says, we'll eat fish on Fridays like the Catholics because that's when it will be the freshest."

"Oh, that seems rather smart of your mother if you ask me." Sarah adjusted her woolen toque pulling it down over her ears more.

"Have you thought about what to wear to graduation?" Helen asked.

"Oh heavens, I have no idea yet. That seems too hard to think of when it is still winter." Sarah kicked at a drift to knock the top off it and stepped into the deep snow. It came up to the top of her boots.

"Have you got an escort?" Helen pushed.

"Have you?" Sarah poked Helen with her finger.

"Well no—but I'm putting some feelers out and scrutinizing my options."

"Helen! You are hilarious! Who have you got your feelers out for?" Sarah laughed.

"Well, that's a secret for me to know and for you to find out!" And with that she bolted ahead and Sarah took chase, both girls laughing and sliding in the snow as they tried to run through the deep drifts.

Christmas was almost here. Libbie was busy shopping, writing cards and letters to family and friends. She had to parcel up gifts to send to the boys. Knox would be coming home to join the family but Oliver was married now and had children so they weren't going to travel in winter weather. Knox was still single and had time off over the holidays. Lyman who had been in Minnesota attending university, studying business, would accompany Knox.

The house always smelled of something wonderful when Sarah came in from the cold. Libbie was making all the traditional things like, butter tarts, shortbread, gingerbread, jam-filled-shorties, Christmas cakes, and rum balls—with rum flavouring only—not alcoholic rum, of course!

"Mother, I'm home! Oh, goodness, it smells wonderful in here.

"We're in the kitchen Dear! I've got hot cocoa for you and a snack. Julia and I made butter tarts today." Libbie called back to Sarah. "You'd better get to them before your father sees them. You know they are his favourite!"

The smell of pine from the Christmas tree and the aroma of the baking were such a wonderful combination, filling the house and adding to the excitement of the season. The radio was playing all the familiar Christmas carols and all the Christmas decorations were up. There was a special red and white lace tablecloth on the dining room table. Libbie had placed a beautiful red poinsettia plant as a center piece with brass candle holders and red candles on either side of the poinsettia.

There would be a feast of sweet potato pie, green beans with toasted almonds, creamy mashed potatoes with gravy, homemade dinner rolls with homemade butter, a jelly mold, cranberries and roast goose stuffed with apples, sweet chestnuts, prunes and onions seasoned with marjoram and rosemary for Christmas Eve. Harvey and his trusty hunting dog, a black Labrador retriever, affectionately named "Mutt", had made sure of a goose. Mutt was supposed to be Harvey's hunting dog. But he loved to spread his doggie love around to each and every member of the family. He had been especially close to Lyman so it would be a nice surprise for him to reunite with his old pal.

Harvey enjoyed hunting with his friend, John (aka: Jack) Powers. Jack had moved to Weyburn in 1908, the year Sarah was born. At that time, Jack was still a bachelor and he was always ready and available to join Harvey on a hunting expedition. They hunted everything from moose, deer, pheasants and geese. Sometimes they would enlist the help of the Powell boys to pluck feathers from the fowl, giving them a whole quarter to add to their allowance. The two men continued their lasting friendship after Jack married Irene Simpson (in 1922) from Carlton Place, Ontario. Before he married Irene, he had spent three years overseas during WWI in France, Belgium and England and had fought at Vimy Ridge; a famous battle in April 1917—one of Canada's most celebrated military victories. Irene, like Libbie, had been a teacher before marriage. Jack and Irene were not Presbyterians but were Baptists. Libbie found them charming and she and Irene shared the same abhorrence for alcohol. She knew Jack and Harvey would be safe when out hunting as neither of them drank, like some chaps.

[19]Jack later went into business selling groceries and then later bought out a hardware business and combined the two things. Eventually, he sold that business to the Co-op. He stayed with the Co-op until 1947. At that time he went into partnership with Ed and,

[19] Hey Seeds! pp 38 – Jack and Irene Powers were special friends of the author, Jan Keating, and her family.

son, Herb Worden selling groceries, and other small hardware items. When Ed passed away, Jack and Herb continued the partnership. Harvey and Jack were also both in Masons, Chamber of Commerce and Rotary Club.

Sarah loved everything about Christmas and she knew there would be much laughter, socializing with young and old, special church services with all the wonderful Christmas music and the joy of family gathered. It was going to be extra special because it would be her last Christmas at home. Once she graduated, she would be heading to university and who knew whether she'd be back for a family Christmas after that? She wanted this Christmas to be something joyful for the family, indeed!

Chapter 5

Sarah was the last of Libbie's chicks to fly the coop and head to the United States for post-secondary education. Libbie suffered the usual moments of loneliness with the empty nest but she had accepted that this was the natural course of life and she and Harvey wanted all their children to seek higher education. The world was still recovering from the war and the best way to survive hardships to come was through education. Also, the boys were all in Minnesota so Sarah would not be lonely. By this time, Oliver was President of the Federal Reserve Bank in St. Paul.

Sarah was a confident young woman. She had seen her brothers and sister all leave home and she felt it was too lonely to live at home without them anyway so now she was ready to spread her wings and fly. She was excited about her new challenge of attending the University of Minnesota. She would be independent for the first time in her life and she was ready. Of course, she would miss her dear mother and father but it was just time for new experiences.

Libbie had accompanied her to Minnesota to help her settle in. They had a jolly time shopping together for new clothes for Sarah. She had brought several things with her but Libbie had thought it best to travel light. She planned it as an extra nice treat to leave her daughter with a good shopping excursion before they parted.

Sarah loved the comfort of the drop-waist dresses. The hemlines had come up to just below the knee. Women were showing their legs more and wearing Mary Jane and T-strap heeled shoes inspired by the Flappers. Mind you, she never considered herself a flapper girl. Her parents would never have tolerated the sort of behaviour that flapper girls exhibited. They smoked and drank and partied with little care of what the establishment would think of them. The modern women of the "Roaring 20s" were bobbing their hair and getting permanent waves. Sarah wanted to be in fashion and she did have her hair bobbed when she was in high school. She had a bit of natural wave so it was easy to make "finger waves" on the crown and soft natural curls coifed her fine featured face.

Her parents had given her a long string of pearls for Christmas which she loved to wear when she dressed up. She kept her jewelry simple and elegant, nothing overstated or gaudy. Tailored, sportswear for daytime dress was now acceptable not just for men but women as well. Sarah chose long soft sweaters worn loose or sometimes belted for a more feminine look. Soft fabrics such as jersey were a favourite of Sarah's influenced by Coco Chanel's designs. These soft fabrics and simple designs were comfortable and stylish.

Libbie suggested Sarah purchase several long, tunic-styled blouses to wear with a pleated skirt. It was a sensible solution to make laundering easier. This way Sarah would only need to launder a blouse rather than a whole dress. The skirt could be taken to the dry cleaners when necessary. She added a double-breasted jacket as well for a more sensible business look. One could always use a jacket to wear on chilly days when a long coat would be too much. She also added a midi-length, straight cut, tweed skirt that would be suitable for colder weather. She had a full-length, wool plaid coat with a shawl collar and wide cuffed sleeves. She bought a cloche-styled hat to go with it. She and Libbie had thought of everything possible to make Sarah's new wardrobe appropriate.

The first few days around the campus were busy and exhausting. Sarah had to find her way to all her different classes and make each class in time. She didn't want to be embarrassed by walking into anyone's classroom late. She managed to be on time for her classes and everyone seemed friendly and willing to be of assistance if she needed directions. It was a whirl-wind time trying to figure out what each professor wanted from the students and trying to decide which classes she liked or disliked.

Although she was never boisterous or forward, but rather a little quiet, she certainly was capable of making new friends. Growing up with all those siblings had given her the strength to stand up for herself when need be. She was bright and confident. All in all, she felt things were going well.

Sarah achieved her Bachelor of Arts at the University of Minnesota. She then set her sights on heading to the University of Chicago. She returned home to Weyburn for the summer and had a glorious time visiting some of her friends. Many had married by now and were starting families. She was happy to be single and felt in no panic to be tied down. She wanted to further her education and pursue a career first and. besides—she had not yet met anyone she would consider that seriously.

1928 - 1930 Chicago & Fadhel al-Jamali

While working toward her Master of Arts degree in English, at the University of Chicago, Sarah decided to attend an International Students event. There was to be a tea at the Cosmopolitan Club in Ida Noyes Hall, the student union building. Little did she know that this one event was about to change her life. While at this tea, Sarah encountered a young Arab student wearing circular, dark-rimmed spectacles. They struck up a pleasant conversation. Sarah thought nothing more about this first encounter with the young Arab, named Mohammed Fadhel al-Jamali. In fact, she later recalled that she didn't remember his name and said all she could remember was that there seemed to be a lot of Ali's in it.

Mohammed Fadhel Jamali was an Arab Muslim who was born in Kadhimain, near Baghdad. His father, Sheikh Abbas al-Jamali, was a well-respected religious leader in the Shi'a community. His mother, Alawiya Khadija was a highly regarded poetess. Young Fadhel was an ambitious student who had attended Teacher Training College where he graduated at the top of his class in 1920. It was a two-year course but he was admitted in the second year so he completed the course in one year. He taught at an elementary school, entering into a new era of self-support and independence. He rented a home on the bank of the Tigris River in the Bustan Kubba quarter where he enjoyed rowing on the river with friends. However, his thirst for further education pushed him on to petition the government to either send him abroad or open an institution of higher learning in

64

Baghdad. At this time, there was no university in Baghdad for him to attend. He won his petition and the government agreed to send him and five other fellow male students to the American University of Beirut. This was the first educational mission Iraq had ever sent abroad. It was the beginning of the world opening up for Fadhel.

The day he left for his journey to Beirut, he shaved his beard for the very first time and put on Western dress. At this time, he left home as a vigorous orthodox Muslim. He writes about his attitude and state of mind toward non-Muslims:

> "My prayers were performed on time, and my attitude towards non-Muslims was one of abhorrence. This continued for two years at the American University of Beirut. I attended the required chapel with a tense feeling. Whenever the hymns were sung, I either refrained from singing or I substituted Mohammed or Allah for Jesus or Lord.
>
> Two big factors helped in changing my attitudes. The first was the Brotherhood Society, an interreligious organization where I learned that the realm of things in which we share is vastly larger than in which we differ; and the second was the study of science and especially zoology with its emphasis on the theory of evolution under Dr. Van Dyck, who had a most important influence on my life. Gradually I developed a spirit of tolerance, of open-mindedness and critical-mindedness. I began to look at our life at home more critically and to

reexamine our social institutions. I was a new man and the new man cherished the brotherhood of man; I was a pacifist and a nationalist. Great aspirations for developing Iraq in particular and the Arabic world in general began to dominate my whole life."

A lot had gone on in Fadhel's life before this first meeting with Sarah. Aside from his education and change in attitude, he had become ill and contracted tuberculosis. He spent a year in a sanatorium in the mountains above Beirut run by American missionaries. While recovering in this scenic retreat overlooking the Mediterranean, he spent hours enjoying books and nature and composing love poetry. A friendship had blossomed into a serious love between him and the head nurse, a bright young Muslim girl. He wanted to marry her; however, her family objected to her marrying a man that she had met outside the Muslim customary way.

The good thing about youth is that a broken heart can heal quickly when attentions turn to someone new. Fadhel met and fell in love with a Christian girl from a nearby village. This was an insurmountable and doomed relationship from the start. At that time, the separation between Muslims and Christians was too wide. This posed a serious problem for the couple and it ended when she decided to marry a rich relative.

That was then and this was now. Once again he was smitten with a beautiful, bright Christian girl. Her name was Sarah Powell.

ജ©രു

"Jamali, old chap! What are you looking at that has you so intense. I see you checking this bulletin board every time I walk past here," a fellow classmate questioned Fadhel. Classmates, often would refer to him by his last name.

"The Cosmopolitan Club is sponsoring a picnic. I'm just checking to see who is on the list to attend it."

"Oh ya? Where's the picnic?"

"It will be held in the dunes beside Lake Michigan."

"Hm! Sounds like a good chance to meet some interesting people of the 'gentler sex', wouldn't you say?" the classmate winked at Fadhel as he signed his name to the list and walked away.

Fadhel finally spotted the name he was looking for. When he saw "Sarah Powell" inscribed, he quickly added his name and whistled a happy tune as he walked down the hall.

Although Fadhel had one purpose only to be at the picnic, he did his best to make his approach to Sarah seem perfectly innocent and by chance. Sarah was delightful and his interests only grew more with each encounter. Soon they were seeing a lot more of one another. Sarah recalled:

> "After our meeting at the picnic, Fadhel began coming to the Library to walk me home, and there was a dear old flat-footed biddy in charge of the rare books. In a very motherly way, she advised me to have nothing to do with that young man—to no effect! We used to go for walks, to organ

concerts in the chapel, and then he went back to Teachers College in Columbia."

Sarah completed her Master of Arts in English and decided to go on to Columbia Teachers College. She decided that the University of Chicago was not for her any longer since they seemed to feel that "anything after Shakespeare was not really literature." She wanted to broaden her scope of literature far beyond Shakespeare.

It pleased her very much that Fadhel would also be attending classes there. She was sure they would continue their growing relationship.

Chapter 6

Sarah and Fadhel saw a great deal of one another during the next academic year at the University of Columbia in New York. Sarah had her own little apartment and Fadhel enjoyed meals that she would prepare for them. They took part in activities at the International House where they shared an active social life with many new friends.

Sarah achieved her second Master of Arts (MA) in Educational Guidance Counseling. After receiving her MA in Columbia, she accepted a teaching post in Prospect Park, Pennsylvania. Her sister, Lydia, was now married and living there.

Fadhel and Sarah continued their relationship and on one occasion they went to the University Museum to see artifacts from [20]Ur of Chaldees, situated not far from Iraq's port city of Basra. By this point, they knew they were in love with one another. There was no denying it. They knew they wanted to get married but Fadhel felt he must return to Iraq and serve his country. With all his time spent abroad, he was becoming a world citizen, but he never lost his affection and concern for his homeland. He felt he needed to hold true to his convictions and the

---

[20] Wikipedia - **Ur** of the **Chaldeans**, is a city mentioned in the Hebrew Bible as the birthplace of the Israelite and Ismaelite patriarch Abraham

goal he had set for himself long before he met Sarah. His love for Sarah was strong but his commitment to accomplish great things for his country was something he could not set aside, even for love of a woman.

Sarah was despondent and missed him terribly but they wrote and his letters were always full of his promises and his intent to marry. That would have to suffice for now and so Sarah threw herself into her work. She loved teaching and felt happy to be using her education after all her years of hard work to achieve her degrees. She had wonderful times with her sister. Lydia kept her included in some social events when possible.

ℰᏡᏟᏒ

In Iraq, Fadhel had been appointed to the Educational Survey Commission by his mentor, Dr. Paul Monroe, a prominent member of the Teachers College faculty in New York. They had traveled from New York to Baghdad together and had stopped in Marseilles and Naples to sight-see. They also stopped in Egypt where Fadhel spoke to a Cairo University Student Assembly on the educational situation in Iraq. He stressed the need for education to serve the rural and tribal sections of the population which were the majority in the country. Fadhel strongly believed that all people should have opportunity for an education; not only the rich, but even the Bedouin (poor Arabs). He felt the objective should be to broaden civic loyalty.

He believed that "Citizens of the same country, whether Muslims, Christians, Jews, Sabites or Baha'is should learn to live together in peace and harmony, each respecting the others' creeds while following his own."

He also strongly advocated for equal rights and education for women. He stated it should be one of the main objectives of education to raise the status of women and give them emancipation which he believed to be their right. This was very progressive thinking at this time for a man from his generation and culture. This attitude toward women held high with Sarah and made her feel even more confident that she was choosing the right life partner. Not many men around her in her own country would have been so outspoken and encouraging toward women's rights.

To Sarah's delight, she soon received a letter from Fadhel asking her if she would like to come to Baghdad to teach in the Women's Teacher Training College. He felt it would be wise for her to see if she could accept life in Baghdad before they went forward with wedding plans. He had taken the liberty of consulting with his friend, Abdul Hussein Chelabi, the Minister of Education, about the possibility of a position for Sarah to teach. The Minister agreed and a post was arranged for her accommodation in the Home Economics School.

Fadhel explained that Sarah and the Headmistress, Miss Beuna Hickson, would each have a room and they would be provided with the services of a Persian servant woman. Sarah was aching to be reunited with Fadhel and this was a thrilling opportunity to visit his homeland and meet his family. She accepted immediately.

Now, it was time to go home and tell her parents. She would want to spend some family time with them before she left the country because at this point, she had no idea whether she would be returning from Iraq. She gave her notice and began packing to return to Weyburn.

Summer 1932 Weyburn & the Dirty Thirties

It was nice to be home. Sarah had been so preoccupied with Fadhel and teaching that she had little time to miss her parents, but now that she was with them, she realized how much she had missed them and how happy she was to be with them now. They had missed her as well. Libbie had set to baking and fussing to prepare some of Sarah's favourite foods before her arrival. She would make sure to invite some of the ladies and young women over for tea one day so Sarah could catch up with her friends. She had Julia cleaning and doing all the extra jobs that would make the house sparkle. A vase of roses was placed on the dining room table in Sarah's honour. This was especially lovely because it was the Dirty Thirties and keeping flowers blooming was no easy feat. It was hot, dusty, windy and dry. Libbie had all but given up on growing too many varieties of flowers. Instead of larger flower beds, she had opted to have a few potted marigolds and petunias. She placed them on the front step to brighten up the front entrance for Sarah's homecoming. Harvey had gone to the train station to pick her up.

Times were tough in Weyburn area and, in fact, the prairie provinces of Manitoba, Saskatchewan and Alberta were the hardest hit provinces in Canada with the Great Depression. There was drought and dust storms that reduced some farmland to sand dunes. Although Sarah was aware from her mother's letters, she wasn't quite prepared for what she saw. The wind would howl relentlessly for days at a time. Dirt and dust and debris blew and sifted and formed drifts of sand and dirt. Tumble weeds bounced across the prairie and through the streets. Days of darkness from the heavy dust in the air prevented any sight of much sunlight. It was eerie and unsettling. She wondered how her mother could endure this. Julia was continually required to dust and polish. She would dampen rugs and roll them up and place them in front of the door thresholds and window sills to keep the dirt from sifting into the house. The smell of dust in the air would make one cough and choke; Sarah had to cover her mouth with a scarf if she ventured out. It was easier to stay inside for the most part. At least it gave her ample time to have discussions with her parents.

"Are you sure you needed to quit a perfectly suited teaching position to go traipsing off to Iraq on a whim?" Libbie was putting the last batch of biscuits in the oven. She had a large pot of stew simmering on the stove for their supper. Sarah loved her mother's soda biscuits with stew but she especially loved the biscuits with homemade jam for tea. She had just sat down in the kitchen and was waiting for the tea to steep. Harvey came in and joined them.

"I have made the decision to go, Mother— and I have accepted another 'perfectly suitable' teaching position in Baghdad. I'm still going to have employment that will utilize my years of training. I am really looking forward to teaching young women at the college level."

Libbie poured boiling water into the teacups to warm them before pouring tea for each of them. She placed some biscuits and jam on the table. Sarah could see the tense jaw and tight-lipped expression on Libbie's face. She knew that look all too well!

"Well, I just wonder if you've thought this all out carefully. You may not realize what you are going into over there, you know. It will be very different than what you are used to over here." Libbie handed them each a cotton napkin. She only used the linen napkins in the dining room.

"Of course, it will be completely different than what I'm used to. I have thought it over carefully. I expect that there will be vast differences but that doesn't mean all the differences will be things I can't adapt to or accept. I hope there will be many things that I will love. I'm excited about having the opportunity to see this ancient part of the world, quite frankly." Sarah took a bite of her biscuit.

"Where will you be staying?" Harvey thought he should change the subject slightly to ask some technical questions about logistics.

"I'll be staying in the Home Economics School. I won't be alone as the Headmistress will also have a room there." Sarah emphasized this to assure her parents that she was not going to be doing anything indecent. Not that they would think that of her but she just wanted them to feel secure that everything was above board and proper.

"I see. Do these people speak English? Are you going to be able to communicate and teach students who are Arabs?" Harvey sipped on his hot tea and put his cup down and added some cream.

"Yes, Father, they speak English. I am thinking that I might try to learn Arabic while I'm there.

"While you are there? So, are you thinking you may not stay indefinitely?" Libbie's eyes were questioning and hopeful.

"Well, I don't know for sure about anything right now. I just know that I love Fadhel and I want to marry him. I would have married him here but he had to return and wants to serve his country. I'm the one who is ready to make the commitment now. I miss him terribly."

"But you don't really know him well enough to make a commitment now, do you? I mean, Sarah, darling, do you realize that his culture and religion will be so vastly different from yours. You will be the odd one in a community of people who dress, eat and live very differently than the way you were raised." Libbie was not giving up. Sarah didn't really think this was going to be easy. She had expected it.

"We have had many long discussions about this topic, Mother. Fadhel believes in the same values as I do. We are very simpatico on topics of religion, food, politics, music, art and we find our family values have much in common. His parents were strict and yet loving just as with you and Father and how you raised us."

"I'm not convinced that you fully realize what you are doing. I think 'love is blind' as they say and I think we need to consider the many factors that may be unforeseen at this point. You know when things get difficult, and believe me there will be times—you cannot just run home or have a friend or family member come rushing to your side." Libbie jumped up to take the last batch of biscuits out of the oven. Julia had the day off so Libbie was in charge of the cooking for today.

"Well, perhaps we can enjoy our tea and biscuits for now and let Sarah enjoy the rest of the day with us. We have a lot of other things to talk about. I'd like to hear about how things have been with Lydia. I'm sure you have some things to share about your time with her and Ed." Harvey smiled and patted Sarah on the hand. She smiled back at him and sipped her tea but she knew well enough that the topic was not completely closed. She knew her mother was far from finished with her on this subject. Maybe this was going to be more difficult than she had anticipated.

She got up and went over to pet Mutt who was sleeping close to the oven. His old bones seemed to need more heat than usual these days, according to Harvey. His hunting days were nearly over and, yet, Harvey couldn't think of going hunting without him. Mutt looked lovingly up at Sarah and she was glad someone seemed to love her without the need for words. Mutt was just there to love everyone and he accepted things without question. The conversation had exhausted her and she missed Fadhel even more at this moment. She was thankful her father was not attacking her with too many questions. Trying to convince her mother was going to be more difficult. It would have been so much easier to have fallen in love with someone that her mother could have hand-picked for her. There were many nice chaps available and willing, of course, but who knows what direction the wind will blow or why we fall in love with someone when we least expect it to happen? Do we choose or is it chosen for us? All Sarah knew was there was no changing it now. Her heart was with Fadhel and if that meant going to his country to live his life in his customs, she was going and she was giving it her all.

Libbie did have a social tea party in honour of Sarah and she and Julia had made sure everything was perfect. The dainties had been arranged on serving platters and little cucumber and mayonnaise sandwiches had been made with one slice of brown bread and one slice of white bread. The crusts had been trimmed away and then the bread was cut with a cookie cutter with scalloped edges. The cuttings of bread would be saved to make bread pudding for dessert for the supper meal. Although fruit was not always easy to purchase, due to the depression and supply shortages, Libbie had managed to get some grapes and she had her own strawberries growing in a pot. There was enough to make an attractive fruit and cheese platter. Julia had made a refreshing batch of iced tea with sugar and a few lemon slices. Adding sugar to the iced tea was a Canadian thing it seemed. Sarah noticed it was never added in the United States.

Sarah was enjoying reacquainting with her Weyburn friends. Ruth Leroux was one guest that Sarah was overjoyed to see again. They had lots of laughs and things to chatter about as they reminisced. When they had chance to speak privately for a few minutes, Ruth got right to the heart of her curious mind.

"So, is this trip to Iran or Iraq—I'm sorry, I don't know which one it is—are you excited? Are you scared? I'd be terribly afraid to go on a journey like that by myself. You're either very brave or very . . ." She trailed off, thinking better of what she was about to say.

"It's Iraq. I'm going to Baghdad where Fadhel and his family live. And, if you promise not to tell anyone— truthfully, I am a little nervous. However, I've done some travel on my own already and I've been living independently for a while now. So I'm pretty confident that I'll cope. And of course, once I get there, I won't be alone."

"So, what is he like? He must be pretty handsome to have swept you off your feet like this."

"I think he's very handsome. I wouldn't exactly put it the way you have, though. I wasn't swept off my feet. I didn't really take much notice of him on the first couple of meetings. We were very casual with one another at first. I think we were both very focused on our studies. We never saw much of one another on a one-on-one basis. There were usually other friends included."

"But you are serious now, aren't you?"

"Yes, of course, but it grew over a few years. We have a wonderful time together. We love all the same things. He has a great moral fibre to him that I admire almost as much as I am attracted to his physical attributes." Sarah smiled and closed her eyes for a brief moment as she thought about his handsome face and how much she loved him.

"In what way, for instance?" Ruth was still very curious about this stranger.

"Well, for instance, he is an Arab Muslim who loves a Christian woman for starters. That is something his parents would not consider in their day and many Muslims today still wouldn't accept a marriage to a Christian. He also respects women and believes in equality for women. He is an advocate for people of all ranks in life to have the right to the best education possible, whether rich or poor," Sarah explained with pride.

"That does make him sound very attractive and interesting, indeed. It would be nice if more men had the same attitude toward women. I'm sure you will be very happy. I hope you will be at least and I hope you will be able to come back here for visits sometimes. I've missed you so much while you were in the States."

"Well, of course I'll do my best to come back for visits, but it is a very long journey and it won't be something I will be apt to do very often," Sarah smiled and put her arm around her friend as they headed back to join the others.

ℰℛ

There were further discussions between Sarah and her parents. Libbie sought outside advice. She wrote to a well-known missionary who replied, "I'd rather see my daughter dead than married to a Muslim." Libbie then turned to another missionary living in Baghdad to ask about the proposed marriage. The missionary replied that she had met Fadhel Jamali and that he seemed like an upright young man. This annoyed Libbie and she asked, "What kind of a missionary is that?" She had expected support for being against the marriage due to some religious aspect that she hoped the missionary could provide.

Harvey tried to remain neutral and stated that he'd rather see his daughter marry an Arab Muslim than to see her move to Hollywood.

Sarah was quoted as saying:

[21]"My parents warned me against marrying, but there were no threats or crises. My father was neutral, but my mother did everything to point out the dangers, which was nothing against her. It was quite right for a mother to do that."

It would be very natural, as Sarah pointed out, for a mother to have concerns about her daughter marrying into a different culture, in a foreign land, so very far away, to a man whom the parents had never yet had the opportunity to meet; however, it may have been compounded for Libbie by her own deep-seated regrets and the anguish she had experienced with her own separation from her parents when she was a young bride. Perhaps she felt she knew only too well what her daughter could not yet possibly know. Perhaps she needed to remind herself that although this was true, she had overcome her depression and doubts and it was the love of her husband and family that had saved her in the end. She had accepted the changes in her life and had moved on. It may not have given her much comfort at the initial time but she would have to have faith in her daughter's ability to make her own life decisions, just as she had done for herself.

---

[21] Iraqi Statesman, by Harry J. Almond

Chapter 7

Sarah returned to the United States and booked her passage on the SS Excalibur from New York to Beirut, Lebanon, where Fadhel had promised to meet her and help her arrange the last part of the journey by car across Lebanon, Syria and the desert. Back home in Canada, Sarah's parents were moving to Regina, Saskatchewan. Harvey had decided to retire when the Weyburn Security Bank was purchased by the Imperial Bank of Canada.

In September of 1932, Sarah had settled into her new accommodation she found that she was very happy teaching and making new friends. Her love for Fadhel had been sustaining and was now blossoming with each new day. Fadhel took some time to escort Sarah around the city, showing her all the highlights and taking her to art galleries, museums, and some of his favourite restaurants, introducing her to new and exciting cuisine. Baghdad, the capital city of Iraq was known as a centre for learning and tolerance. Fadhel explained that the Baghdad, also called Dar el-Salam, means "City of Peace". Sarah loved the sound of that for starters.

Sarah was truly amazed at the ancient architecture of the mosques and palaces with their columns, arches, onion-shaped domes, spires and minarets. The white stucco buildings seemed to gleam and sparkle against the contrast of the bright blue sky. Fluid molded shapes and designs made from concrete and covered with stucco, were used in decorative ways on buildings and columns. Some stucco buildings were coloured in red or blue incorporating colourful glass mosaics. Hand-painted ceramic tiles and stained glass windows added art, beauty and a kaleidoscope of dazzling, jeweled-coloured light to the inside and outside of buildings everywhere. Persian carpets gave a softness and sense of luxury under foot. Palm trees, ancient cypress trees, red junipers added a majestic frame of greenery to many buildings.

Red roses, the national flower of Iraq were prominent and added royal beauty everywhere. Mounding red yucca flowers in shades of coral and red with their sword-shaped leaves and tropical hibiscus flowers attracted humming birds and butterflies. And, of course camels! Sarah had never seen a camel other than in National Geographic magazines. She was amazed at how gentle and placid these great creatures were; unless, of course, they ever became distressed and then they could be known to spit at the object of their distress. She wondered about lions but she was told that the last lion had been killed on the south end of the Tigris River in 1918; he assured her that none had been seen in the area since then. Sarah absorbed the beauty of all the different plants and colourful birds. Sarah was feeling very enchanted by her new surroundings.

Sarah introduced herself to her new pupils by drawing a map of North America and then pin pointing where she grew up in Weyburn, Saskatchewan, Canada. She enjoyed telling her pupils a little about where she had originated. She felt life was very pleasant both at work and in her personal life. She wrote to family and friends:

"I could come and go to school and the market and shop with new friends in the *arabanas* (the carriages that served as taxis). There were quite a number of teachers from Lebanon and Jordan. People were accustomed to seeing teachers coming and going. We visited homes, we went on hikes, we went on picnics, but we could not go to hotels. Some of my teacher friends taught me Arabic. So, after a year I found I liked Baghdad."

ℰℚ

After four months, the young couple formally announced their engagement at a New Year's Eve party at the end of 1932. Fadhel had been appointed to the Ministry of Education and he was confident that they would live comfortably enough. On July 11, 1933, they were married. Harvey Powell and Elizabeth Powell did not attend but they did send out their announcement of the wedding:

Mr. and Mrs. Harvey Oliver Powell

Announce the marriage of their daughter

Sarah Hayden

To

Dr. Mohammed Fadhel Jamali

on Tuesday, July the eleventh,

nineteen hundred and thirty-three

at Baghdad, Iraq

The marriage formalities were traditional. Friends gathered at the home of their good friend, Abdl Karim al-'Uzri (who later became Minister of Finance in the Jamali government). Fadhel had a friend act as his agent and his father, Sheikh Abbas, acted on Sarah's behalf, in place of her own father, a bridesmaid or family member. His participation in the ceremony was a great gesture of kindness toward his new daughter-in-law in view of the fact that he had not been in favour of his son going to Beirut for a Western education. He, like Sarah's parents, had his own reservations about some of Fadhel's ways of thinking.

The bride and groom were asked separately by their respective agents if they agreed to marry. Each replied, "I do" and the agents announced their agreement to the guests. The celebration began with a sherbet (a sweet drink). It was a modern event with a small party of men and women dining together at the Tigris Palace Hotel.

When Fadhel went to register their marriage at the Shi'a religious court, he learned that the judge at the time would only recognize his marriage to a Christian woman as a temporary marriage; therefore, Fadhel refused to sign the documents and went to the Sunni court, which was more open minded. By doing this, he was then considered a Sunni of the Shafi'I branch. Although he signed the required document, he had this to say:

> "This registration was a formal act and had nothing to do with my religious tenets. I am a believer in universal Islam, and I respect all leaders of Muslim schools of theology. I shun denominational

quarrels and squabbles, so I cannot be called Sunni or Shi'a. I am purely and simply a Muslim."

Sarah and Fadhel began their married life together in his rented home facing west and overlooking the Tigris River on Abu Nawas Street, in the Bustan Kubba quarter, Baghdad. Sarah and Fadhel loved the beautiful sunsets and enjoyed rowing on the river. There was a park nearby their house along the riverbank where families would picnic. On summer evenings they would go up to the flat roof of the house to sit and enjoy the wide panoramic view of the river. The moon setting on the far side of the river cast a wide, rippling path of copper and purple coloured light across the water. They would carry their old hand-wound gramophone up to the roof so they could play their records of classical music. They listened to their favourite composers like: Bach, Beethoven, Brahms, Tchaikovsky, and Mozart, as well as a series called His Master's Voice; a 78 speed record with a variety of opera, big band orchestral and choral music. Sarah described it as: "A delicious enchantment of music, river, moon, and refreshing coolness that kept us spellbound till long past midnight."

Sarah was pleased with the house which was framed by Eucalyptus trees with beautiful green and purple leaves that emitted a most refreshing fragrance as you approached. Stairs with ornate, concrete, baluster railing led up from the ground level of the street to a tiled, first-floor front entrance. A second staircase led from the front landing to the roof top which was considered extra outdoor living space often used in summer. The front foyer and entrance hall was spacious and welcoming. To the right of the entrance hall were two bedrooms connected by a large living room with two very large windows offering a splendid view of the Tigris River. To the left of the entrance hall was a guest bedroom and the dining room which opened with French doors to the back-garden area. There was a library, siesta (or den) room, storeroom and kitchen across the back with a lovely view of the garden. The garden area's focal point was the tiered fountain situated in the centre of a tiled patio. Trees, bushes, and flowers made a lush, and beautifully-scented, colourful framework adding greenery and a sense of added privacy to the garden. Sarah loved to sit with Fadhel in the garden and listen to the sound of the water and the birds.

Sarah admired the great sense of taste in the decor of the home. Fadhel had put great effort into his library and his vinyl record collection of classical music. However, she felt it needed a bit more of a "woman's touch". She explored markets and bazaars alone some days and on other days Fadhel would accompany her. Again, she was experiencing something new and wonderful. The markets where open with vendors selling vegetables, meat, fish, fruits, dates, figs, raisins, nuts and spices. There were open sacks of allspice, black pepper, cardamom, garlic cloves, coriander, cumin, nutmeg, red chili peppers or paprika and dry lemon. There were barrels of olives and pickles. The vendors were cheerful and always willing to let you taste their wares. With the luxury of two rivers, the Tigris and the Euphrates, Iraqis ate fish two to three times a week. Sarah learned to prepare several recipes using fish with ancient grains like bulgur or quinoa. She was familiar with rice but she had never heard of the ancient grains before.

They found many little shops with interesting household items such as brass ornaments, urns, rugs, art and other home décor. She thought if she just bought a few new things, like a couple of Persian rugs and some pillows of her choosing, it would be enough to brighten the place and liven the rooms up a little more. Fadhel was pleased to let her do this and to allow her to put her stamp on things to make the home feel more theirs rather than just his.

Fadhel's parents had welcomed Sarah with open arms from the beginning. Abbas had a very soft spot in his heart for this young girl—in spite of the fact that she was Christian. Fadhel's mother, Alawiya took Sarah under her wing. [22]Of the seven Jamali children, only two had survived, Fadhel and his brother, Abdur Rasoul, who was born seven years after Fadhel. Although it is not known what terrible fate took the lives of the five siblings, Usameh (Sarah's son) is quoted as saying: "one could safely assume that they died in infancy. Cholera, tuberculosis, the plague, and other pandemics were ever-present around Baghdad. My father was tough enough to survive them."

Perhaps Sarah was like a daughter Alawiya always wished she could have raised. People in the community revered Alawiya as someone whose prayers were answered by God. Sadly, Alawiya grew old and infirm so Sheikh Abbas married his cousin, Bahiya, a young widow with two daughters. Alawiya passed away in 1938.

---

[22] Iraqi Statesman by Harry J. Almond – pp 7

In 1934, Fadhel received his Doctor of Philosophy in Education. Sarah and Fadhel were very busy with the first two years of their marriage. They were both busy with their careers in education.

When Libbie wrote to Sarah, she would always ask her if she was "free". There seemed to be a concern that Sarah's freedom may be in some jeopardy in some way. Sarah would constantly emphasize by replying, "I'm free as a bird!"

Chapter 8

When Fadhel and Sarah first married, he told her that he wanted six children—three girls and three boys. Of course, Fadhel had only been raised with one brother whereas Sarah had five siblings. She knew how much fun that had been to grow up with all those wonderful times together but she also knew how busy her mother had been with the task of raising her children. Sarah felt she was ready to begin a family now that she and Fadhel had been married for a couple of years. Their life together had been filled with all the new things that they were experiencing together; especially for Sarah with her teaching position, learning to speak and write Arabic, learning to cook new foods, how to run a household and making new acquaintances at work and in Fadhel's family and circle of friends. Sarah was ready to consider motherhood.

On July 5, 1935 they were blessed with a son, Laith. He was a beautiful child with light brown, naturally curly hair and was the apple of his father's eye. For Sarah it was love at first sight. In fact, it was love before sight. She loved him before he was born. She gathered baby clothes, blankets, a crib and other necessities in preparation of his birth. She would fold the clothes and then unfold them again and look at them as she waited in anticipation wondering whether she'd have a girl or a boy.

℘℃

"What are you busy with there," Fadhel came in from outside. Sarah was sitting at the kitchen table writing in a book.

"I'm making some notes in Laith's Baby Book. He said his first word today. I'm sorry you missed it. He said the word so clearly—airplane."

"Oh what a smart little fellow he is! I thought his first word might be Daddy or Mummy, but 'airplane'— how brilliant is that? Maybe our little boy will be a pilot one day when he grows up or an aeronautics engineer." Fadhel paused to look over Sarah's shoulder at the Baby Book.

"Well, it's likely because you are always holding him up and pretending he's an airplane flying around in the air," Sarah smiled up at Fadhel.

"He does love it when I do that, doesn't he?" Fadhel beamed with fatherly pride.

"Yes, and you can always make him stop crying when you do your wild Arab dance," Sarah laughed.

"You should dance with me. Come on—I'll show you how to do the 'camel trot." Fadhel started dancing in circles around the kitchen table. He made Sarah laugh out loud.

"I'd love to, my handsome prince, but I must get ready for your parents. They are coming over for supper. Your stepmother is going to teach me to make Masgouf. I got fresh carp yesterday at the market. I want to prepare some vegetables before they get here while Laith is having his nap."

Fadhel's stepmother, Bahiya, was a wonderful mother-in-law to Sarah. They got along very well and

Sarah came to rely on this woman for insight as a woman. Bahiya taught Sarah to make many of the family favourite dishes like kebabs, a dish consisting of grilled or broiled meats such as lamb, beef or chicken, on a skewer or stick. Bahiya had a wonderful talent for telling folktales. She was very animated and expressive. Sarah continued studying Arabic so she could understand the folktales which people told on many occasions. She wrote: "I was impressed by the amount of folklore to be heard on every side, and I longed to collect some of the stories before they died or were forgotten."

Sarah loved the way Fadhel took an interest in their son. One of her favourite photos was of Fadhel and his father, Abbas holding Laith—the three generations. Abbas was also very fond of his little grandson and everyone was so amazed when Laith took his first steps at age 11 months. Sarah recorded this momentous event in the Baby Book.

1936 Usameh

On September 23, 1936 Sarah gave birth to her second son, named, Usameh. He was born in Lebanon in a Quaker hospital located in the mountain town of Broumanna. At this time, Sarah added both boys to her passport at the US consulate in Beirut in case anything should happen to their father. Three days later, with Usameh in a wicker basket, they flew back to Baghdad.

Another beautiful baby boy with curly, fair coloured hair and the face of an angel, made both parents very happy. Two sons now—with four more to go, that was if Sarah was to fulfill Fadhel's wishes for six children. For now, these two little boys were quite enough for Sarah to handle. She adored her sons. They were good playmates for one another and got on reasonably well with only minor spats as siblings will have from time to time. Sarah felt they were almost like having twins. She sometimes had fun dressing them alike. She found the cutest little matching safari outfits for them and had their portrait taken at the photography studio. She would send a copy to her parents.

She had received a letter from her parents telling her that brother, Oliver, had just been selected as First Vice President of the Federal Reserve Bank in Minnesota. He was married now and he and his wife, Ada, had three children. Knox was engaged to be married soon. As Sarah read the letters from her mother telling her the latest news about her brothers and sister, it made her a little homesick.

ℬ⃝ℛ

"Fadhel, could you give me a minute to talk to you about something, please?" Sarah had just finished reading the boys a bedtime story from *The Christmas Carol*, by the author, Charles Dickens and put them to bed for the night. Fadhel put his book down.

"Certainly, what's on your mind?"

"Well, I've been thinking . . ."

"Oh my—will it cost me much?" he smiled teasingly at her.

"Yes, but I think you'll agree it is necessary. I'd like to take the boys to meet my family."

"I see. I suppose it would be best to have you go there rather than for them to come here."

"Yes, I fear that Mother's health is not so good. You know she had that gall bladder operation and she has had problems ever since it seems. She suffers a lot of joint swelling and pain so I think travel would be out of the question for them." Sarah frowned. "I want to take the boys to my sister's in Philadelphia first and then make my way to Canada."

"That seems an awful journey on your own, but you know I cannot afford to leave my position at this time."

"I know, I have thought about it. I will ask my sister to accompany me to Canada."

"Yes, I think you should make arrangements and you should contact your family to give them the good news."

Sarah was relieved that Fadhel understood about her desire to make this trip. Of course, if it had been the other way around and he had wanted to make a request to visit his family, she knew she would have understood for his sake too. That was how they were with one another.

1939 Vacation in Canada

That summer in 1939, Sarah made the long trip with the boys by bus and then by boat. It was already feeling like a wonderful vacation as she had time to entertain the boys with reading stories to them from their favourite books, helping them colour, and walking around the ship pointing to things and explaining about all the things on the ship. Sarah was more relaxed now that she was away from the day-to-day tasks of cooking, cleaning, going to market, and such things. It felt like much needed pampering to just sit on a deck chair and breathe in the sea air while she watched the boys at play. The only thing missing was Fadhel. She would have loved for him to be able to have some time to relax too. He had serious responsibilities that kept him in Iraq. That was understood; however, it didn't stop her from wishing it were otherwise. Sarah thought it best to turn her thoughts forward to more pleasant thoughts of how wonderful it would be to see her family in the United States and Canada.

ဆာလ

Lydia Powell and Edward (Eddie) Johnson had met when Lydia was attending University of Minnesota. Eddie was an Agriculture student who became good friends with Lydia's brother, Louis Powell. After Louis and Eddie graduated, they went on a tour of Europe together. Eddie had tried to pursue a career in forestry after getting his degree. However, he developed an allergy to trees so he abandoned this for a desk job with General Electric. During the Great Depression, he had been laid off from this position. During World War II, General Electric scaled down their workers and supplied the United States military with executives and equipment manufacturing. Eddie decided to open his own laundry business, called Eddie's Economy Laundry. When the war ended, General Electric, went back to manufacturing and selling household appliances. There was a postwar boom that required more jobs for men returning from the war. Eddie was once more hired by General Electric. But at this point, in 1939, he was self-employed at his laundry service.

Lydia had studied Chemistry and Medical Technology. After graduating, Lydia worked at the University of Pennsylvania as a Medical Technician. Once she began having her family, she left the work force. She later took further training to do Electrocardiogram testing and returned to the work force when her children were older. Eventually, Lydia and Eddie had two daughters (Gladys and Karen) but at this time, in 1939, they only had the one little son, Harvey Oliver Johnson, born in 1937 and named after Lydia and Sarah's father, Harvey Powell. Sadly, their first son, Bruce Lanier Johnson, born in 1933, had passed away from crib death on January 3, 1934 before turning six months old. Having another baby boy to care for was something the couple both needed. Sarah knew her visit would also bring cheer to Lydia. They would both be thrilled to meet one another's children.

Lydia and Eddie had some wonderful things lined up to entertain Sarah and her boys. They had arrived in the United States just in time to attend the Fourth of July celebrations at the Liberty Bell in Philadelphia. They had a grand time hearing the bands play. Laith and Usameh waved little flags and ran gleefully after the candies being tossed from the parade floats. When they returned to Lydia and Eddie's place in the suburbs, they all dressed up in Arab costumes to take part in the local parade. Sarah was almost giddy with girlish excitement to be with her sister. She realized now more than ever that she had been missing her family. It was almost as if being with them now was like a tonic to her soul. The sisters would sit up late some nights after the children were nestled in their beds and talk and talk. They had so many things in common to talk about now that they were both grown women with husbands and sons. Eddie let them have their time together and would offer to give the boys a bath before bed or read them their bedtime stories. He knew this time was just as good for Lydia as it was for Sarah.

Sarah bought a second-hand car. Eddie helped her pick it out. It was a 1936, grey, Chevrolet and it was in excellent condition. He made sure the tires were good and he had the mechanics give it an oil change. The women packed sandwiches, cold chicken, cookies and hot and cold thermoses to have snacks along the way. Then they loaded up the little boys and headed across the continent to visit their brothers living in Minnesota. Oliver's wife, Ada, organized a family gathering at their home in Hennepin County, Minnesota. Oliver had been selected to be First Vice President of the Federal Reserve Bank in Minneapolis. He was a lecturer at the Graduate School of Banking at Rutgers University. He and Ada now had three children, Ellen, Richard and Robert.

The Powell family had two reasons to celebrate: their sibling's reunion with everyone's children and Knox's recent wedding. He had just married Elizabeth Annette "Beth" (nee: Polley) Hacking in May 1939. Beth had a teen-aged son, Earl Leslie Hacking Jr. The day was memorable for everyone and Ada had even made arrangements for a photographer to take several family photos in the back yard. A photo was taken of the six Powell siblings to commemorate the first time in a long time when they were all in one place at the same time. It was a perfect day with all four brothers and their wives and children.

Sarah's brother, Louis and his wife, Virginia Wetherbee, by now had two children; Louis Harvey Jr. and Mary Elizabeth "Betsy". The couple had met while attending university. Louis had attended an event at the Cosmopolitan Club where he heard Virginia play the organ. She majored in classical music at the university. Louis (while travelling with his pal and future brother-in-law, Eddie Johnson) had spent time in Africa in the bush country of northern Rhodesia before his marriage, working with a British copper surveying corporation. He brought many photographs of his trip and even some excellent charcoal drawings he had drawn of zebra, antelope and other wildlife. He gave the drawing of the antelope to his mother and father and Libbie displayed it on her living room wall ever after. Louis also wrote a series of short stories about his time in Africa, called Mojambe. He brought copies which he distributed to his family. Everybody was impressed with his creative talents. He had achieved his degree in civil engineering and a PhD in Paleontology and was the Director of the Saint Paul Science Museum in Minnesota.

Lyman and his wife, Catherine, had one little girl, Arlene. Lyman had received his Bachelor and Master degrees at the University of Minnesota and was now a Bank Examiner. Catherine, who was a Canadian, had grown up in Regina, Saskatchewan and became a registered nurse. Lyman's career in banking had taken him from Minneapolis to Los Angeles, California and eventually to Canada. They had been living in Regina since their marriage in 1933, but had recently moved to Minneapolis. For Lyman it was a move he welcomed to be reunited with all his brothers; for Catherine, a Canadian, it was a change that was still quite new. Lyman was well read and took his Christian faith very seriously.

After spending a few days with family, Lydia and Sarah drove northwest from Minnesota, through North Dakota to Canada. Harvey and Libbie, were now residing in Regina, Saskatchewan. The trip seemed to pass fairly quickly as the boys would fall asleep in the back seat. It was hot so they had the windows rolled down and they had to talk above the roar of the wind gushing through the vehicle. When they stopped for gasoline, they were relieved to have an attendant wash and squeegee the windshield to clean away the dead grasshoppers. They agreed that as much as the prairies had good memories for them, grasshoppers were not one of those. The sisters would chat about everything from fashions, to recipes, to child rearing, to the grand time they'd had with their brothers and sisters-in-law, and even to personal things that only sisters would share about their marriages and their happiness.

ℂℂℂ

The time with Harvey and Libbie was a wonderful reunion. After all the late nights, long talks and hectic fun time spent with their brothers, Lydia and Sarah were quite content to have a little more subdued time with their parents. Lydia and Sarah kept the children entertained and playing outdoors so Libbie could rest inside. She suffered a great deal with lame shoulders and sore joints in her hands. She loved to hold her grandsons on her lap and read to them but she was reluctant to try to lift them. She was relying on the use of a cane more these days. After the three boys were laid down for their nap, the adults had tea and chatted.

Sarah could see the changes in her parents since she had last seen them. They still seemed to be in reasonably good spirits in spite of Libbie's frequent ailments. Libbie's ankles were swollen and she moved much slower. Her hair was not completely grey but rather a salt and pepper version. Harvey's hair was almost completely white now—a beautiful silver white that made him look even more distinguished. He always had such a great head of hair, Sarah thought. Sarah and her siblings were concerned about Harvey. He had trouble from time to time with heart spasms from angina. Their worries were valid and were telling of things to come.

Their visit made the social column of the Regina Leader Post, dated July 24, 1939. The paper reported how fascinated the brothers (Laith 4; Usameh 3) were with real working tractors. The paper also reported that Laith had a pet gazelle at home, that he was coaxing his parents to get him a mongoose, and that seeing the fireflies in the eastern states, swimming in lakes, riding street cars and going up elevators had delighted the lads. Libbie invited Sarah's best friend, Ruth Leroux to come for lunch one afternoon. Ruth was now Mrs. Hartnett and was living in Regina. Ruth looked quite radiant, Sarah observed. She had smooth olive coloured complexion, beautiful thick curly black hair and dark brown eyes—a beauty passed down from her French descent, most likely. Her smile gleamed white against her full ruby lips.

They spent a lovely afternoon reminiscing with one another about the "good old days" in the neighbourhood. Libbie smiled and nodded and Harvey laughed as the girls told stories of things that they had done together. Some things Harvey and Libbie were hearing for the first time!

"Remember that time that you wanted to learn to drive a car, Lydia?" Sarah started to giggle.

"Oh—do I?! Yes, indeed. I talked Lyman into taking me out into the country one day to teach me. The only problem was, I hadn't asked for permission to take Father's car! I didn't tell Lyman and when he found out, he was fit to be tied with me. He fretted that we wouldn't get the car back before Father noticed it was gone. He made me help him wash the car off so Father wouldn't see all the dust on it from the dirt roads," Lydia chuckled.

"Was that my model A Ford?" Harvey asked.

"Yes, and before he would let me try to drive it, he made me change a tire! I was only about twelve at the time," laughter Lydia.

"Well, maybe I'll send you to your room now," teased Harvey.

"It's a few years too late now Father but I would likely have had worse punishment than that if you'd have known at the time. Sarah, you are naughty for telling on me!"

"Maybe this is a good time for me to change the subject to save you from having to confess to any more of our shortcomings," laughed Ruth. "I have some news that I was going to write to you about but when I heard you were coming to Canada to visit, I decided to wait to tell you in person."

"Ruth, don't keep us in suspense! Are you going to have a baby?" Sarah was hopeful. She thought it would

100

be wonderful news if Ruth was expecting a first child. She had been married for a few years already. It seems often that when one woman starts her family, she wants all her friends to join in to share the great experience—or maybe, to share the misery at times when motherhood becomes somewhat trying.

"No, it would be nice, but that's not it," Ruth paused to give effect to the moment. Everyone stopped and waited for her to go on.

"We're moving to the United States! My husband had an offer he couldn't refuse to work as Head of Medicine at the university hospital. We'll be going there in a couple of weeks to find a place to live. I might be your neighbour, Lydia!"

"Oh—what a great surprise this is, Ruth!" Lydia jumped up and gave Ruth a hug.

"I know; I couldn't wait to tell you all. I'm going to open up a shop there as well. There is a little candle and gift shop for sale and we've decided it will be an excellent way for me to meet people in the community. I don't have any children so I need something to get me out of the house. I'm so excited about it all. Of course, my parents aren't too thrilled. I can understand it. They will miss having us here but my twin brother and his wife and children are all here so they won't be too lonely."

"We're happy for you, of course, Ruth, but I can relate to the emotions of your mother. No matter how many children we have, if one is missing, we never quit missing them," Libbie made her point as she began setting the picnic table. Sarah looked at Lydia and they both jumped up to help Libbie.

Harvey started telling Ruth one of his funny stories. He was a great conversationalist and Ruth loved to listen to him talk. They shared stories about the depression and how they had survived the Dirty Thirties.

"It certainly hasn't been pleasant but they say adversity is good for the soul. The 'dose' has been rather severe and we hope our souls have been well strengthened!" Harvey chuckled.

"Yes, indeed!" Ruth agreed.

"I know Father won't tell you this, Ruth, but I will. There have been times during this depression that he has given his salary to certain employees rather than laying them off." Sarah was proud of her father's kindness to others and she knew he was too modest to tell anyone of his generosity.

"Oh Sarah, there's no need to talk about that. I'm sure if it were the other way around, those people would do the same for someone else." Harvey tried to change the subject with another one of his jokes and then Libbie announced lunch was ready.

Libbie had prepared a tasty lunch of cold, fried chicken, Waldorf salad, devilled eggs, and potato salad served with refreshing lemonade. There was carrot cake and watermelon for dessert. They ate outside in the back yard. Libbie had borrowed two baby high-chairs for Usameh and Harvey. Laith was a "big boy" and could sit up to the picnic table. He had a great time running around in the back yard. Libbie had made a dish of soapy water for him to blow bubbles through a ring into the air. Little Harvey Jr. and Usameh laughed as they watched Laith run after the bubbles and try to catch them and make them burst. Libbie snapped a photo to capture the day to be long remembered in years to come. Little did anyone know what shocking sorrow lay ahead in the near future.

୨୦(ଓ

"Mother, how did you ever manage with six of us? I am nearly exhausted after a day of running after these two boys," Sarah heaved a sigh as she let herself fall back into the comfort of the sofa and kicked off her sandals after saying her good-byes to Ruth. [23]The boys were down for a nap. Sarah had read a chapter from *Moby Dick*, by Herman Melville. She had bought the book before their voyage and the boys were now all about boats, ships and the sea. Harvey was puttering in the back yard tidying things up and putting the lawn sprinklers on. The house was quiet. Lydia brought iced tea and a platter of fruit in for their afternoon snack. This was a time to relax and have a chat with their mother.

"We did have our struggles from time to time. I am glad now that I did have some time as a young woman to experience life on my own," Libbie took a sip of her iced tea.

"I remember," she continued, "a friend once told me that she remembered me saying that after I had Knox, that this baby would be my only one. I never remember feeling cross when a new baby was coming. Your father

---

[23] Quote from Usameh Jamali to the author, Jan Keating: "Sarah would take advantage of the obligatory rest periods to read us novels of Scott, Dickens, Melville and others. I owe much to this practice." (Email message, dated July 21, 2020).

and I were alone as far as developing them was concerned, so I made it my duty to be a mental and spiritual mother as well as physical. This was my greatest work and my career."

"You certainly have done an admirable job of it Mother. I mean, just look at how wonderful we turned out!" both girls broke into laughter.

"But seriously Mother, do you ever have any regrets about giving up your profession to raise us?" Lydia asked as she passed the fruit to her mother and Sarah.

"I think there are always some little regrets about things that could have been handled differently, perhaps, but they all fade into insignificance. But. . ." she tilted her head to one side and paused. "I do feel the loss was to you, Lydia in a sense."

"How so?" Lydia asked.

"I feel that just after you came along, I began the missionary work with the call to organize our own and other societies. I think you would have been much further along if I had poured my own mental life into you as much as I did with the other children."

"Oh, Mother, I don't hold that against you at all. I do remember feeling sorry for myself at times when you had to go out to one of your church or temperance meetings but I soon got over it and one of the boys would get me interested in a game or a story while you were out. Sometimes one of them would make us a bowl of popcorn and I'd soon be having a grand time. Please do not have regrets on my account for anything. I have happy memories of growing up in Weyburn. I had friends, church and school activities and lots of good times."

"Thank you Dear. I'm glad to hear that. I am so thankful for all my children and I am thankful that the Lord blessed me with two lovely daughters. I'm so happy to have this time with you girls. It seems we so infrequently had time together just us women. I must say, I am wondering how you are doing Sarah. Your letters always indicate that you are totally free to come and go as you please—how was it you put it?—you were 'free as a bird', I think was how you put it. I hope you feel content with your life over in Iraq," Libbie just had to ask when she could see her daughter face-to-face. This would be a chance to really judge for herself. Letters were one thing but now she could judge for herself by how her daughter responded.

"Mother, I can't tell you enough how **free I am**," Sarah emphasized the words.

"Fadhel's family and friends are so lovely to me and to the boys. I have many friends from contacts of Fadhel's and some from when I was teaching. I am not restricted from making my own decisions. Some things we decide together and some things I am in control of for myself. However, if I am honest with you, I will admit that having the boys a year apart has been rather taxing. However, they are getting older and soon they'll both be in school. Laith will start Kindergarten when we get back this fall. It is hard to believe how fast they are growing up on me." Sarah smiled and sipped her iced tea.

"Well, I hope you both have freedom in your marriages. I don't believe that men have the right to take all their enjoyment from the bodies of us women and leave us to drudge in the home with never a peek into the social world with our husbands."

Libbie surprised Sarah and Lydia with this statement. Perhaps Libbie was remembering how stressed she had felt at times when she had all the children and was not getting out socially; except for the times she took her leave and went back East to spend time with old friends and family. Or, could she just be giving insight into her life to warn her daughters not to go down the same path without paying attention to their own needs from time to time?

"I know what you mean about the drudgery in the home, Mother. It can become boring and tedious and no one ever notices much of what a woman does in a day. As you know, in your day women didn't have careers after marriage. It just wasn't acceptable, it seems. I think that is changing in our generation. There are more women who look after a home and family but are also working outside the home. It all stems back to WWI, I think. Men had to go fight and women were forced to take jobs that were normally done by men."

"That's so true, Sarah. I sometimes wonder about that but then I think—not for me while I'm raising my son. I want to spend every moment of motherhood that I can with Harvey." Lydia stopped smiling and her eyes dropped for a moment. Sarah felt a sudden pain for her sister's loss of Bruce. Of course she understood Lydia's feelings wanting to be with her young son.

"Yes, there's nothing wrong with that Lydia. I think we all enjoy time with our children and I'm not saying working outside the home is for everyone. I know you may not want to work but you do like being involved in your church. So, I think we all find some interests that are set apart from spending every moment at home," Sarah paused.

"I'm not exactly staying home every day. I help Eddie at the laundry business. I used to go there to clean and now Eddie does all that so I can be at home. I do the books though. Of course that doesn't get me out in the community. I plan to go back to take some training to learn to do Electrocardiograms and some other updates. I will eventually go back into the medical field that I've trained in. For now, I have a hobby that keeps me well entertained."

"Oh, tell us about it," Sarah smiled.

"I'm making puppets. I've joined a puppeteer club, called Quaker Village Puppeteers, and we put on puppet shows in the community. I've learned to make marionettes, hand puppets and humanettes."

"Humanettes?" Libbie asked. "I'm sorry—I'm not sure what those are like."

"They're quite amusing. You make part of a puppet and then the puppeteer uses part of their own body incorporated into the puppet. For instance, maybe the arms and head will be the puppeteer's or maybe just the legs. They can create quite the comedic performance."

"So, in some respects, your life is similar to mine. I found social causes to occupy my mind apart from family life and you have found something creative with your puppets and the club offers you some social outlet apart from your family," reasoned Libbie.

"Mother, I loved that you were always home for us when we got home from school. I'm also glad you had the opportunity to do some of your other activities and attend your meetings. I think those things were very stimulating for you. You were an intellect and you probably needed things apart from us and Father. I can relate to that and I am seriously considering going back to teaching." Sarah hadn't intended to say that out loud. Until now, it had just been an inner thought of hers but now—there it was.

Libbie decided to open up and share what she had on her mind for many years but had never discussed up to this point. However, her daughters were grown women now with children and husbands. She knew that she may not see them again for a very long while, if ever. She was not going to hold back her honest thoughts now. The discussion was already going this direction so she continued.

[24]"If men would be less selfish and give their wives a bit of freedom to do the things that would relieve the monotony of home—and not demand too much from them in the way of their own physical wants—I believe women could develop themselves right in their own homes. As we are equal in right, it may be that some women will be the ones to have careers; but the largest career I know will always be for women, is the development of themselves through the sacrificial life as wife and mother."

---

[24] Quoted from Elizabeth "Libbie" Powell's memoirs – contributed from her granddaughter, Mary Elizabeth "Betsy" Powell Polglase

Sarah and Lydia exchanged wide-eyed looks at hearing their mother discuss men's physical wants. They knew they didn't dare look at one another too long for fear of getting the giggles. They knew this was straight from their mother's heart and they loved her dearly. They did appreciate her being so candid with them and having a woman-to-woman discussion. It was just not something they had ever heard her make a reference to before.

"Your father and Oliver do not at all approve of a young woman for a wife who is devoted to a career and who finds homemaking dull and distasteful. I know women who brace up and do it well, but these days the risk is great. A child garden is the most exacting of all, and the weeds do grow unmercifully at best and need constant care." Libbie rested her hands in her lap as if to let her body come to rest and be at peace. She was finished what she felt she needed to say to her daughters. The truth was out. She had never spoken her heart so earnestly with anyone else. She wanted her daughters to be willing to sacrifice as she had done to ensure that family came first above all else.

However, there was evidence from her words that was telling of how she must have had deep feelings at times that she did not feel appreciated for much more than her body and her homemaking skills. She fully understood the want and need to fulfill one's own desire to achieve and make a mark in the world, to be heard, to be admired, to be valued beyond being a homemaker and mother. But with her last breath, she would defend putting family first. Giving up something she had wanted as a younger woman had taught her about herself and for this she had no regrets. It had made her stronger.

Unfortunately, their wonderful summer vacation came to an early end in 1939 with the outbreak of World War II, and the sinking of the SS Athena, a boat trying to carry British children to safety in the USA. Sarah had the grey Chevy car shipped to Baghdad and began the journey back home. She and the boys boarded the SS Excalibur and began the long trip home for fear that the Mediterranean would soon be closed to neutral shipping. The ship that preceded them was torpedoed which gave Fadhel great anxiety as he awaited them in Beirut.

Chapter 9

Sarah had given up her teaching position when she and Fadhel started their family; now she wanted to return to her profession. She began to feel the need to use her mind again for more than just being a housewife and mother. She loved being a wife and mother but she felt it was time to get back to work. She thought a great deal about her mother's words and she didn't take it lightly. But her mother was from a different generation. And, from her own mother's lips, she had said that Harvey would not have tolerated a young wife insisting on being a career woman. Her mother had use the word "sacrifice" in terms of being willing to make a life commitment to doing for others. Sarah understood and loved her mother for this but she still felt that a woman of today's generation need not sacrifice her whole self for an entire lifetime. She believed that there could be balance in life between home and career.

Well, that was her parents; she was not married to a man like her father. She loved her father beyond words but Fadhel was a totally different man. He wanted her to be happy and they had had many conversations about this before they even married. She knew Fadhel would be supportive as long as the home and the children were looked after. He had always advocated strongly for women's rights and applauded those who sought furthering themselves through education and careers. Maybe the trip back home had helped to energize her and to convince her to move forward. She hired a cook and a nanny to take care of the house and the children and a driver to transport Fadhel. The one time he had tried to drive the car, he put his foot to the accelerator instead of the break and put the car in the ditch so a driver was hired. Sarah could drive when alone. She's had plenty of driving experience.

In the spring of 1940, Usameh became very ill with sore throat and fever. He became so ill that a doctor was called and the diagnosis was given as measles. Not surprisingly, Laith soon fell ill as well. Sarah thought he must be getting measles as well and she had them both in bed. Usually, Laith would seem to take illnesses harder than Usameh. Sarah expected Usameh to recover but after ten consecutive days he was still running a low-grade fever and was complaining, "Mamma, I can't breathe, I can't breathe." His voice was gone all but for a whisper. Sarah consulted the doctor again but she told Sarah that it was just the effects of the measles.

Fadhel was not satisfied with the diagnosis and wanted to call a throat specialist. Sarah recalled: "We had quite an argument about the matter because I wanted to follow my western ways and rely wholly on the doctor in charge. My husband, accustomed to local ways, wanted to call in several doctors to get different opinions."

Fortunately, Sarah gave in to Fadhel and a throat specialist diagnosed the child with diphtheria and administered a dose of an anti-toxin. Almost at once, there was a change for the better. Fadhel was still not satisfied and called a third doctor. This doctor, named Sa'eed Dajani, said the case was critical and telephoned the Royal Hospital to arrange for an emergency operation.

The driver immediately drove them to the hospital and Sarah was allowed to lay Usameh on the operating table. As she did this, she noticed Usameh seemed to be breathing much better. She was hesitant to interfere but felt she needed to speak on behalf of her child. She spoke up.

"Doctor, don't you think Usameh's breathing is a little easier now? Do you think it would be possible to postpone the operation just a little while to make sure?"

"Yes, we can wait awhile and see. I will remain in the hospital in case there is a crisis." Sarah was relieved for this doctor's patient and kind attitude. She took Usameh from the operation room to a bed in the next room and she stayed with him all night with her face close to his because he could not speak above a whisper. The kind doctor spent the whole night in a chair in the waiting room, but no crisis came. If it were not for this devoted mother's love for her child, he may not have fared as well through the night. Sarah's vigilance, staying close by Usameh's side, giving her mother's love and support to the little boy must surely have been calming and reassuring for him. Sarah was thankful to this doctor for his kindness and consideration that saved Usameh from a needless operation.

Feeling uplifted, Sarah and Usameh returned home only to find her husband and the servants in a panic. Laith was calling for her and she took one look at him and said, "Diphtheria." Throat swabs taken from Laith and Sarah both proved positive for diphtheria. Sarah felt she had most likely contracted the disease while hovering over Usameh all night. Anti-toxin was prescribed for Laith and a prophylactic dose was suggested for Sarah but she refused to take it when she learned that she may suffer a severe reaction to the injection. She decided that she needed to be able to nurse the children and couldn't risk having a reaction to the drug. Fortunately, the next time a swab was taken, Sarah tested negative and was not contaminated.

There was no hope to hire a private nurse as there weren't enough trained nurses to work in the hospitals so Sarah had to take an indefinite leave from her teaching position and stay home. Fadhel's father, Sheikh Abbas, was a great support to Sarah at this time. He came every day in his flowing robe, white beard and turban to sit with the boys and pray for them. His presence was much appreciated by all.

Sarah wondered how the boys could have contracted this deadly disease. There were no cases in their school or in their neighbourhood. Because of measles going around, Sarah had kept them from playing with other children. Years later she learned that the first doctor she had tending to the boys had been treating a case of diphtheria. Could this doctor have brought the dreaded disease into their home?

Laith began refusing his chicken broth and milk saying that the milk was green and other odd things like "put me in my bed", when he was already in his bed. His temperature dropped to 35° Centigrade. Sarah called the first doctor and she prescribed brandy. It was delivered to the house by special messenger. Sarah poured it into the spoon and stood by Laith's bed but couldn't bring herself to administer it. She had been brought up by Libbie to believe that alcohol is unnecessary as a medicine.

114

A friend, Dorothy Litten, who was the matron nurse at the Children's Hospital dropped by to check on Sarah and the children. Sarah was quick to relate Laith's strange behaviour and low temperature. Dorothy looked at the child and said she felt he was nearing unconsciousness. She asked what the doctor had said. Sarah told her about the brandy, explaining why she hadn't administered it. She asked if Dorothy thought she should have. Dorothy said she had also grown up in a temperance home but assured Sarah that hospitals often used brandy in cases of pneumonia.

Sarah, near tears said, "Dorothy, he doesn't smile anymore." Laith had such a wonderful smile and had been such a happy little boy. Dorothy could tell Sarah was near having a breakdown.

"How would you like me to stay with you tonight? I have to go back to the hospital now, and I have to have my supper there, but I could come back before long and stay with Laith so you could get some rest."

"That would be wonderful. I've nursed fevers before, but never anything like this. I really don't know what to do."

"You'd better put a sweater on him and an extra blanket. Do you have a hot water bottle? You've got to get that temperature up. Try giving him hot chicken broth. And if you do decide to give him a little brandy, mix it with water and sugar or you'll burn his stomach."

When Fadhel came home, Sarah explained the day to him. He was so concerned that he called in a fourth doctor who said he doubted that the condition was diphtheria. He asked to be allowed to call in a fifth doctor to consult further with. The fifth doctor made a brief examination and then said, "I think this is a case of encephalitis. Notice the rigidity of the neck and the eyes fixed and staring, indicating pressure on the brain. I saw 2000 cases like this in Vienna in 1918 following the epidemic of Spanish influenza."

"What is encephalitis?" Sarah asked.

"Many things about it are still a mystery. We know it is one of the very rare complications of measles, but I hope we can cure it." He then made a lumbar puncture to relieve the pressure on the brain. He instructed Sarah to take Laith's temperature again.

Meanwhile the two doctors stepped out into the hall and Fadhel spoke with them. He asked if Sarah should have listened to the first doctor and administered the alcohol. The doctors explained that alcohol goes unchanged into the blood stream and then to the brain. It penetrates the brain tissues, making them inactive and causing congestion.

"With this disease, it would be very bad to have that reaction," the doctor explained.

"So you think brandy would not have saved him?" Fadhel asked.

"No, in his case, it might have harmed him."

Laith's temperature had come up to 35.5°C. The doctor advised Sarah to put Laith in a dark, quiet room by himself and to feed him liquid nourishment from a spoon. He warned her to be very careful that the child must swallow properly to avoid choking.

"Is the disease contagious?" Sarah asked. The doctor told her there was no possibility of anyone else in the house contracting this disease.

When Dorothy came back, Sarah was happy to report Laith's temperature had come back up to 36°C.

"See that's the brandy!" exclaimed Dorothy.

"I didn't give him the brandy. I think it was due to your good advice," Sarah smiled. It was a relief at the end of the day and now she could finally have some rest now that her good friend was there to take charge.

ഇറ

There is a saying that things happen in threes—this is what happened when suddenly poor Fadhel became ill as well. Sarah, following doctor's orders, had placed Laith in the back bedroom that had the least amount of daylight. She had left Usameh in the front bedroom normally shared by the two boys and she had the third bedroom. Fadhel had been sleeping on a day bed in the living room. A sixth doctor, and a personal friend who had come to see the family, diagnosed Fadhel with an advanced case of diphtheria requiring immediate treatment. Sarah was nursing three patients now.

The good news was that when lab results came back they showed that Fadhel tested negative and, therefore, he did not have diphtheria after all. The bad news was that the injection that had been administered was causing terrible joint pain. It took two people to move him and it became evident that he would now need round-the-clock care. An ambulance was called and he was carried out of the house weeping. He had a terrible fear of hospitals and cried out to Sarah, "You are sending me away to die!" Sarah had little energy left to worry about her husband and as it turned out, Fadhel got wonderful care and after 11 days, he had come to love hospital care. After that, any time he became ill with so much as a heavy cold, he would ask Sarah, "Don't you think that I should go to the hospital?"

Shock sets in

A visiting matron nurse, employed by the Ministry of Education as the matron of a boarding school, had been sent to give some nursing relief to Sarah when Fadhel had become seriously ill. She had brought her nursing manual with her and so Sarah picked it up and looked up encephalitis. A short passage described it as a viral disease of the spine and brain which causes brain damage.

Her first thought was, *"Why didn't the doctor tell me this?"* However, on second thought sometime later, she realized that it was likely wise that he hadn't told her because she was so exhausted from nursing everyone and was, admittedly, depressed. If the doctor had given her the full truth at that time, she may have had a serious break down.

She had asked how long to expect Laith to be ill with the encephalitis. She had been told two weeks. Sarah thought she could manage two more weeks. The hidden truth was that Laith would remain in a comma for three weeks, keep to his bed for three months, and need special care for the rest of his life.

ଛୀଔ

There was no medicine for encephalitis but a medicine to kill germs in the spinal fluid was prescribed and given to Laith by injections. Also, glucose injections were given to absorb excess fluid surrounding the brain to relieve pressure. Encephalitis causes inflammation on the brain, bruising it and causing death of brain cells in a certain area. A third treatment given was injections of mother's blood once every three days. A few milliliters of Sarah's blood was taken from her vein and injected into Laith's buttock. This continued for months and would continue as long as there was a visible improvement seen. The improvement detected was that once Laith became conscious, he had quicker and more varied reactions in his movements and words on the day he received an injection of his mother's blood.

Sarah received some backup from two wonderful nurses; one was a young Lebanese nurse who taught Hygiene and Child Care in a government secondary school for girls. This nurse came for a month to cover night duty so Sarah could sleep. The other was her good friend, Dorothy Litten, who came for a few hours on Sundays so Sarah could go for a walk. She later reported, "Their help was a great encouragement and comfort for me."

Advice from a Mother

Now that Sarah was beginning to understand that Laith would be permanently brain damaged, she began to question whether it would have been better if God had just taken him. She knew that life for him would never be what she and Fadhel had dreamed possible. He would be mentally challenged for the rest of his life. She tormented herself by questioning whether it would have been better if she had taken him to the hospital. One nurse had brusquely advised it. Perhaps if she had, he may have died and she would not have had to witness his death. However, if that had happened, she would surely have blamed herself for his death and would have felt responsible for abandoning him. Over and over it tumbled around in her mind but the answer always came down to knowing, that as Laith's mother, she had to stand between him and death.

Of course Sarah had notified her parents and her siblings about Laith's and Usameh's illnesses and how Laith was ultimately afflicted; whereas, Usameh had recovered. But now, Sarah felt it was time to speak with her mother to let her know the full extent of the seriousness of things. It was a conversation she was dreading for several reasons. Of course, no one wants to deliver upsetting news to grandparents about the children. Sarah had always tried in her correspondence to spare her parents the full details of the situation. After all, what good could it possibly do to have aging folks put into a depression over a sick child for whom they could do nothing?

But it was even more than this. It was also that nagging thought that kept raising its ugly head over and over. The warning words from her mother that were spoken at the time of Sarah's engagement to Fadhel. Would her mother say something like, "Didn't I warn you that there would be problems and now here you are living so far away that I cannot be of any help to you." Sarah knew if her mother took this path, it would be a devastation that she would not bare easily.

"Hello, Mother, it's Sarah calling. How are you?"

"Oh Sarah, it's so lovely to hear your voice! Is everything alright?" It was so like Libbie to be able to almost read Sarah's mind before the conversation had even started. But because they usually wrote letters, perhaps the telephone call set off an alarm in Libbie's psyche. Or, maybe it was just another case of 'mother's intuition'; Libbie seemed to have a lot of that!

"We're doing alright but progress with Laith is still very slow and we're not sure how much brain damage he has incurred yet. He's struggling, Mother, and he's really starting over like a baby. I . . . well, I . . ." Sarah began to lose her composure and fought to hold back the tears. She cleared her voice and started again, "We've been told that the damage is permanent."

"Oh, Dear, I'm so sorry. Is there any hope of progress over time?"

"Well, we hope so. We are being encouraged by medical people to give it time and to work on things but to not have too great of expectations for now. For now, it is a case of survival and recovery."

121

"Sarah, hang on to your faith. The Lord moves in mysterious ways. He always has a plan for every human being. I don't mean that He planned for Laith to become ill but he may have a plan for you and Laith that you cannot understand or see right now. You are doing your best, Dear, and you are doing the right thing to just get him back to better physical health at this point."

"I think you are right, Mother, but I cannot help having so many questions about it all. It drives me to distraction and I feel so helpless right now."

"You are not helpless. You are never alone. Remember that. And do not let this event in your life make you bitter against God, Dear. In time, His message to you will come through. For now, you just have to put your trust in Him that He will show you the way. Take it one day at a time and keep doing what you are doing. Concentrate on the little things for now. Get as much outside help as you can and take good care of yourself so you can spend time teaching Laith things day by day. Focus on the moments and let God worry about the bigger picture."

"Thank you Mother. I know you are right and it's good to hear your voice. I just had to call. I didn't want to write to you about things. Today I just needed to hear your voice."

"Of course, sweetheart—that's what mother's are for. I'm here and if we can't be together in the flesh, we are always together in the spirit. When you are weary, as I am sure you must be these days, take it to the Lord in prayer. He listens. He's ever present and some burdens are just too heavy for us mortals. If you turn it over to

Him, I promise He will lift you. There is power in prayer and I will keep you all in my prayers. I will talk to my prayer group at church and ask them to join with me in special prayers for Laith, and for you as well."

"I would appreciate that Mother. I have been praying and others here have also given support and prayers. Fadhel's father, Abbas, has been keeping vigil and praying daily. Of course Fadhel reads the Quran daily and he prays earnestly. Although I don't read the Quran, I do pray in earnest as much as Fadhel."

"That brings to mind another thing I will leave you with before we end our chat. Try to be thankful for the blessings in each day. When I feel down, I make a mental list of all the blessings. You can start with the one that God has given you a strong life partner in Fadhel. He is a loving husband and a very good father. You have his family there and they are loving and supportive. Praise the Lord for these great blessings!"

"I know. I will try to look on the bright side and be thankful for something each day."

"Yes, it can be one simple thing. It might be simply the blue sky or the still of a starry, moonlit night— or a smile from your little boys, a hug from someone who is kind. And also, try to find the good in this because I truly believe that there is something good to be found in every situation. It may not be apparent now, but it will come to you in time. Just remember—no experience is a total loss."

They ended their conversation with the strongest love between mother and daughter that anyone could expect. Sarah was moved to tears when she hung up the

123

phone but they were tears of love and thanks. Her mother had not said one word that she had dreaded might be spoken of the warning given years ago. Why had Sarah doubted for a moment that her mother would be anything but loving and supportive? This conversation had lifted her and she would carry on with a mission to take things as they came and to do what she possibly could for Laith and leave the bigger issues in God's hands. Maybe her mother was right. Maybe there was something good that could come from this.

Baby Steps & Recovery

Feeding Laith was a slow process while Laith was still in the comatose state. Sarah had devised a way of wedging a tablespoon between his teeth and, using it as a funnel, she would pour a teaspoon of liquid into his mouth and wait for him to swallow. This took an hour to complete a feeding and he was to be fed like this every three hours. By the third week, he began to regain consciousness and no longer had starring eyes, which was a sign of pressure on the brain.

Laith was once again in his infantile development. The sucking reflex appeared; if one put a finger to his lips, he would suck at it. A smile reflex could be simulated by a touch to his chin. Later came the reflex of grasping with hands and feet. Soon his hearing returned and he would turn to respond to the faintest sound. Later a true smile and a laugh developed. One of the doctors made an assessment one day and declared, "Now he is human." Sarah was shocked by this comment because she had never thought of her son as other than human.

As speech slowly returned, Laith developed a rather curious habit of repeating a line from a book he remembered called, *Tim and the Brave Sea Captain* by Ardizzone. He would repeat the words, "No, I am not too bad for a stowaway." The problem was, he couldn't stop once he started unless he heard the sound of another human voice. Sarah learned that if she spoke to him, he would calm down. So, she recited the stories and nursery rhymes from memory from Mother Goose.

Getting Laith to his feet was also a slow process that had to be taken in stages of raising his head a little at a time by lifting his head by placing a hand under his pillow. At first he would turn very pale. Each day this was done a little more until he was almost able to sit upright. Next when he could sit upright, Sarah held him on the edge of the bed with his legs dangling over the edge. Finally, he was able to stand and took steps hanging onto Sarah's hands.

At first his speech was jumbled and he would parrot anything that someone said to him but, eventually, he spoke English or Arabic and could make sense; the only problem was—he talked very loud and he spoke to anyone about anything and everything. Laith even managed to recover his verbal ability to a level of his own form of jokes. One day while listening to a religious service on the radio, he asked, "What are they singing?"

Sarah answered, "They are singing hymns." To this, Laith replied, "Why don't they sing hers?" Another day he said to Fadhel, "You are drinking chai (tea), so that means you are Tchaikovsky." Things like this were humorous and uplifting. It showed intelligence, the ability to coordinate a thought and, perhaps, even a sense of humour.

Eventually, he could count his fingers, tell a simple story, name colours, button and unbutton his shirt, buckle and unbuckle his sandals and he recognized people very well. His appetite was good and he slept eight hours at night. In spite of this progress, the doctor warned Sarah that it would only be by a miracle that Laith would ever have a complete recovery. Although a complete recovery would have been desirable, Sarah would have to wait and see. She believed that miracles do happen and she would pray for a miracle for Laith.

Chapter 10

1941 Lebanon Retreat

While the Jamali family was seemingly over the worst of the battle with the encephalitis for Laith, there were other things happening. For Sarah, her battle and war was fighting the effects of the disease with Laith at home. In one way, Sarah may have envied her husband who continued going to work each day, spending time with his peers and having a distraction from the day to day agony that plagued Sarah. He could spend his day speaking to adults, giving lectures, attending meetings, eating lunch with interesting people. He didn't have to watch Sarah trying to teach Laith the simplest task over and over only to fail time and time again. However, Fadhel was facing other demons in his personal and political life as well. His beloved father, Shikh Abbas Jamali had died that spring, at age 74, and the country was in a state of serious unrest.

It was 1941 and World War II was still raging. In the years before the war broke out, Arab resentment was strong against British domination. The British, however, considered their influence to be a continuation of their tutorial responsibility under the League of Nations mandate, which had legally ended in 1933 when Iraq became a member of the League of Nations. A revolution eventually broke out in Iraq led by four colonels who installed Rashid Ali al-Gailani as Prime Minister. This coup d'etat brought about the evacuation of British and

American wives of Iraqis men to India. There were riots and looting in Baghdad.

"Sarah, I'm afraid it isn't safe for you to remain in Baghdad," Fadhel spoke calmly and quietly one evening after the children were in bed for the night. "You know that many wives and families of other government officials have already begun to flee the country."

"Yes, I know but where do you suggest I go? And do you really have to stay? Or would you accompany us?" Sarah reached for his hand as they sat quietly together on the roof top. They had been enjoying the moonlight and their beautiful classical music in peace. Why couldn't things seem to settle down? It seemed to Sarah that she just barely got through one crisis before there was yet even another to face.

"I want you to take the boys and go to Lebanon. No, I will not be able to accompany you. I know you are capable of this short journey in light of what you were able to deal with when you and the boys went to Canada. For now, it is a precaution we must take for your safety. You will need to make arrangements immediately and you must get passports. I'll send word when it is safe for you to return."

For now, Sarah just wanted this one last peaceful evening to never end. She looked at the beauty of what God had created with the stars above, the moonlight rippling on the water of the river and a tiny moment of her love shared with her husband. How could men keep fighting and destroying?

ഌരഃ

Sarah, Laith and Usameh flew to Beirut, a flight lasting three hours. From the airport, they took a taxi up to Ain Zahalta to a quiet hotel standing under pine trees. This retreat in the mountains of Lebanon was good for Sarah and the young boys. They went for long walks. Laith grew taller and started gaining some weight. He had been so thin and waif-like in appearance. His hair was long as he had not had a proper hair cut in five months due to the fact he was not well and when his health did begin to return, he would not sit still long enough to have a barber cut his hair. Sarah had used her sewing scissors to trim the ends as best as she could. But this was the least of her worries now. Her son was being a little boy out in the fresh air of the mountains.

He learned how to climb up and down the mountainsides, how to collect pine nuts and crack them, how to make a fire to roast pine cones, how to play in the sand in a mountain cave, and how to pick blackberries along a stream. He survived falling off a footbridge and getting wet, and being stung by a wasp. He sang marching songs as he walked up and down the mountains and he could run faster than Usameh. Seeing her child do all these simple boyish things may not seem like great accomplishments to many but, to Sarah, these were great accomplishments. When she thought back to where he had to start from just five months ago and how far he had come, she felt maybe there was hope that he could learn even more. She prayed it would be so.

At the age of six, Laith's abnormality was not immediately evident. Although, he had regained a lot to this point, Sarah knew he was still lacking in many ways.

One day in kindergarten, after going to the toilet, the teacher reported that Laith returned to the classroom without his trousers. He had no sense of what was appropriate but, then again, didn't small boys do odd things like this from time to time? Although in her heart, Sarah knew other boys would learn not to do such things and she feared that Laith may never learn this.

He had difficulty with learning directions. He would start out and perhaps find his way to a place but had no idea how to retrace his steps to return. It was a fear of Sarah's that he might get lost very easily. Although he had been learning how to play with other children in his neighbourhood, Sarah worried when he was with children that didn't know him. Their neighbours were all familiar with Laith and his existence there was insulated to a degree. However, now they were in Lebanon and Sarah knew she must watch over him very closely.

She tried to watch him carefully at all times. However, even the most watchful parent cannot possibly have eyes and ears on their child every waking moment. In one of those unfortunate moments, while playing with two other children, one of them hit Laith on the head with a hammer. Children can be cruel at times; they sometimes strike out at the unsuspecting child who is too different. Usameh never forgot the incident and remembers his feeling of helplessness in not being able to protect his brother. Even at this tender age, Usameh realized that he needed and wanted to help protect his older brother. It hurt him to see anyone ever hurt Laith. One begins to see that siblings of a child such as Laith can be affected at times. But this is brotherly love—it is not a bad thing.

ഇൽ

By autumn of 1941, the British military forces from Jordan had overcome the situation and had gained re-occupation of Iraq. Nuri es-Sa'id, who had been forced to flee into exile, had been reinstated as the Prime Minister of Iraq. Sarah and the boys returned to Baghdad and Sarah returned to her teaching position. Both Laith and Usameh returned to kindergarten. Sarah was a determined young woman. She felt confident enough that Laith was physically healthy now and the rest would just be a work in progress. She was a teacher and a mother. She would carry on with both careers.

The doctor had urged Sarah to teach Laith to read and write. He believed that pushing Laith would help to eventually overcome the deficiency left by the illness. Kindergarten was in Arabic so Sarah decided to wait until summer vacation before teaching him more English. She did read bedtime stories to the boys in English.

That summer, Sarah taught the boys to ride a bicycle. She would hold them by the back of the neck of their shirts and eventually they got the knack of it. They had a birthday party for Laith. He was now seven. All the children in the neighbourhood and two of Sarah's friends, who were chemists, gave the children a magic show. They made white water change from white to brown, then to blue and then back to white. They made the corner of one cloth turn from white to blue and another from white to yellow. They blew into water through a pipe and made smoke rise from the water. They did several other tricks that amazed the children and kept them well entertained. The highlight came when ice cream and cake was served.

It was a hot summer so every afternoon, the children and Sarah would seek relief from the heat in the basement and would take a nap with added coolness from the electric fans. After their nap, the boys would play in the fountain in the back yard. Sometimes, Sarah put on her bathing suit and got in with them to cool off as well. Fadhel had rented a rowboat so he could take the boys rowing. Evenings were for relaxing on the rooftop when it was cooler. Just as Sarah and Fadhel had enjoyed their romantic rooftop evenings before they had the children, they continued to enjoy this time as a family. The boys loved to fall asleep to the music of the masters. A lasting appreciation for music stemmed from this experience for the boys.

ℰℭ

During this summer, Sarah set out to follow the doctor's suggestion that she teach Laith to read and write in English. She began with words printed in block letters and used the phonetic system. He struggled and never seemed to quite be able to understand it all. Usameh, on the other hand, had no difficulty and if Sarah read him a line three times, he could read it back to her. In no time Usameh could read and write. As parents, we often hear that we should not make comparisons between our children. Sarah was not doing this out loud in any way to draw this to anyone else's attention; however, she couldn't help but observe the differences between Laith and his younger brother. It was somewhat of a "measuring tool", if nothing else, to see what Laith should have been able to comprehend and at what speed he should have been able to learn. By observing the differences and how vast they sometimes were, she began to see that Laith was falling behind. Well, she determined—they would just keep trying and Laith would make his own way in his own time.

Laith never learned to read and he could only write by copying. However, there was an incident that astonished Sarah. Laith looked at the hot water tap one day and said, "I can spell HOT!"

"How do you spell HOT?" Sarah was amused and decided to test him.

"It is two anti-aircraft guns, a zero and an airplane," he said proudly. This showed his ability to observe and associate shapes of objects to explain his line of thinking in regard to the letters. It was again observed when he noticed that if you move a stick back and forth very quickly, it appears as though the stick becomes divided. When things like this happened, Sarah could see that there was intelligence still in there and she felt encouraged to work at finding the key to open up more of Laith's mind.

She would cut things out of magazines and trace them onto cardboard cards. Then she would punch holes along the outline of the drawing. Laith would sew with thick, bright thread or wool following the outline with his stitches. He would spend hours doing these. He also loved to construct simple airplanes from his Meccano set which is a model construction system consisting of reusable metal strips, plates, angle girders, wheels, axles and gears, and plastic parts that are connected using nuts and bolts. This was a popular toy that was a learning tool and of great value to growing boys. It helped to develop creative building ideas and dexterity. Laith's airplanes may have been simple in construction but he was happy making them. Who knew, maybe one day he'd be able to build something more.

Laith understood language at a normal level. He loved to listen to stories and Tom Sawyer was a favourite. He loved words and would make up little rhymes like: 'a slave in a cave,' 'be quick or I'll beat you with a stick,' and 'There was a little fire that went higher and higher.' These signs of development and of cognizance were encouraging; however, they were not the whole picture. Sarah would never tell her mother about the negative things that happened when she wrote to Libbie. This, of course, would be a normal thing as no one wants to write a letter that will be full of depressing news about their child. Somehow, writing it or saying it out loud seems as though you are criticizing or giving up on your own child. Sarah never wanted to give that impression. She wanted to stay as positive about Laith as she could. After all, no one knew for certain at this point what he might eventually be capable of learning. Also, she didn't want to cause her aging mother any worries.

There was that little nagging thought way at the back of her mind; how her mother had warned her about marrying someone different and moving so far away from family. She remembered Libbie's words that there would be tough times and she would not be able to run home or have family come to her rescue. She never wanted to sound like she was complaining about her life. She loved her husband, her children and their life. It was just better to try to be positive. Giving in to depressing thoughts was just so defeating and would do no one any good.

Something new raised its ugly head in Laith. As if he didn't have enough to deal with in his young childhood life, something else had to inflict itself upon him. He would have spells where he said, "I'm afraid," or "I think I'm going to vomit." Sarah would hold him and the spell would pass. This would happen in clusters on consecutive days and then disappear for months but, over the next two years, it happened more often and as many as twelve times in one day. No one seemed to know the cause or the significance of these spells.

Chapter 11

Mistaken Identity

After the 1941 coup attempt, the British controlled the schools and removed all foreign languages other than English. They removed mention of Germany, Japan and Italy from textbooks. As Director General of Education, Fadhel had introduced the teaching of German and French to the school system, and had hired a German to teach that subject. English was already being taught. His introduction of German language was viewed with concern by the British educational advisors and they did away with his innovations promptly.

To add to the negative feelings toward Fadhel by the British, there was a case of mistaken identity that caused him grief. An Iraq Army Colonel, named Mohammed Fadhil Janabi, was responsible for para-military training modeled on Hitler's *Jugend* (the youth organization of the Nazi party in Germany). He had taken a group of students to Germany to attend the Olympic Games. At the same time, Fadhel was in Berlin to settle an issue between Iraqi students and their Legation in Berlin. While there, he toured Europe in search of textbooks and curricula.

Colonel Janabi had been photographed shaking hands with Hitler. Unfortunately, the Iraqi in the photograph was mistakenly identified as "Jamali." Rumors were spread and later in an Israeli newspaper, while Fadhel was attending meetings in Cairo, Egypt, it

137

was falsely reported that Mrs. Jamali (Sarah) was German and was educated in Britain and USA and that Fadhel had ordered Hitler's picture be hung in Iraqi schools. This false news created a flurry of ill feelings toward Fadhel. The confusion remained until US Minister, Loy Henderson saw to it that the record was set straight.

೫ಞ

"What a delicious supper you've prepared tonight, Sarah," Fadhel smiled as he viewed the plate before him.

"I'll relay your compliments to the cook," Sarah smiled as she took her first bite. Sarah could cook and she often gave meal plan suggestions to the cook but in this instance, she had not prepared the supper. But no matter, the compliment was well received.

"I like how you are wearing your hair these days. You've let it grow long and it is most attractive how you swirl it into that twisted bun. It amazes me how you can do that." Sarah had adopted this new hair style as it was easy and meant fewer trips to the hair salon to keep up a short bob style that she had maintained in her high school and university days. Life with a teaching career and looking after Laith and Usameh left little time for too many salon trips. It was a style that was to become her signature look in the years to follow.

"How observant and how kind of you my sweet but, you are making me suspicious with all this flattery. Is there something behind it all?" Sarah winked and batted her eyes in jest as she poured some water for the boys.

"Oh, dear—am I that transparent?"

138

"I'm afraid so—what's on your mind?"

"Well, I might as well just spit it out. I have to go to Egypt. I'm being sent to recruit 400 men and women teachers for all the schools and colleges in Iraq."

"I see. What is so bad about that? You've been there before."

"Yes, but this time I'll be gone for a couple of months. I know this will be difficult for both of us. I know that most of the responsibility of running the house and caring for the boys rests on your shoulders. But at least when I am home at night and on weekends, I hope that I have been some help to you."

"You are a help and we will certainly miss having you here but you must do what you are expected to do. And, to look on the brighter side, this is a wonderful thing for our education system. We need more teachers and you are the best person to have a say in who shall be best suited for the job. I am proud of you and know that this will be all for the good. Really, two months can pass quickly. I will keep myself busy. Maybe I'll read in bed at night," she laughed, "and, maybe I'll invite some of my teacher girlfriends over some evening. The time will fly for both of us. You'll see!"

ೞಆ

Fadhel was gone for two months and he gave lectures at the University of Cairo and to the Teachers Association. He met with the Rector of the University. They discussed the condition of Islamic education and the need for Islamic revival and unity through Muslim education.

During his past ten years in the Education Ministry, Dr. Fadhel Jamali had sent hundreds of young students abroad for university education, offering them the same opportunity that had been given to him. Many of those scholars rose to responsible positions in government and private sectors.

While Fadhel was away in Cairo, Sarah received a call from her sister, Lydia. Their father, Harvey, was in the hospital.

"What's wrong?" Sarah grabbed for a chair to take in the rest of the news sitting down as she felt weak at the knees as soon as she heard that Harvey was in hospital.

"Well, apparently, he has been suffering a lot with a bloated stomach and gas and tests showed earlier this year that he has an enlarged heart. I think you already knew this, though," Lydia explained.

"Yes, go on."

"I got the call from Oliver and he told me that Father has been having dizzy spells lately and it was during one of these dizzy spells that he felt a tightening of his heart. He had chest pains so that's why he's in the hospital now," Lydia heaved a sigh.

"Poor Mother—have you spoken with her?"

"Yes, I called her before I called you because I knew you'd want to know how she is taking things. She seems calm and she has friends near-by so she says she'll be fine."

"I hope so. It is times like this that I feel so helpless and the distance seems such a barrier—and it is!" Sarah had a flash back thought of her mother's words of warning many years earlier when she predicted that Sarah would have times of difficulty being so far away from her family but, actually, all her siblings were far from Harvey and Libbie. On second thought, they were all on the same continent, whereas Sarah was not.

"Well, you can pray for them Sarah. That is about all anyone can do for them now. They are in their twilight years and we can expect more of this in the future, unfortunately."

"I know you are right. I will pray for them both. I'm so glad you and I made that trip to see them. Wasn't it wonderful? We can remember the good times."

"We certainly can! Good-bye for now my little sister. I'll be sure to keep you informed if there is any change. Chin up!"

"Thanks Lydia. Give my love to all there."

1943 Abbas

On April 21, 1943, Sarah gave birth to a third son whom they named, Abbas, after his Iraqi grandfather. Before the birth of this baby, Sarah had stipulated that she didn't want another name that meant "Lion". Both Laith and Usameh mean lion in Arabic. After she agreed to name the new baby Abbas, she found out from an erudite scholar that Abbas also means lion. [25]Sarah was now the

---

[25]In a letter to the Author from Usameh Jamali (Sarah's son): "It is estimated that Arabic has over 400 names for lion. My father was aiming to have seven lions. Unfortunately, Laith's illness intervened.

mother of three little lions! And Fadhel was Abou El Leeyouth (the father of lions).

Just before the arrival of Abbas, Sarah had hired a new cook by the name of Um Sania. Sarah had stipulated that she was not interested in hiring a cook that would go from house to house or that would up and leave after a short time. She wanted a cook that would stay. Um Sania had only worked for one family and stated that she was an 'honourable woman' and would not go house to house. She was true to her word and a faithful servant who became a beloved family member. Sarah gave permission to Um Sania to bring her little granddaughter to live with them. Um Sania did the shopping and the cooking. Every morning, summer and winter, regardless of sun and boiling tar pavements, rain and mud, her stubby bare feet carried her to the market. She bargained for meats, vegetables, and fruits brought in on donkey back early each dawn. She packed everything into a deep basket made of palm fronds, balanced it on her head and with arms swinging at her side and her cloak flowing, she walked with swift ease on the road home.

Um Sania was a great help to Sarah. She took charge of the baby, Abbas. She bonded with him and treated him as if he were her own son. She had lost a son who died as a child. Very quickly she became known in the neighbourhood as Um Abbas which means Mother of Abbas. As soon as Abbas could sit up by himself, Um Sania took him to market with her. He strattled her shoulders and balanced himself by putting a hand on her

---

Nonetheless, he had three which qualified him to be called Abou El-Leeyouth.

head. On the trip home, he again sat on her shoulder and the basket of food balanced on top of her head. At home the old woman took Abbas into the kitchen and weaned him on rice and stew fed to him by her fingers instead of a spoon.

Laith was turning eight on July 5, 1943. Sarah decided there would no longer be any birthday parties. It was becoming clear that there was too large a gap between him and other children his age. In spite of this, there were some happy events where Laith was included. On one occasion Laith and Usameh were invited to visit the young King Faisal II of Iraq who was only two months older than Laith. It was quite well known that Laith was not normal, but he was included in the invitation. A car from the palace came for the boys and brought them back.

The palace, Qasr Az Zuhoor, (Palace of Flowers) was not far beyond West Baghdad. It was a modest palace with only two turrets to indicate that it was more than a private home. The garden was young and still very desert-like in landscaping details.

On arrival, the boys were taken around to see the young King's miniature golf course, his miniature roller coaster, and movie house where Walt Disney cartoons were shown. Then it was time for tea and biscuits supervised by the English governess. After tea the King took the boys to greet his mother, Queen Aliya, who was a beautiful Arabian woman with long dark shiny hair that she wore parted in the middle and symmetrically coifed in rolls that framed her face making her look like a porcelain sculpture. Her face was heart-shaped and her large almond-shaped eyes had a way of drawing one in even if you were just a small boy like Laith and Usameh. They then went outside again to examine the King's toy armoured tank. Next they took turns riding around on a tricycle, a push-pedal motor-car and a push-pedal airplane. This was particularly of interest to Laith as he loved airplanes so much. At last they decided to make an expedition to the house of the HRH the Regent, and the three boys pedaled in a cavalcade accompanied by guards. The Regent's house was an hour and a half to make round trip. Although the children had been told to stay one hour only, it was three hours before the palace car brought them home. Sarah breathed a sigh of relief to hear all about their day and that there had been no mishaps.

Summer days were often spent on the river. Fadhel rented a row boat and staked it on the riverbank in front of their house. The water was low in summer so an island sandbar rose up from the water every summer in front of their house. Sarah would row the boys over to the island every day where they would swim, collect shells, feathers, bottle caps, rocks, etc. They looked for water beetles and once saw a small crab. Sometimes they chased birds and other times they just sat and felt calm and peaceful and far removed from the troubled world. The world was still at war; however, when Sarah sat or played on the beach with her boys, she felt thankful for the peace that she could give her children.

ℰℭ

In September, the boys went back to school. Usameh took a special examination and was admitted to Grade Two. Laith remained in Grade One. Laith would tell visitors

144

that came to the house, "My brother is younger than I am but he is in Grade Two and I am in Grade One." He was fully aware that Usameh could do things that he could not. He never seemed jealous but Sarah was sure he must have felt frustrated to be falling behind his younger brother.

In Baghdad at this time, there were no special schools for children like Laith. There was no alternative but to place him in with normal children. Sarah was not happy about this and in her words she stated:

> "It is a heavy drag on the teacher and the class as well as a strain on the child who is mentally handicapped. A child who is mentally [26]retarded should not be accepted for education with normal children, but it sometimes happens as a personal favour to the parents, or out of pity for the child, or because the degree of backwardness is not recognized. This is an unsatisfactory solution for a sad state of affairs. In my opinion, the right solution is to give the child who is mentally retarded his own school or his own class where he can be trained and helped by special teachers."

These were the words spoken from the heart of a woman who knew both sides of it all. She was a teacher with years of experience and also a mother with an ache to see her son accepted and in an environment where he would be able to learn at his own pace. She knew the

---

[26] Retarded – a word considered appropriate at this time in the 1940s but is outdated today.

145

frustration for him as she understood that he himself knew he was not keeping up with his peers.

Sarah was frustrated too. What was she to do? Employ a private teacher? No one wanted to work in private homes. The work was considered too menial. There were no special schools or classrooms in the schools and no one wanted to build a private school because they said it was the responsibility of the government. In turn, the government said their first duty was to normal children.

Sarah and Fadhel were still hopeful that they could do something to help Laith. They still had a team of medical doctors whom they consulted. One doctor suspected that defective vision might be part of the reason why Laith could not learn to read. So, Sarah found an eye specialist who examined Laith and determined that glasses would not help her son since his vision was quite normal. On one hand Sarah felt elated that her son had normal vision but on the other hand, it would have been a comfort to learn that all he needed to learn to read was a pair of eyeglasses for defective vision.

Chapter 12

Dr. Fadhel Jamali was transferred from the Ministry of Education to Foreign Affairs in 1943. The order was from Prime Minister, Nuri es-Sa'id. Before this, Fadhel had refused an appointment to the Embassy in Washington as Counsellor, sensing that it was a move to get him out of the way. He was then appointed Director General effective July 19, 1944. The change from Education to Foreign Affairs did not please him at first because education had been his special field of study. He had spent his life, up to this point, working on something he loved and to which he felt dedicated. However, even once he was Director General of Foreign Affairs, he kept his hand in teaching by giving lectures on moral philosophy and [27]Plato's *Republic* at the Higher Teacher Training College.

When asked why he was transferred, he replied, that perhaps the British advisors were concerned with what effect a man with alleged Nazi sympathies, however unsubstantiated, might have on the youth of Iraq. This remark of his was in regard to the previously mentioned ordeal of mistaken identity and the false reports that he was a friend of Hitler's and that Sarah was German, etc.

---

[27]The center of Plato's *Republic* is a contribution to ethics: a discussion of what the virtue justice is and why a person should be just. (Stanford Encyclopedia of Philosophy)

This career change took place during the war and was surely the influence of the British. The British had just had difficulties in putting down the revolt in Iraq. They knew that Fadhel was a strong nationalist. Having him in Education was not considered to be wise. They did not want him influencing the minds of young students. Of course, Prime Minister Nuri Sa'id didn't put it that way. He said to Fadhel, "We need you in Foreign Affairs. We need a man of your qualifications."

It was true that Fadhel Jamali had the education and the overseas experience, making him a logical choice for the appointment to Foreign Affairs. Other older statesmen also had vast experience; however, their experience was more limited to Middle East and Europe. Fadhel, with five years in the American University of Beirut's western atmosphere and three more years at Columbia University in New York, was quite at home in the West and in America.

Once his transfer was effective, Fadhel set to work to implement his Pan-Arab and patriotic convictions. In his new position he could make sure that the Iraqi government took every chance to convince the British and American allies of the urgent need for liberation of Syria and Lebanon from the French authority.

1944 Jerusalem

One of Laith's doctors suggested to Sarah that she take him to the Hadassah Hospital in Jerusalem for an X-ray treatment which could possibly stimulate the brain cells. Unfortunately, Laith had come to develop a pattern of behaviour that was concerning. When he was annoyed, a dark look came over his face, and then he would become somewhat violent and would push, pull or nudge the person with whom he was annoyed. With time this mannerism became more and more troublesome. He also was very fidgety and had difficulty sitting still. He would talk to strangers, fidget or pick at things. If Sarah tried to stop him, he would become angry and throw a tantrum tearing buttons off his clothing. To avoid embarrassing situations like this, Sarah carried cookies and candies to pacify him. She would tell him stories or play quiet games to distract him from his angry moods.

A trip to Jerusalem would be difficult for Sarah and it would be expensive but, if it could help Laith, she felt she must give him that chance. With the career change for Fadhel it became more evident that the responsibility of the children, and Laith in particular, would fall on Sarah. Although Sarah understood the new position for Fadhel made it impossible for him to join her on this mission, she surely would have liked to have his company.

It would seem that just as Fadhel's career was soaring upward, Sarah's career needed to be put on pause. After the birth of Abbas, she felt that something had to give. It was like being the ring leader of a three-ring circus—balancing and juggling teaching, running a home and being mother to three active children—not to mention trying to be the best teacher and mother to Laith she possibly could. So, it was determined that Sarah would take a year off from teaching English to stay home with her little den of "lions"!

That summer, she left Usameh and Abbas in the care of Um Sania and flew to Ghaza. From there, she and

Laith drove to the Arab section of Jerusalem where they took a room in an Armenian hotel called Almas.

After a long wait, the doctor finally did a consultation and Sarah had to continually work at calming Laith with her usual methods during this preliminary meeting. They were then told to return in three days. Much to Sarah's disappointment, the doctor was of the opinion that the X-ray treatment would not be advantageous for Laith. He said that the spot on the head where the X-rays are applied would become bald and this would be an additional handicap for Laith. Also, he informed Sarah that it was imperative that a patient remain totally still during the procedure; otherwise, the brain would be overexposed to the X-rays. He added that the treatment had been tried in Berlin and discontinued due to lack of positive results. Although disappointed, Sarah appreciated his honesty. She would rather have straight answers than to be lulled into false hopes.

Not wanting to let Sarah completely down, the doctor recommended she take Laith to an internist. The internist advised her to see an oculist (eye doctor); the oculist referred her to a psychologist. They saw the psychologist several times. He spoke broken English with a very heavy accent. He asked Laith, "What is a hoghz?" He repeated this several times and Sarah could see that Laith could not understand the doctor so she repeated the question to Laith saying, "What is a horse?" Once Laith understood the question, he was able to answer well enough. The psychologist turned to Sarah and said, "He doesn't understand English very well, does he." Sarah had to restrain herself from laughing in his face.

The psychologist suggested that Sarah leave Laith with him to live in his home as a boarder so he could administer psychological treatment. Sarah said she would consider the matter and let him know. She agonized over what to do. She wanted suitable treatment for Laith and she knew it would be a relief to know he was going to receive treatment that she herself could not provide. She reasoned that the whole purpose of this trip to Jerusalem was to find a source of help for Laith and now here was someone offering help. Should she not just accept it?

However, the next day as she and Laith approached the psychologist's house, Sarah noticed his two young children, of elementary school age, standing at the gate. They were the sons of the psychologist. Sarah greeted the boys with a smile and a friendly, "Hello." They just stared back at her and made some derogatory remark in Hebrew. Sarah knew at once that this was not the atmosphere she wanted for Laith. She realized that placing him in a small home with these two boys would certainly not be beneficial to Laith. Her mind was now made up that she needed to continue her search.

℘℆

One day when Sarah and Laith were in a bakery in the Jewish section of Jerusalem. It was crowded and noisy which bothered Laith. He disliked crowds and loud noises disturbed him and made him nervous. As the crowd seemed to swallow the boy up, he apparently punched a man with his elbow. The man turned around and slapped Laith in the face very hard. Sarah grabbed Laith by the hand and they left the bakery. This incident was not only

151

a shock to Laith but it devastated Sarah. Laith would forget the slap in a short time but Sarah felt the sting of that slap deep in her heart for a very long time. It kept her awake at nights. How could she possibly protect her son from further abuse at the hands of others when things like this could happen when she stood right beside him? To give the perpetrator a piece of her mind would have felt good but a man who was that volatile would likely have done something even worse had she tried. She was smart enough to know that she had to protect herself and Laith by removing themselves from the situation. If she got hurt, Laith would be alone. She wondered what would have happened if Fadhel had been at Laith's side. She doubted that Fadhel would have just retreated like she had. No, he would have taken a stand and made that horrible man apologize. Oh God! Why did children like Laith have to be subjected to this from some unkind stranger? No child should ever be mistreated in this way.

Not all days were as terrible as the day at the bakery. Sarah and Laith took some pleasure visiting Arab friends and a Jewish communal farm. Friends told Sarah about a couple of schools for mentally challenged Jewish children. She tried to visit these schools but they were closed for the summer. Another disappointment; however, she looked on the bright side thinking that she had seen a lot of the city of Jerusalem and that was a good experience on the whole.

Every day before going for a walk, Sarah gave Laith lessons in arithmetic and English. She had some psychology education training which she tried to apply. These techniques made Laith eager to please his mother and he tried hard. He learned to recognize some words and numbers, though he never really learned to read. He liked making up rhymes so Sarah filled a notebook with his two-line sayings. Again, it was disappointing that she couldn't help him master reading but she tried to focus on what he could do and to make the child feel a sense of pride for his accomplishments. Sarah smiled as she thought about how maybe one day Laith could be a poet. He certainly knew how to make words rhyme.

Kidnapped

Upon returning to the Almas hotel after their morning walk, Sarah and Laith passed a photography shop where there were long strips of film hanging outside the door to dry. Laith reached out and took hold of a strip of negative with his fingers. Sarah reacted with a sharp reprimand, "Don't do that!"

Laith scowled at Sarah and began running away from her. She called out to him, "Laith stop! Wait for me. Please stop running. Laith!" Laith kept running.

She didn't chase him because she thought he would run to the hotel. He knew the way as they had been living in Jerusalem for almost a month. However, when she got to the hotel, there was no sign of Laith. She thought he may have gone past the turn to the hotel and continued down the hill toward the Damascus Gate. Behind the hotel, was a vacant lot where she came upon a band of boys who played there everyday. She had seen them there often as she and Laith sat in this area together while Sarah told stories to Laith. She asked the boys if they had seen her son. She told them he was lost and that she was looking for him. They told her they were sorry but had not seen him that day.

Sarah walked to the Damascus Gate and walked amid the crowd of people, donkeys, and camels but there was no sign of Laith. Weaving her way through the noisy crowd only added to her feeling of frustration and growing anxiety. She walked back to the hotel where she spoke to other guests about the situation and began asking if someone who could speak Arabic better than she could might be willing to accompany her back to the market. One kind man offered to go with her back to the Damascus Gate. The gate—one of eight gates in the wall that surrounds the city of Jerusalem, was most beautiful and impressive. It was a place where trade and bartering was conducted. The gate might have been beautiful but the market area was crowded and dirty. People squatted to rest or carry on business and it was a colourful scene with men and women in all manner of dress. Sarah and the gentleman spoke to many people asking about Laith. No one had seen him. No one knew anything. They returned to the hotel.

At this point, Sarah decided it was time to contact the police. She took a taxi to the police station and filled out a report describing Laith. The police promised to let her know if they found him. She felt reassured that someone would find Laith and contact the police. Laith could speak both Arabic and English so if someone questioned him, he could respond. His speech was limited but surely if he was found, he would respond properly to direct questions. She returned to the hotel and sat down to a lunch. Other guests were shocked at her seemingly uncaring behaviour. How could this woman sit there and eat when her child was missing? Sarah herself came to question her own behaviour when recalling the incident years later:

> "I should have telephoned some of my Palestinian friends who might have obtained real action. However, at the time I thought that it would be only a little while until a lost boy would be reported to the authorities."

There may be another explanation for Sarah's behaviour at this time. She had been living day to day with a great deal of anxiety and stress. She had been up early, walking around the city for hours by this point with very little sustenance. She was fatigued no doubt and eating lunch, though it seemed odd, was likely the best thing she could do at that moment to carry on. Obviously, she was not thinking as clearly as she should have been so it is possible that she was in a state of shock which might explain her rather odd detached behaviour.

Sarah called the police station to check but they said they had nothing to report. She returned to her search walking up and down blind alleys and talking to anyone she came in contact with asking about her son. Laith had been missing for a few hours by this time. By now, the seriousness and fear of what might be happening was beginning to sink in a little more. She pushed herself to move on and keep searching.

Meanwhile, the young gang of boys that she had spoken to earlier, behind the hotel, decided to take things into their own hands and play a bit of detective work. They went to the Damascus Gate and made enquiries. They found a man who said he had seen a boy by the description of Laith who had left the city, heading out into the desert, with a Bedouin riding a donkey. The boys ran home and got their bicycles and started out on the desert road—something the police should have done by now but had not bothered to do. Some distance out from the city they found the Bedouin man riding with Laith on a donkey. The boys called to him telling him that he had no business taking Laith away with him. The man ignored them. The boys told the man that they knew Laith and his mother and that he must give the boy over to them immediately. The man argued that Laith had told him that he would rather go with the man and learn to drive a donkey than return to his mother. The boys would have nothing to do with this and, finally, the man surrendered the child. They put Laith on the back of one of their bicycles and returned him to Jerusalem.

As Sarah stood in the lobby of the hotel consulting with people about what she should do next, in walked the gang of boys with Laith, who looked very hot and dusty. Sarah embraced her son and tearfully thanked the boys. She questioned Laith, who seemed unhurt as she quickly examined him from head to toe, but all she could get out of him was that the man had given him some food. Sarah wanted to give the boys a rich reward but all she had to give them was a little token baksheesh (small monetary tip money) and her most heartfelt thanks. In the days that followed, Sarah had frightening thoughts about what could have been Laith's fate with this mysterious man had the boys not managed to find them. She had felt alone and, yet, she now realized that she was never alone. God had intervened. He had been with her and Laith. He had sent the gang of boys to do what the police were not doing. She gave thanks to God for saving her son once

156

again. His life had been spared from encephalitis and now he was saved from his kidnapper; God must have a purpose for her son.

There was nothing left for her to do in Jerusalem. She had exhausted all hope of finding treatment there. It would be in God's hands. Sarah lost all hope of a recovery for Laith. She would have to trust that God would hold the future.

Chapter 13

Resignation and Acceptance

After the trip to Jerusalem, Sarah and Fadhel began to face the fact that Laith was not improving. His mental development seemed to have stopped. Of course, they were thankful for the many things he had accomplished as he made his way back from a state of unconsciousness to a healthy boy who could run, laugh, tell little jokes, climb trees, play games, recognize and write numbers up to 100 in Arabic and English but, the truth of it was—he was nine years old and he was still at the kindergarten stage. He continued to have tantrums if things didn't go his way. He would strike out or rip the buttons off his clothing at the least annoyance. He disliked bad table manners and noisy eating, so his younger brother Usameh was always being told to behave in order not to upset Laith. Thus, Laith began to dominate the lives of the family members. His presence developed into a kind of tyranny. Sarah admitted to be the one who always gave in to Laith's demands to try to keep him calm and to avoid a scene. Using cookies and treats to calm and distract him just enforced the bad behaviour and ended up being a reward for his demands and tantrums.

It is easy for anyone to look in and make a judgment call; however, it is not so easy when you are the one living through the kind of struggles that Sarah faced each day. This was her son, her own flesh and blood. He was like this through no fault of his own. Every day that she watched him falling farther behind his peers and his younger brothers, her heart broke for him a little more. To see his face go dark and to witness his frustrations turn into violent tantrums, hurt her because all she ever wanted for Laith was for him to feel good and to be happy. As a mother, she felt a certain amount of guilt. After all, is it not up to the parents to save the child? If she had known about the serious affect that measles could inflict, or if she had known about encephalitis, would she have been better equipped to save her son? If . . . if only . . . what if? Why?—these were the questions that rolled around in her head relentlessly. As a loving parent, she wanted to try to give her son every chance to thrive in some way and to regain as much of his true self as she possibly could. Truthfully, she was too emotionally attached to be able to think of any other approach other than to try to sooth him by giving in to his demands. Her approach was to be patient and loving and, as commendable as this was, it was not as effective as she had envisioned.

ℰℂ

Sarah's year off from her teaching position was up. It was time to go back to work. The issue was what to do with Laith. It was impossible for him to return to his elementary school because he was mentally too abnormal. God seemed to answer her prayers because she was appointed to teach at the Elementary Teachers College where there was a Practice School. It was agreed that Laith could go to school with Sarah and sit in the Grade One classroom of the Practice School while Sarah taught.

160

"How are things progressing with Laith's new class and teacher? It's been a month now so what have you or his teacher been able to conclude?" Fadhel enquired after the boys were asleep one evening.

"His teacher and I have both tried to help him learn to read and write in Arabic. Any time I have a break between classes, I take him to an empty classroom and work with him. His teacher tries as well but I'm afraid it is no use. It is always the same."

"But his doctors tell us to keep trying to stimulate his brain. You must not give up on him."

"Forgive me, Fadhel, I have not given up on him. I'm just telling you the truth of the matter. He is not learning! I think you of all people know full well how hard I've tried. If I weren't a teacher, he would likely be even further behind."

"Calm down Dear. I know you have tried very hard and I'm sorry I've upset you. I just keep hoping and praying that we will make a break through again. He has learned so many things and I want to trust that the doctors may be right. Maybe he can still learn more."

"No, Fadhel—we're just going to have to accept that there's a part of Laith's brain that is dead. He can't be pushed or prodded any further to learn to do the things we want him to do. I'm sorry but you and the doctors are not with him every single day. I am the one who has to help bathe him because he cannot complete the task properly, I'm the one sitting with him daily to try to teach him the tiniest thing over and over again. I will never give up on him, but I am to the point of accepting that he cannot develop as far as we had hoped. It is just not going to happen," Sarah broke down and wept quietly.

"I hear you and I know you are right. I just have difficulty accepting it as you say we must. I don't know how to accept it, but I know I must," Fadhel patted Sarah on the back and kissed her forehead.

"I'm sorry, too, Fadhel. I am just frustrated and tired. Today wasn't a good day. Laith threw one of his tantrums in his classroom. He was rude to his teacher. He picked up a drinking glass and threw it on the floor and broke it," Sarah wiped her eyes and blew her nose.

"Oh my goodness, I'm so sorry. How did the teacher react?"

"Well, she was rightfully upset and she went to the head mistress and said, 'It's impossible to put up with things like this in the classroom.'

"I see. Hmm. . . So, does this mean Laith may no longer sit in her class?"

"No—at least, not for now—the head mistress calmed the teacher down and said, 'I don't think it has reached the unbearable stage yet.' She told her to carry on," Sarah heaved her shoulders in a heavy sigh. Fadhel hugged her and they sat there for a long time just holding on to one another. They had both been holding things in and everyone, including the doctors, had not wanted to say the words out loud but this was a point of admitting what they all had to face. Laith was not developing further and he was becoming a problem at school and at home. He could not be left alone. He was not naughty, he was simply an abnormal boy becoming more and more maladjusted.

Chapter 14

Epilepsy

One morning, without warning, Laith lost consciousness and began to jerk. Sarah had no idea what was happening so she called a taxi and took Laith to the hospital. Tests were run and the diagnosis was static epilepsy. A sedative was given by injection and tablets were prescribed. Sarah took Laith home and he slept late into the day. He awoke later, pale and tired but with no recollection of the event. A few weeks later, when walking home from school with Sarah, he collapsed into unconsciousness and fell hitting his head on the pavement. Some men rushed to Sarah's aid and helped her get Laith into a taxi and she took him back to the hospital. He was given another injection and returned home to his bed.

The doctor diagnosed the spells that Laith had been having—the sensations of fear and desire to vomit—as petit mal seizures. Laith had been having these spells for two years. They came in series lasting a few days, with rest periods of one or two months. The frequency increased until he had as many as twelve in one day. The spells only lasted about a minute. There was only one occasion where Laith had a grand mal seizure. The doctor thought Laith's case to be somewhat odd because he never dropped anything he had in his hand at the time of the seizure.

As frightening as this had been, Sarah was glad that it had finally been diagnosed. There was medication to help but now, she felt she needed to watch over him even more closely than ever before. She worried about further brain damage from the falls and trauma to his head. She remembered the child who hit Laith on the head with the hammer and the cruel man in the bakery who slapped Laith in the face hard. And she wept when no one was there to witness her despair. She prayed for strength and patience. She knew God had a purpose for every human being. Surely this included her son.

Problems at Home

"I don't want to go, Mother. I was there once already this week and I feel awkward eating at their place," Usameh was upset that he was being sent to the neighbours' place for supper again. It was a friendly arrangement made between Sarah and her neighbour to avoid Laith's tantrums during mealtime with his younger brother.

"Come on now, you're always behind just like the old cow's tail!" Sarah cajoled Usameh by tousling his hair. "Get ready to go. Wash your hands and face and put on a clean shirt. You will have a lovely time, I'm sure of it!"

"You're just pushing me out onto the neighbours to please Laith! Why don't you send him somewhere else to eat? I want to stay home. It's not fair!" Usameh turned and went to his room to change.

Sarah knew he was right. He was being pushed out to keep peace with Laith. The whole family regulated their conduct to Laith's whims. Laith wanted all the lights in the house turned out when he went to bed. Sarah allowed this and many other demands as well.

164

Um Sania had brought another granddaughter to live with the family. This was, of course, with the approval of Sarah and Fadhel. How could they deny this kind and helpful woman who had become like a beloved family member? Sarah found the two young girls to be quite a help to her. They would sometimes take Laith and Usameh to the movies which gave Sarah freedom and an afternoon to relax or visit a friend.

Abbas was still a baby and was still consigned to the kitchen where Um Sania reigned and watched over him. She taught him her dialect, and her ways while leaving Sarah to tend to her more difficult child—the nervous and demanding Laith.

ℰᗅ

"Laith, comb your hair, Son. Try to do your whole head, Dear. Remember to do the back part too," Sarah was instructing Laith one morning. Laith liked to be clean all the time and he wanted to do things for himself. However, he couldn't wash himself completely or comb his hair completely. He would miss parts that he couldn't see. The back of his hair would get tangled and sometimes Sarah overlooked this and would just tell him he was a good boy and had done a fine job to encourage him rather than to upset him. But this morning she wanted him to look proper because they were going out in public.

"Oh, I see you've missed the back part Laith. Let me comb it for you, shall I?"

"No! Laith pushed Sarah's hand away causing her to let go of the comb and it fell to the floor.

"Laith, come on now. Be a good boy. Let's not quarrel over this, please."

"Don't—you hurt me!" Laith kicked the comb across the floor as Sarah had bent down to pick it up.

"Laith, I'll give you a cookie if you let me comb your hair. Would you like that? I have your favourite biscuit in the kitchen for you."

"I said NO!" At this point, Laith pushed Sarah and she lost her balance and fell to the floor. Fadhel heard this commotion and came into the room and grabbed Laith by his arm and shook him.

"Pick up that comb and listen to your Mother! You will do as she says, do you hear me Laith?" Fadhel's face was red and his tone was sharp.

"Don't upset him, Fadhel! Please, I'm alright," Sarah was up on her feet and trying to smooth things over. She knew Laith would go into a frenzy. And he did. He began screaming and pulled away from his father and began tearing at his clothing. He hit Fadhel. Fadhel smacked him across his shoulder.

"Stop—you're making him worse, Fadhel! I can handle him. Please just let it go!"

"I will not allow this child to rule over this house like this every day, Sarah. He needs discipline. You coddle him and reward him for bad behaviour."

"I want a biscuit!" Laith yelled and slapped at Fadhel again. Fadhel grabbed him hard by the arm and sat him in a chair. Laith jumped up and started screaming again like a banshee.

166

"You will not get a biscuit. You will stop hitting people. Laith stop screaming!" Fadhel's face was even redder now. His temples seemed to be pulsing.

"Please Fadhel! Just go get ready to go to work. I can't stand all this noise and clearly it isn't helping one bit."

"Sarah, you want me to go to work, you want Usameh to eat at the neighbours' house, and our baby is living in the kitchen with the cook raising him. Do you not see what is becoming of our family? You push us all away so you can keep Laith calm. He will never be able to live with anyone except you if you keep this up." He shook his head and walked away to leave for the office.

Sarah knew there was truth to what Fadhel had said. She was fiercely protective of Laith. She couldn't seem to help it. The instinct was always there to try to keep Laith happy and calm. It had been that way from the beginning of his illness. There was a deep feeling of guilt in her over his illness. She was his mother and it was her duty to know what to do when her child was sick. She felt she had failed to save him from the encephalitis. This was not true, of course, but she felt it sometimes. When she rationalized it, she knew that she and the medical people had done the very best they possibly could for Laith. However, the need to protect him came from something that she just couldn't control.

The tantrums continued. Sarah would forcibly remove his clothing when he was having a severe tantrum to prevent him from ripping buttons off and tearing his shirts. She would lock him in an empty room and let him howl until he was quiet again. She didn't do this to be cruel; she just knew that physical restraint or a slap would only make things worse so she did this for lack of knowing what else to do. One day when this was happening, Laith was screaming and crying in a room and Sarah saw a British soldier walking past the house. He was plainly distressed by the child's screams and kept turning to look back at the house. He walked back once or twice to stop and look at the house. Sarah knew he was contemplating whether to intervene to save this child from brutal treatment.

Sarah began to fear Laith's tantrums. She worried that this might develop into a violent mania as he got older. His punches were already strong enough to hurt. She wondered how she would cope as he became stronger. She spoke to the doctor about this and he told her to wait until after puberty. At that time they could assess whether he was going to become calm or more violent. If he was to become violent with the strength of a man, he would have to be locked away. In the meantime, he recommended that Sarah continue to try all possible forms of treatment.

Problems in Society

Laith loved the water so Sarah would take him every morning in the summer to the local swimming pool near their home. They would go early in the morning and would leave before anyone arrived. Sarah tried to teach Laith to swim but he panicked when she tried to get him to put his face in the water. So, she just let him paddle in the shallow end while she took a leisurely swim. She loved the exercise and it brought back childhood memories of swimming in the Weyburn public pool as a child. . . the carefree days of childhood bliss and freedom!

Sarah never took Laith through the main entrance of the swim club. There was a side entrance that she used so no one would take notice of them. She wasn't ashamed of Laith but people stared and it was uncomfortable. Laith was a very nice-looking boy with handsome features. He had thick, wavy, dark-brown hair and gorgeous dark brown eyes. He had a beautiful friendly smile but, from his expressions, his walk and manner of speaking, one could instantly recognize that he was mentally abnormal. Sarah was aware of members of the swim club looking at him with disgust and fear. This bothered her, of course, but mostly, she wanted to protect Laith from any taunting or negative behaviour toward him.

Sarah wanted to socialize but it was difficult. She did see friends that shared her interests in education and social welfare. Sometimes when the boys were at the movies with Um Sania's granddaughters, Sarah would visit such friends. When Laith was asleep, she would attend social outings in the evening with Fadhel. One evening at a dinner party, she met a woman who seemed very engaging and they had a friendly discussion about their interest in classical music and art.

"Sarah, I heard a rumour that you have been instrumental in getting a symphony orchestra from Minneapolis to come to Baghdad. Is it true?" The woman, was a wife of a British diplomat. She smiled at Sara as she sipped from her glass of champagne. She was very elegant holding her glass with her slender hands covered with long champagne-coloured evening gloves, a diamond bracelet dripping from her tiny wrist and a large diamond ring on her finger. Sarah always thought that wearing jewelry over gloves was rather ostentatious, but

169

she couldn't help but admire this woman's beauty and dazzling sequined floor-length evening gown that shimmered in the same champagne colour as her gloves and her drink.

"Yes, I have family members back in Minneapolis and—thanks to their assistance—I made contact with the conductor, Antal Dorati. Are you familiar with him?" Sarah sipped from her crystal cup of fruit punch.

"Of course—he is the Hungarian conductor. My husband and I had the privilege of seeing him in Paris, in 1940. He was conductor and music director of the Ballet Russe de Monte Carlo, which he took on a tour of Australia in 1938. My sister saw the ballet in Australia that year. I must admit I have lost track of him since then."

"Well, he's recently moved to Minneapolis and is the conductor of the symphony there now. I heard that he was planning a trip back to his native home in Budapest to perform there with his symphony. They are planning a tour of France, Italy and Greece. I wrote to him and invited him to extend his tour to Baghdad and he accepted!"

"I must attend the concert and I'm sure the word will spread quickly amongst the music lovers here in Baghdad. You really must come to tea mid-week so we can discuss it further. I have connections and will be happy to help promote this event."

Sarah graciously accepted the woman's invitation.

ℰℭ

It was a hot summer day and Sarah, foolishly decided to include Laith on this visit. She was quite sure that he would enjoy the outing and he could sit down to tea without a fuss. He was in a good mood and she was enjoying his company. She felt guilty for always leaving him out of social outings. She was greeted by her hostess who was wearing a handkerchief tied around her breasts and a pair of shorts. Although it was a very hot day, Sarah was a little shocked by this appearance for afternoon tea. Sarah, always immaculate and appropriately dressed for any occasion, wore a light-cotton, mid-knee length, sundress with matching bolero jacket and white sandals.

The house boy served tea while the two women looked at lovely art objects in the room and discussed Japan and Japanese art. Sarah was pleased with how quiet and polite Laith was; however, she took notice that the woman never once took any notice of Laith. She completely ignored him. Sarah didn't know how to take this. She wondered if the woman was uncomfortable looking at Laith; obviously she could tell he was mentally affected in spite of how well behaved he was at the moment. She also wondered if the woman was a little annoyed and perhaps thought that this was a breach of etiquette. At any rate, it was uncomfortable and Sarah felt the afternoon tea was a let-down.

This incident reminded Sarah of her childhood in Weyburn and an incident concerning one of Libbie's friends who had a feeble-minded child. She took her child with her everywhere she went. She had no choice but to do this as there was no place to leave him. Later, she did get him accepted into a ward for retarded children at the Weyburn Mental Hospital. One day the woman brought her son to Libbie's house in Weyburn. Sarah recalled her mother looking out the window and saying, "Here comes Mrs. Gerrard with that idiot child of hers." Libbie was always kind and welcoming and she never ignored the child. Mrs. Gerrard must have felt welcome because she came to call quite often. Sarah thought how it would have never occurred to Libbie that one day she would be the grandmother to such a child herself.

Whether right or wrong, Sarah felt that Western associates and friends were less comfortable with Laith than were Iraqi friends. It seemed that people were inclined to accept and enjoy only healthy, normal people and they shunned those with handicaps. Sarah became sensitive to this and was careful how she chose her friends and who she would invite to her home. It is possible that Iraqi friends were more at ease with such children as Laith because many of them likely knew someone in their family or associates who had a family member with some disability. There were no special schools or homes for such children with any sort of affliction so such children were more apt to be seen and known in their communities.

Chapter 15

1944 – 1945 Dr. Jamali & Foreign Affairs

[28]The Palestinian Arabs felt ignored by the terms of the British Mandate. Though at the beginning of the Mandate they constituted a 90 percent majority of the population, the text only referred to them as "non-Jewish communities" that, though having civil and religious rights, were not given any national or political rights. As far as the League of Nations and the British were concerned, the Palestinian Arabs were not a distinct people.

Fadhel had watched developments in Palestine with deepening concern. He was sympathetic to his "Arab brothers." He began to write a series of newspaper articles to warn the public of the Zionist threat. Due to his position as Director General of Foreign Affairs, he used the pen name of "ibn al-Iraq (son of Iraq)." These were eventually collected in pamphlet form and printed in Cairo under the title, *The Zionist Danger*. Fadhel feared that because the Arab people were focused on WWII, they were not likely alert to the intent of the world [29]Zionist program.

---

[28] Wikipedia – During the British Mandate

[29] Zionism - is the nationalist movement of the Jewish people that espouses the re-establishment of and support for a Jewish state in the territory defined as the historic Land of Israel (roughly corresponding to Canaan, the Holy Land, or the region of Palestine).

King Abhdul Aziz ibn Sa'ud Arabia and Crown Prince Abd al-llah, on behalf of King II of Iraq (who was only a young boy at this time), wrote letters to President Roosevelt. Fadhel Jamali translated the Crown Prince's letter into English. The letter reminded President Roosevelt of Arab friendship, and referred to the Covenant which the Caliph Omar ibn al-Khuttab addressed to his Muslim army when they undertook the conquest of Palestine in early Islamic history. In that [30]Covenant, he commanded his conquering army to treat the Christians in a just and humanitarian manner.

The Saudi and Iraqi letters emphasized that Palestine having passed through so many historical developments, belonged to its legal inhabitants, the Arabs. They asked President Roosevelt to uphold the principles of the Atlantic Charter of which he himself was co-author. Mr. Roosevelt's reply, dated April 12, 1944 was as follows:

> "In the view of the Government of the United States, no decision affecting the basic situation in Palestine should be reached without full consultation with both Arabs and Jews."

---

[30] "In the name of Allah, the Merciful, the Compassionate. This is the Covenant which Omar ibn al-Khuttab, the servant of Allah, the Commander of the Faithful, grants to the people of Aelis (Jerusalem). He grants them security of their lives their possessions, their churches and crosses . . . they shall have freedom of religion and none shall be molested unless they rise up in a body. They shall pay a tax instead of military service. . . and those who leave the city shall be safeguarded until they reach their destination."

Although this statement left the Arabs feeling dissatisfied, they were at least relieved to be considered important enough to have their voice heard in equal right to the Jews. President Delano Roosevelt passed away exactly one year to the day after the above-mentioned statement.

In December, 1944, Jamali, as Director General had submitted a memorandum to his Minister which laid out a plan to present the Arab cause in the United States through a network of information offices. Later, the Arab League, having heard Jamali's proposal, resolved to establish Arab Offices for Palestine in Britain and America. In New York, the Zionists were worried about this venture and their protests eventually prompted police inspection of the Arab Information Office premises. Jamali protested vigorously to the US Embassy in Baghdad and threatened to have a police inspection of the US Information Offices in Iraq if such a breach of diplomatic immunity was repeated. It never was. However, due to lack of financial support from Syria (Syria stopped contributing after the first year) and eventually Iraq, the offices were ultimately closed.

Fadhel and his associates worked hard to make sure that Syria and Lebanon were invited to the 1945 San Francisco Conference for the organization of the United Nations. This was Fadhel's debut in a major world conference. As the Conference opened, the French were bombarding Damascus, and Jamali denounced the assault, asking the French if the attack was in harmony with their principles of liberty, fraternity and equality. The Lebanese delegation included, Charles Malik, an old friend and classmate of Fadhel's from the American University of Beirut (AUB). In fact, there were more graduates from AUB than from any other university in the world at the San Francisco meeting. Jamali felt right at home.

Although Fadhel was the junior in the delegation at San Francisco, he signed the [31]Charter for Iraq because Nuri es-Sa'id and the others had left early to protest America's refusal to apply the principle of self-determination to Palestine. It was a mark of confidence on the part of Prime Minister Nuri.

A few months later, on August 4, 1944, Sarah's beloved father, Harvey Oliver Powell passed away at age 76 after a battle with pneumonia. He had been ailing and suffered pain and cramping in his hand as well as a bout with skin cancer. In more recent years, he had suffered with heart issues. He had a high pulse rate, kidney and bladder infections and finally succumbed to his heart failure and died peacefully in the Regina General Hospital. Unfortunately, due to the war and Sarah's quest to find suitable placement for Laith, Sarah was unable to attend her father's funeral. Harvey was returned to his home State of Wisconsin to have his final resting place alongside his ancestors in the Greenwood Cemetery in River Falls. He would be fondly remembered by his family and friends as a pleasant man with a mischievous smile and a marvelous sense of humour. As his daughter, Lydia stated, "Father was an expert on anything he cared to set his mind to."

---

[31] UN World Charter signed by countries agreeing to uphold world peace

1945 Laith & A Special Teacher

While Fadhel and his fellow delegates were striving for Arab rights in Palestine and world peace at the UN meetings, Sarah had been looking for a special teacher for Laith. It had become clear that there was no place for him in a regular school any longer. She realized that her teaching skills, although exemplary by her effort and her training, were not enough for Laith. She knew she was too emotionally connected to him. She felt he may do better with someone other than his mother as his teacher. It would have to be someone who could devote themselves to Laith during the day. She tried hiring an Iraqi woman to take charge of him during the day but no one would accept. No one wanted to work in a private home. Professional pride and local traditions stood in the way of this idea. It was far too expensive to hire a European woman.

Finally, a young man who was an elementary school teacher with some experience took an interest in Laith's case. He suggested taking Laith to his village in the north of Iraq for two months during the summer vacation. This young man was exceptionally good at managing children and Sarah felt she could trust him to look after her son. The teacher had no difficulty with Laith. The child had a healthy, happy summer in the cool hills of northern Iraq. He played with his Meccano, walked a great deal, and paddled in the swimming pool near the village.

For the first time in years, Sarah felt like she was on vacation. She and the rest of the family were able to live a normal life. Sarah paid more attention to Usameh and Abbas. She knew she had been putting most of her mental and physical energy into caring for Laith. It was heartening to be free to play and teach the other two little boys things that she was happy to share with them. It was also a much-needed time of reconnecting with her husband. Both had been far too busy and involved in serious matters of great importance but, now—it was a time to enjoy being a couple and a family again. Fadhel took them rowing on the Tigris and they played in the park and had picnics without any tantrums from anyone! It was glorious. Of course, Sarah was thinking of Laith, but she knew he was content and that allowed her to also be content.

Laith returned home in the fall looking very fit, but on his second day at home, he threw one of his worst tantrums. He smashed his fist through a window pane and cut his wrist, so Sarah removed his clothing to prevent him from tearing at it and locked him in an empty room once more. She called the teacher and asked him to please come and see Laith. He told her, "You don't know how to manage him."

She asked him how he had managed Laith all summer so well. He told her that he used a system of rewards and punishments and suggested that she adopt this system into their everyday life. She knew that she could not carry it out with any sort of consistency, so she reverted back to the old way of doing things. And, of course, the tantrums carried on.

Advice from Others

People who may have good intentions sometimes make the most incredulous suggestions about how one should live their life or how to raise their children. One such thing happened when the Jamalis' chauffeur suggested that Sarah take Laith to a famous Mullah (a respected teacher or healer) who was credited with many cures. He said that Laith could be treated by this man with prayers and talismans, and by chaining him to a shrine for a whole night. Another person had suggested that Sarah should lock Laith in a room, feed him food like a wild animal and let fate take its course. It was difficult to keep a straight face and not scream at these ridiculous suggestions.

Sometimes when we least expect it, help comes out of the blue. Or, perhaps, as Sarah thought— it could be considered a Divine intervention. This was the case when Sarah received a phone call from Mr. Lampard, Secretary of the YMCA.

"Mrs. Jamali, I have a wonderful man here, a psychologist. He is in Iraq giving lectures to the British Army. I have heard him speak and I think he is great. I want you to meet him because I think he might be able to help Laith."

Sarah thanked Mr. Lampard, as she knew him to be a very kind man and knew his intentions were for Laith's best interest; however, she had serious doubts that anyone was going to be able to help Laith. But she reminded herself that she had always vowed to keep an

179

open mind when it came to finding help for Laith. She would see this psychologist. What could it hurt?

Sarah was immediately impressed by this psychologist. He surprised her with his learning and his understanding. She asked his opinion about the epilepsy and he told her that it might be caused by the strain of the environment. He went on to tell her that certain kinds of epilepsy ceased when the patient was put in a suitable institution where there was less strain on the nervous system. Sarah began to have a feeling of hope.

"Why don't you put your son in a special school? It would be the best thing for him." Sarah nodded in agreement but stopped short at what the doctor said next.

"A mother—even the best mother in the world, can never do for her child what a school can do."

This remark cut Sarah like a knife and she bit her lip for fear of letting him know what she really felt. She found the remark extremely irritating. After all, was she not a trained teacher with years of experience? Could she not teach her son whatever he was capable of learning? Besides, she loved him and no one on God's earth could love Laith more than she did. How could her care be considered not good enough or bad for her child? She was filled with wounded pride. She was sure the psychologist was wrong but she remained silent because she didn't want to expose her conceit. All she could do was ask, "Where can I possibly send him? There are no such schools in Iraq, or anywhere in the Arab world."

To add to Sarah's shock, the doctor replied without hesitation, "Send him to England."

"England? Will an English school accept an Iraqi boy? How long would he stay at such a school?"

"There will be no difficulties, believe me. Your child will be accepted to any special school in England."

Sarah thanked the doctor and promised to look into the matter further. Before channeling all her effort into a school in England, Sarah enquired to her brothers and sister in the United States to see if there were any such schools there. It turned out that the private schools were too expensive and the government schools would not accept Laith because Sarah was not a tax payer.

The psychologist sent Sarah a list of schools for children with mental deficiencies as well as of colonies for epileptics. She began the tedious procedure of writing and receiving replies from these schools. Due to this time-consuming process, nothing more would be done that year.

Chapter 16

1946 Trip to England

"Where's my new suit, Sarah?" Fadhel was searching in his closet. He was packing for another business trip to England. He was preparing to attend the London Conference on Palestine.

"I steamed it for you; it's right here hanging on the back of the door. I wanted to let it air out."

"Thank you. Will you please pick out ties to go with those shirts I've laid out? You are so much better at that than I." Fadhel was grabbing socks from his sock drawer and packing things into his suitcase.

"Fadhel, I have a favour to ask. If I give you a list of schools, will you please take some time to check at least some of them out while you are in England?" Sarah took a folded piece of paper from her pocket and handed it to Fadhel and then selected some ties to match his shirts. She mused at how his collection of shirts and ties was growing.

"Well, they usually do allow us some free time at these conferences so I'll do my best. I may not get to them all, but I'll try." Fadhel took the paper and put it into his suitcase.

It was September of 1946. As Fadhel was flying to London, Laith was getting injections of Calcium Sandoz for decalcification to his teeth which had been noticed by one of his doctors. Another of his doctors suggested that Sarah get tablets of glutamic acid from the USA. Sarah contacted her sister, Lydia, who was able to get a supply. In the meantime, Sarah had found a medical leaflet that explained that the drug had been used to experiment on rats. It was observed that the rats that received the drug learned faster than rats that did not receive the drug. Sarah administered the drug to Laith for many months, but unfortunately, there was no improvement. It was so disheartening to think that a rat could improve its ability to learn by taking the drug and, yet, it was useless to a young boy who could benefit so much in his life from just a little help.

ഇ൫

Fadhel returned from his trip to London and told Sarah of a small boarding school not far from London. He had spoken to the administration and they had agreed to take Laith.

"I saw children outside raking leaves in the garden as I drove up to the school. There were a number of pets as well. From what I saw of the place, I think you would approve. You will have to determine that for yourself, of course. I didn't have time to go to many places but I managed to see two and this one was the best in my opinion." Fadhel seemed hopeful in his report of this news to Sarah.

Although the government schools were about to open, Sarah once again took a leave of absence from her teaching job and began making preparations to go to England with Laith. The flight from Baghdad to London followed the route from Baghdad, Cairo, Castel Benito, Marseilles, London with an overnight in Cairo. Laith seemed content during the first part of the journey. Sarah kept him well amused with playing games, telling stories and taking naps. However, after the night in Cairo and during the flight over the Mediterranean, there were some turbulents. Laith became disturbed and frantic to get off the airplane. There was no calming him or making any sense to him. He became violent, tearing at Sarah's hair and her hands, pulling the handle off her purse and slapping her. Passengers and stewards pretended to not see but clearly they couldn't help but witness the goings on. When they reached Marseilles, Sarah found a doctor on duty at the airport and asked him for some sleeping medication for Laith. He was very reluctant until Sarah explained a little about Laith's history and his violent tendencies. Finally the doctor relented and gave Sarah half a pill which Laith took without any problem. He liked taking pills. The rest of the journey went without further incident.

The First School

At times like this, Sarah was thankful for some of the perks afforded her through her husband's position. Arrangements had been made for her arrival for someone from the Iraqi Embassy to meet her and Laith. They were able to forego the formalities at the airport with ease and were driven toward London where a lovely hotel room had been reserved for them. Their accommodation was at the Claridges, a four-star hotel. They had a comfortable evening with dinner served to their room. Although the luxury of this hotel was much appreciated, Sarah called a

185

friend and asked her to find them a room in a less expensive hotel. They settled into a small place at Queens Gate, near the Iraqi Embassy. As soon as possible, Sarah called to make an appointment at the school recommended by Fadhel. That same afternoon, they took a train to the town where the school was located and found a hotel for the night since the appointment was for the next morning at nine o'clock.

The next day, they arrived at the school, which was privately owned and run by a woman doctor. They were ushered into her office. The woman seemed surprised to see them which struck Sarah odd since she had booked an appointment. The woman took them to a classroom where there were young girls with Down syndrome sitting at desks having a writing lesson. Once seated in the office again, the woman explained, "I'm sorry but we cannot accept your son in our school as he is too old."

"Perhaps you think he's older because he is rather tall for his age. He's only just turned eleven, you know," Sarah explained.

"Well, I know how old he is but you see—we only plan to accommodate young [32]Mongols."

"I see—I guess that's it then. Thank you for your time. We can see ourselves out," Sarah took Laith by the hand and they made their way back to the train station and returned to London to their hotel.

Once again, Sarah had to hold her tongue. She couldn't believe that this important age criteria wouldn't

---

[32] Mongols - the term used for Down syndrome children at that time

186

have come up when Fadhel visited the school. Or, at least it should have been mentioned on the telephone when she booked the appointment. There was no use fretting over it now. She would just move on to selecting another school to visit. What else was she to do?

The Second School

There had been some correspondence between Sarah and a large school in London. She called to make an appointment. When she and Laith arrived at the school, Laith stayed with a teacher while Sarah took a tour with the head matron of the school. She was shown sleeping rooms, single rooms, clothing storerooms, some lovely American dresses of a girl from the USA, costumes for fancy dress parties, the central hall where the children would meet and play together. Everything was pristine and quite lovely but devoid of any sign of the children that lived there.

"I think of this as a chosen vocation, not simply a job. I love my work so much and would choose the same type of service if I had to choose my life work all over again," the matron said with great pride.

"That's very commendable, indeed. I wonder, would it be possible to see some of the children?" Sarah asked not wanting to sound too pushy, but after all, it was important she felt.

"I'm sorry—it is against the policy of the school to allow someone to see the children." The matron was very matter of fact about it and Sarah could tell there was no use in pushing. However, this made her feel quite uneasy about this school and she began to have serious doubts. The matron then escorted her to see the director, a middle-aged man who said that there was an opening and they could take Laith. All she had to do was sign a few forms. One form informed her that she should not visit her child for a week to allow him time to settle into his new surroundings. Another form stated that the school could request the removal of the child if management found at any time that he was not fit for the school. Another form was for the deposit of fees in advance. Sarah signed the paperwork and agreed to bring Laith and his belongings to the school the next day.

As she left the school, she noticed a young woman in a wheelchair being taken away. Sarah asked the doorman who she was and he told her the woman was a resident that was deemed unfit to stay in the school any longer. Apparently, she caused too much trouble. This also worried Sarah as she knew only too well that her son was quite capable of causing a ruckus if he got upset. She hoped that the caregivers would be well trained people who would know how to work with children like Laith, even when they might have tantrums, but she had more doubts.

As she and Laith walked on the sidewalk alongside beautifully manicured, sprawling lawns that stretched down to the elegant wrought-iron gates, where huge old trees extended their shade over the lush grass, Sarah noticed that there wasn't a single sign of a living soul anywhere. It seemed a shame to have all this beautiful garden space going to waste on such a lovely day. Sarah had a sinking feeling that the director and matron had not been completely open with her about the conditions of the school. She would keep searching for another school; however, she could not take Laith with her while she continued hunting for other schools so her plan was to leave him at this London school for the required one-week's trial basis. The next day she took him back to the school, hugged and kissed him and then left him. As she walked the long sidewalk to the gate, tears filled her eyes and she felt broken hearted. But it was only a week and this would be a test to see what she could learn.

Next, she visited the Council for Mental Health in London and asked their advice about a school for a child like Laith. They gave her a list of private schools. She set out to visit some of them but quickly found out that all of these schools closed over vacations throughout the year. This would not work for Laith. He needed to be in a school that could keep him all year. Unfortunately, the only school that offered that service was the London school where she had left Laith for the week.

When the week ended, Sarah went to visit Laith. Before she saw him, she went to speak with the head matron. She asked her how Laith had behaved. The matron told her that once when all the children were playing games, he had caused trouble, but that he was getting along better now. Sarah knew how crowds and noise upset Laith. She was not reassured that if in the same situation, he would not cause trouble again. Finally, she was taken to meet Laith and they went for a walk alone. Again, she noticed that no one else was enjoying the beautiful grounds around the building. What a shame she thought. She was glad she was there to give Laith a little outing in the fresh air.

"Have you been a good boy, Laith?" Laith just looked down at the ground and made no response. So Sarah tried again, "What did they do to you when you were naughty?"

"They put me on my bed. They shook me."

"What did you do then?" No reply from Laith.

"Do you often play outside?"

"No, they never take us outside."

Greatly disturbed by this, Sarah took Laith back into the school and turned him over to the matron. She wanted to say something but decided it was wise to hold her tongue. She went back to her hotel room and put in a long-distance call to Fadhel who was in Cairo on business. He was presiding over the Council of the Arab League.

"How are your meetings going? I got your message this morning that you are in Cairo. This must have come up quickly after I left. I didn't realize you were scheduled to meet in Cairo." Sarah kicked off her shoes and perched on the bed. It had been an exhausting day but she imagined it was the same for Fadhel.

"Yes, it was rather in haste but I did know it might be in the works. I met today with President Truman's personal representative, a chap named George Brownell. He's just been to India negotiating traffic agreements."

"Oh, that's interesting. What did you discuss with him?"

"I told him that there is great danger of revolution throughout the Arab world if Arab rights are violated. He sent me an enquiry just a week before asking about the

190

possibility of obtaining a civil aviation agreement. I told him it is now up to the President to think whether he really wants to become the cause of international instability and insecurity in this part of the world."

"Oh dear—it all sounds so intense and stressful. I'm sure you must be frustrated."

"Yes, at times I certainly am but let's not talk about this anymore. I'm anxious to hear how you have made out with the search for a school," Fadhel let out a sigh as if to expel all the tensions of his day.

"I've cancelled my plane reservation and I don't know when I'll be returning to Baghdad. The first school you recommended to me won't take Laith because he's considered too old! Can you believe that? A mere child who's barely turned eleven is too old for their school! They only want young Down syndrome children. I've left Laith in the huge London school but I'm not comfortable with the situation there," Sarah broke the news to Fadhel.

"Sarah, you are likely just letting your emotions get the better of you. . ."

"Fadhel, don't—just don't, please. You would feel exactly the same if you were here and witnessed what I've seen. Trust me."

"Leave Laith in the school and come home Sarah. He'll adjust. Nothing will ever be perfect. Come home. I'll soon be home and we both know our situation at home will improve once Laith is settled there."

"No, I've got to stay until I find a better school. I'm not leaving my child until I am convinced that he will be in good hands."

191

"As you wish, Dearest— I do trust your judgment. I am just concerned about you and want you back home as soon as possible. Everyone misses you there."

"I know, I miss you and everyone too," Sarah hung up and went down to the front desk to extend her stay at the hotel. She explained to the owner of the hotel that she would be staying a little longer to continue looking for a school for her son. The housekeeper overheard her and approached her later. She told her that she was an [33]anthroposophist, and that she had heard of a new school in Scotland. Sarah began to enquire about anthroposophy and the [34]Rudolf Steiner schools.

Sarah learned about Rudolf Steiner. In 1913, he founded anthroposophy. He believed that in man—body and soul form a unit. He considered a person as a whole to be physical, emotional, mental and spiritual. The teacher and pupil form a unit. Together, they should both progress. The teacher should believe in the Creator of the Universe, and practice his religion, just as he introduces prayer to his pupil. Emotionally, the teachers and the pupils should feel united. Physically, they should spend as much time as possible in the open air.

Life in a remedial school combines all the things necessary for the development of a normal child. In addition, it gives treatment designed to correct deficiencies found in each individual child. Rudolf Steiner did not use

---

[33] Anthroposophy - a formal educational, therapeutic, and creative system established by Rudolf Steiner, seeking to use mainly natural means to optimize physical and mental health and well-being.

[34] Rudolf Steiner 1861-1925, Swiss philosopher, educator, and naturalist

the term 'mentally retarded' or 'mentally handicapped'. He thought that children learn about the world in stages. In the first seven years the child learns through imitation. In the next seven years, the child develops his speech and body. Educational material includes music, art, emotions, and body rhythms. For the first time, Sarah was hearing something and learning about something that excited her. She knew she needed to look into this further and find the school that was using these new techniques. The housekeeper told her the name of such a school in Scotland was Garvald.

The Third School

Sarah made an appointment with Garvald School. She spoke to a Dr. Schroeder who explained that there was an opening but that they would need to meet Laith in person before accepting him. Sarah decided it would be wise to leave Laith registered in the London school until she was sure that she could move him into Garvald. She wanted to inspect Garvald first and then make her decision so as to not be caught without any school for Laith. She contacted the London school telling them that she was making a trip to Scotland (she did not state the reason for this trip). She told them she wanted to take Laith with her. They said this would be permitted and so she bought two tickets for the night train to Edinburgh. From Edinburgh, they took a bus to Dolphinton. From there, they walked for fifteen minutes to the school which was a former manor house situated in the heart of the rolling countryside. The structure was stately and was like an aristocratic home rather than like an institutional building. Sarah was immediately impressed and felt that she had finally found a place that had a homey appeal.

Dr. Schroeder had a friendly approach and welcomed them into his office. He and Sarah talked for a long time about the type of treatment used in the school, the education of mentally challenged children and the application of the philosophy of Rudolf Steiner.

"Now, Mrs. Jamali, I have to ask you—I know you are coming from a very long distance, from Iraq. Are you leaving your son here as a sort of desertion, or do you intend to keep in contact with him? Contact with parents is very important for the development of the child, you know," Dr. Schroeder leaned forward and looked straight into Sarah's eyes with his question. He seemed to be searching her expression and assessing her very keenly at this moment.

"I'm not deserting my child and I will visit him whenever I can. I would rather have him in Baghdad where we could see him often but, as you may know, there are no such schools available there at this time. If it ever becomes possible to have him in Baghdad again, that would be my preference, of course," Sarah looked the doctor in the eye unwavering with her earnest response.

Sarah went on to tell the doctor as much as she could about Laith's abilities, his personality traits—both the good and the bad points. She wanted to be as open and honest with him as she hoped he would be with her.

"Laith loves his Meccano set. He will amuse himself building little airplanes by the hour. I've brought masses of it for him. I just thought you should know how much he enjoys playing with it."

The doctor smiled gently and replied, "I'm sorry but anything mechanical is undesirable for Laith as it will only make him more nervous." Sarah found this to be rather curious but she was willing to accept that the doctor likely knew what he was talking about. Perhaps it was something that over stimulated the brain and might contribute to Laith becoming intense at times. When she thought about it more, she could understand that it may well have contributed to some of his mood swings and tantrums that seemed to come from out of the blue at times.

After further discussion, Sarah and Laith were given a tour. They were introduced to all the teachers and the children at the school lunch. The children all sat down quietly in the dining room and had their meal together, boys and girls and teachers. After lunch it was agreed that Laith should remain at Garvald. Sarah was much relieved that he could stay here and not have to go back to the school in London. However, she needed to return there to retrieve his belongings.

When she returned to the London school, she was met by the Director's daughter who seemed to be a charming young woman. She noticed Sarah was without Laith.

"I see Laith is not with you today, I hope he is well. Will we expect him back to school soon?" she asked.

"Thank you for seeing me today. No, Laith won't be returning. I will be removing my son from the school. I'm just here to retrieve his belongings," Sarah explained.

"I'm sorry to hear this; we were just getting nicely acquainted with Laith. Will you be taking him back to Baghdad?"

"No, actually, I have found a school where he will be taught carpentry and farming—and these subjects, as you know, are not offered here. And furthermore, if you don't mind me being perfectly frank—I cannot bring myself to trust a school where I am not allowed to meet the other children," Sarah wanted to be clear on this because she felt it was important that the school hear it straight from her. They needed to get some feedback and perhaps consider things going forward.

"That policy was established by my father because people who understood nothing about the matter spread the most awful stories after they had seen the children. But, in some cases, the school makes an exception and we will make an exception for you." She went to the door and spoke to someone to ask the head matron to please bring one of the children to meet Sarah. A few minutes later, a healthy young Irish boy was brought in to meet Sarah. He was ten years old and polite. He said, "How do you do?"

The matron who stood with her arms crossed and looking rather dour, spoke up saying, "This young chap has become fond of Laith and keeps asking where he has gone."

All this was well and fine but to Sarah it was too little too late. She had made up her mind—she was going to leave Laith in Scotland. Now she just needed to return to Garvald School with his belongings and say her good-byes to him.

196

Just as Sarah had questioned Laith about the London school, she wanted to question him about Garvald. From his responses, she felt sure that he had not received any physical punishment. The matron told her that physical punishment was forbidden in this school. They never used it; nor did they use any mood-altering type drugs. Sarah watched Laith and he seemed content. She had a strong feeling that this was the right place for Laith, finally. She thanked the Director for accepting him and turned to Laith.

"Son, come here. I have to go home now for a time," she smiled at him.

"Home? I come too?" Laith looked up at Sarah. Laith's speech was often limited to single words or short phrases.

"No, you will stay here at your new school and you will learn many new things here. You are going to learn carpentry and farming. Won't that be great fun?"

"Yes, carpentry. Drive a tractor!" Laith expressed with excitement. Laith still loved tractors and any type of animal. Sarah hoped this opportunity would give him great pleasure in the days ahead.

"Alright, Darling, let's have a hug and a kiss." Sarah bent down and embraced Laith and held him close just long enough to hold him without crushing him and scaring him with her last embrace. She didn't want to let go—but letting go was what this was all about. She had to let him go to be with people who might be able to give him something she could not. She had to let go so she could return to Fadhel, Usameh and Abbas. They needed her too. She stood up and patted Laith on the top of his head and turned with a little wave and made her way out. Her eyes blurred with tears as she walked away from the school.

She had a two-hour wait at the train station in Edinburgh. It was Sunday evening and she knew there was a church near the station. As it was time for the evening service, Sarah decided to go into the church. She was feeling very sad and alone and thought being in church might give her some comfort. She took a seat in a pew near the back of the church to be inconspicuous as possible. She had been praying every day and asking God for guidance. She felt He had guided her to the right school and she would give a little prayer of thanks. She was feeling very emotional and was already missing her son. As soon as the music began to play, her eyes welled with tears and she wept silently through all the hymns, the sermon and the prayers. The tears just kept falling. Even though she knew people were looking at her with sympathy, she couldn't stop the tears from flowing. She was thankful that no one approached her and she escaped without drawing further attention. She dried her eyes and returned to the station.

This was the saddest day of her life. Had she done the right thing? Yes, she knew in her mind it was the right thing and especially the right thing for Laith. As painful as this parting was for her, she loved her child enough to want to give him an opportunity to learn to be independent of her. She could not live with him every day and continue putting him in an empty room every time he had a tantrum. His physical strength was already almost more than she was able to manage. Keeping him with her would only make things more difficult for him when she became too old to care for him.

She had to talk to herself about this as she made her journey home. Other people in Europe sent their young children away to boarding schools all the time. This would be like that, she reasoned with herself. She would visit Laith as soon as possible and as often as possible. Her reasoning made sense, but her heart wasn't listening to her mind. She prayed that time would be a healer and she prayed that Laith would be able to cope with his new home and that the staff there would be able to cope with him as well. She prayed that his endearing qualities would outshine any of his shortcomings. She hoped others would learn to like him even if they could never love him as she did.

Chapter 17

The United Nations 1945

The UN meetings included 48 nations. Among them were five Arab countries: Egypt, Iraq, Lebanon, Sa'udi Arabia and Syria. These Arab delegates worked hard to be sure there would be guarantees in the UN Charter for the independence of Syria and Lebanon, for the rights of non-independent Arab states and to protect Palestine from Zionist invasion. They gained some success in their objectives except for that of achieving self-determination for Palestine. Jamali took part in the committees drafting the portions of the Charter that dealt with trusteeship and with the Security Council. Iraq and the other developing countries insisted on the right of all nations to be free.

An impasse was reached in the Trusteeship Committee when the Arab states asked for a text which would protect the Arabs of Palestine from unwanted immigration and guarantee their independence. There was conflict between the Arab delegates and the American delegates who were pressured by the Zionists seated directly behind them at the conference. This struggle lasted for a month. As a result, Article 80 made no mention of the rights of Palestinian Arabs. This opened the way for President Truman to ignore those rights and to involve the USA in support of what Jamali called, "the ugliest imperialistic operation enacted in modern history."

UN Conference 1946

In September, 1946, Fadhel represented Iraq at the Palais de Luxembourg Conference in Paris. The purpose of this conference was to debate the fate of the former Italian colony of Libya for which he asked immediate independence. Also at this time, things had changed for Syria. It had been under the control of the Vichy Government until the British and Free France invaded and occupied the country in July 1941. Syria proclaimed its independence in 1941 but it was not until January 1, 1944, that it was recognized as an independent republic. Finally on April 17, 1946 the French evacuated the last of their troops and Syria was completely independent.

During the Conference, it was made clear that Britain wanted Cyrenaica; Italy and Russia both wanted Tripoli; France wanted the Fezzan, and United States wanted an air base. Jamali urged that if the conference did not grant immediate independence, trusteeship powers should be exercised either by the Arab League or by a League member. He also asked that Iraq be admitted as a full member of the conference, reminding them that his country had declared war on Italy in January, 1943.

Following these meetings, American President, Harry Truman, asked of Britain that the 1939 White Paper on Palestine no longer be enforced. The White Paper limited the Jewish immigration into Palestine to 15,000 people a year for five years, at the end of which Palestine was to be independent. Britain's Foreign Secretary opposed setting the White Paper aside because doing so would open the door to unlimited entry for Jews into Palestine where tensions were already dangerously high.

Truman asked Britain to permit immediate entry for 100,000 Jewish refugees and detainees. Up to then, emigrant Jews who had left Europe without visas for Palestine at the urging of the Jewish Agency, had been detained in Cyprus as illegal immigrants. Truman's announcement was a bombshell and showed a total lack of teamwork with Britain. Negotiations between USA and Britain followed with the agreement that an Anglo-American Committee of Enquiry be sent to Europe and the Arab countries to study conditions and submit a report as to what seemed appropriate regarding current Jewish immigration and the future of Palestine itself. The Committee's twelve members included several Zionists. Jamali was designated to represent Iraq. He asked the Committee to apply the same principle to Arabs and non-Arabs alike. He cited the Golden Rule, "Do unto others as you would have them do unto you." He invited the Committee to come to Baghdad to hear political leaders there, both Arab and Jew. The invitation was not accepted.

The Committee's conclusion was in agreement with Truman's wishes, and the Report recommended immediate entry into Palestine for 100,000 Jews. The Arab League States were outraged. *The New York Times* reported (February 6, 1947) that the unexpected violent reaction of the Arab League's delegates to any suggestion of a partition of Palestine had shaken Foreign Secretary Bevin and other top officials of the Foreign and Colonial Offices and that the outspoken attacks had forced a hurried reconsideration of plans. Nonetheless, the partition proposal prevailed. Jamali was still holding out a hope for a peaceful solution and on February 4, 1947 he stated:

"There is no reason why Jews and Arabs should not live together amicably, if Zionism gives up its political aspirations and becomes cultural and spiritual Zionism."

Life in Garvald

Sarah and Fadhel were more than pleased with Laith's care at Garvald. The school emphasized speech and gave training in group speech. Developing emotions was encouraged by teaching the appreciation of beauty and nature. Picnics were a frequent treat organized for the children as well as a favourite activity of acting out of familiar stories. Inspiration and a feeling of unity came through the teaching of simple prayers which were recited before meals with a simple grace repeated in unison of, "We thank Thee, God, for our food." At night, the children and teachers held hands and recited an evening prayer which had been written by Rudolf Steiner.

Birthdays of each child were celebrated at the dinner table by placing a lighted candle before the birthday child. A cake, presents and little party were also arranged for the child at some part of the day.

Christmas was a very happy time. The season was well recognized with gifts to send and gifts to receive. Laith was taught handwork and created some baskets using basketry and wool. Each year one piece of his work was sent to Sarah for Christmas. The story of the nativity was taught and acted out with music and acting. Music was a highlight and brought pleasure to all. The teachers all played an instrument such as violin, cello, flute, recorder, or piano. This reminded Sarah of similar family gatherings in her childhood home in Weyburn when Harvey would join in playing his cello with Libbie at the piano or Sarah and Lydia playing a piano duet accompanied by Harvey. It gave her great comfort to see the effort put forth to bring music and the spirit of Christmas to Laith and the other children of Garvald.

In the evening after the younger children were put to bed, the older ones were allowed to sit up to sing and listen to recorded music. Sometimes Laith was taken to Edinburgh to attend an orchestral concert.

All of this was what Sarah had yearned for Laith to experience. From all reports, he was adjusting fine and he was making new friends. The children were treated with respect and given encouragement to allow them to flourish to their best abilities.

There were earnest attempts to teach Laith to read; however, no matter what method was used, he still could not master it.

ℰℭ

As much as Sarah was thankful for Garvald and the exceptional care being given to Laith, that didn't prevent her from suffering great pain of separation from him. She referred to this pain as a form of "amputation and severed nerves." She would suddenly feel sure that Laith was crying and that he needed her. This feeling usually hit her at the end of a day when she had time to think. If she kept herself busy and occupied, she seemed alright. When the agony of this terrible feeling came over her, she managed to sooth herself by figuring out what time of day it was in Scotland and then she could assure herself that Laith would be sound asleep at that time. She would tell herself that her sensations had no validity.

Other thoughts crept into her mind that caused her anxiety. She worried about what might happen to Laith so far away in the case of war. Would he suffer starvation or annihilation? How could she possibly protect him? She would have to force herself to change the subject in her thoughts. Sarah prayed every night and sometimes during the day asking God to take care of her son. She decided that none of us can foretell the future but can only live one day at a time. She would put her trust in the goodness of the Lord.

Usameh & Abbas

When Sarah returned to Baghdad from Scotland, she made an earnest attempt to reconnect with her other two little sons. Usameh was about ten and Abbas was three. The boys had not only been separated from their mother recently by geographical distance but also by emotional distance. This was something Sarah had been aware of but she was not able to split herself equally in so many different directions. This was part of the reason for her search to find a suitable new home for Laith. It was for Laith's best interest but also for the best interest of the other two boys.

As previously mentioned, there had been deep concerns about the increase in violent tendencies with Laith. One such incident occurred one day when Sarah was not present to witness it. Something had happened most likely when the boys were outside playing. Abbas was just a tiny toddler and had likely done something that had annoyed Laith. Laith picked up a stone and threw it at Abbas hitting the toddler in the head. Abbas bore the scar of this for a long time. This incident brought to the fore, the danger of having a mentally deficient child in the home with other children who were put at risk.

In an attempt to protect Abbas from Laith, Abbas had spent his first four years playing in the kitchen under the supervision and loving protection of Um Sania, the cook. Um Sania had allowed Abbas to learn certain habits that were acceptable to her but Sarah found them unacceptable to her way of life. She determined to break Abbas of these undesirable habits. She enlisted the help of Usameh and Fadhel and one habit at a time was corrected over a very long time period. They worked on one habit a year over several years.

Sarah also determined that it was time for Abbas to learn to speak English. She would begin by saying a word to him in English and then say it in Arabic. After a short time, less translation was necessary. She also read bedtime stories to the boys. She would start with a simple book for Abbas and then read from a more difficult one for Usameh. By listening to these stories in English, the young boys acquired a good vocabulary in English. [35]It was at this time that they were introduced to Mark Twain, the author of *The Adventures of Tom Sawyer* and *The Adventures of Huckleberry Finn.*

[36]Much to the delight of Abbas, Sarah loved animals and she seemed to accept that her sons could benefit by learning to care for pets. The menagerie of pets

---

[35] As told to author, Jan Keating, by Abbas Jamali

[36] Abbas Jamali – as quoted to Jan Keating, "Life with Mother was quite an adventure, thanks to Canada, Weyburn, Saskatchewan and USA."

included: cats, a ewe, a dog, a female donkey, chickens, pigeons, and even honey bees! Sarah believed as long as the boys cared for the pets, it would always be possible to add just one more. Abbas also began his love of plants through the early teachings of his mother. She encouraged him to plant things and to learn how to care for them. He remembers having date palms, Christ thorn and mulberry trees—"not bushes", as he stated for clarity.

Often Sarah would stop to think about her mother, Libbie, who had raised six children. Of course, Libbie never had the responsibility of a child like Laith; nevertheless, Sarah marveled at the mothering skills her mother had managed during those days back in Weyburn. Sarah wondered how her mother had mustered the energy for six children when it was taxing to look after just two boys now. However, she did feel a sense of relief in knowing she could now devote more time to Usameh and Abbas.

Libbie had moved back to the United States after Harvey's death. For a short time, she had moved in with her youngest son, Louis, and his family. She had just recently moved in with Lydia and Ed to their home in Prospect Park, Pennsylvania, making this her permanent home. She once again became an American citizen.

Sarah wrote to her mother and family as often as possible. The letters and occasional telephone calls kept them abreast with one another. Sarah deeply regretted that she was not able to join the family at the time of Harvey's death. Of course the family understood. The war was still on at that time. But it was now over and had ended in 1945, a year after Harvey's death. Sarah hoped that now that Laith was in a good school and the war was over, perhaps she and Fadhel might be able to plan a trip to the United States. However, it was too soon yet. She still wanted to visit Laith before she went anywhere else.

1947 Sarah and Fadhel go to London

Fadhel had been attending meetings in New York City and was on his way back, via London. While in London, he made a quick trip to Scotland to see Laith. He found the boy to be in good health and spirits. He was pleased with all the conditions that he noted in the school. Before he could reach Baghdad, he received word that he must return to London in three days time.

℘℘

"I'd like very much for you to join me, Sarah. And, since the government of Iraq has offered to provide tickets for the wives of delegates, it seems an opportune time to consider a trip, don't you think?" Fadhel was at his desk in the study gathering papers to take with him back to London.

"Yes, I would like to go but what about the boys?"

"Well, I'm sure they will be fine with Um Sania and you can enlist the extra help of the neighbours. Their boys are always playing with our boys anyway."

"You're right. I will go. I can squeeze in a trip to Scotland while we're there. I've been longing to see Laith and he'll be so happy to see me so soon after seeing you just days ago. I'll make arrangements. I will need to start packing. I've not much time to prepare."

210

"Could I come too? Oh please Mother, let me come," Usameh had overheard this conversation and stepped into the study. He was a sturdy, good looking lad of eleven now. His hair was sandy coloured with blonde highlighted streaks like his mother's. His aqua-blue eyes seemed to sparkle and were captivating; like windows to his soul, they always betrayed his feelings.

"Me too, Mummy? I want to see Laith. I'll give him one of my new toys! He'll like that," Abbas was a sweet little four-year old with a big heart. His fair hair and beautiful eyes gave him a cherub look and although he was not always the perfect 'little angel', he was Sarah's little angel. He was a bright little fellow that brought so much happiness to the family.

"Oh, darlings, not this time. You both have school," Sarah put Abbas on her knee and hugged him.

"But Mother, up until now, I haven't seen very much of the world!" Usameh implored with a longing look that could melt one's heart.

"Well, don't forget, you did see quite a bit of the world when I took you and Laith to the United States and Canada."

"Oh, yes, but I was only three years old then! That doesn't count because I don't remember it very well."

"Usameh, your Mother has told you why you cannot accompany us so that is enough on the subject. There will be other times, Son. We will take a family vacation sometime."

211

"Yes Sir. . . but Mother always tells me that quote—to not give up if the first response to a request is 'no'," Usameh persisted.

Fadhel stopped shuffling papers and looked questioningly at Sarah over the rim of his dark, round-framed eye glasses.

"It is from Carl Jung. It's one of his inspirational quotes about never giving up. I thought it was character building," Sarah rolled her eyes and grimaced as she shrugged her shoulders.

"I think that quote has come back to bite you. Now you have given our son free license to protest every time we say 'no'."

"Perhaps I should have added—unless the word 'no' comes from your parents. Usameh, I am sorry but this trip is just for adults. Off you go!"

ॐ

Sarah and Fadhel enjoyed the travel time to London. Being together without any children was a rare treat for Sarah. When Laith was with them, it had been difficult to leave him with others so usually one of the parents was always with him. Sarah had been busy devoting time to the other two boys since she left Laith in Scotland and so now she was really enjoying some adult time with her husband.

Upon their arrival to London, Fadhel was immediately involved in meetings. Sarah took advantage of the free time to go to Scotland to see Laith. It was a nice surprise for him even though it was not usually good to spring surprises on Laith. But in this case, he met her with a big smile and warm hug.

"Look how tall you are getting to be now Laith! You look like a very strong young man," Sarah beamed at her young son and noticed how clean and well groomed he looked. She knew he loved to be clean and neat so it lifted her heart to see that he was being cared for and kept the way he wanted.

"I am strong. I work on the farm. I make things in carpentry. I eat my vegetables. Vegetables make me strong."

"Yes indeed. I am happy to see you. Shall we go outside for a nice walk together?"

"Yes, I like to walk outside. I get my sweater first. You come to my room."

Sarah spent three days in Scotland with Laith and then returned to London to attend a gala evening with Fadhel. She promised to come back within a couple of days to celebrate Laith's birthday by taking him to the circus. It was late in July and Laith's birthday had already passed but that didn't matter. Fadhel had brought him a present when he visited earlier that month and now Sarah would top things up with a fun day at the circus.

ℴℹ

Back in London, Sarah was dressing for the gala evening. She wore a floor-length evening gown with a white, Chantilly lace, bodice with scallop-edged capped sleeves matching scallop-edged neckline, and black peau de soie, strait-cut skirt. She had been to the hair stylist earlier in the day and he had styled her hair into a loosely curled pageboy with the sides neatly rolled back from her face. She chose a simple drop-pearl earring and necklace set to compliment the Chantilly lace. She wore white, full-length evening gloves and carried a small silver clutch evening bag and matching silver shoes.

"Oh my . . . you look stunning," Fadhel looked at Sarah with loving eyes. "I love your hair like that! It reminds me of what you looked like when I first met you as a young university student."

"Thank you, Dear. I thought it would be something special for this evening. I'm glad you approve."

"I do indeed," and he extended his arm to her and they made their way to the dining room. They were a striking couple and heads turned as they made their entrance—he in his black and white tuxedo and she in her black and white evening gown. They joined the other Iraqi delegates for a delightful social evening. It was a romantic get-away and a time they would never forget. At the end of the evening, they sat on their balcony and watched the moonlight—love was in the air!

1947 Sarah and Fadhel go to New York

In the autumn of 1947, Sarah had the privilege of accompanying Fadhel on another UN trip to New York. She was a delegate in her own right, accredited to the UN Social, Humanitarian and Cultural Committee. While attending a luncheon at the Waldorf Astoria where they were staying, she was interviewed by a New York Times reporter. She pointed with pride to the fact that Iraq "has the strongest representation of women in the United Nations." In the interview, she also warned that, "There is

214

great danger of a popular uprising throughout the Arab world" if the UN accepted the partition plan for Palestine.

On October 6, 1947, at the request of Prime Minister Nuri as-Sa'id, Fadhel gave a summary of the Arab position to the Ad Hoc Committee. His speech concluded that the Palestine problem would appear to be very simple if it were considered according to the principles of democracy, justice and international law. The partition of Palestine passed in spite of the Arabs best efforts. The vote came up just before the long weekend recess for the American Thanksgiving Day (in November) which is always on a Thursday. When those in favour of partition saw that they did not have the required two-thirds' vote, they managed to rally the simple majority required to postpone the vote until after the holiday. This allowed them time to persuade enough delegations to ensure the passage of the partition plan by the required two thirds.

The United States and Russia competed in speedy recognition of the newly proclaimed state of Israel. Although the Soviets later switched their support to the Arabs, the Arabs did not forget that initial recognition and the aid they (the Russians) had given the Zionists. Fadhel embarrassed Vyshinsky (the Soviet Foreign Minister) several times. He is quoted as saying:

"Mr. Vyshinsky, I want to ask you one question. You people always spoke of Zionism as a reactionary force, and I have in Baghdad some books in English published in Russia against Zionism as reactionary. How is it that you supported this movement and you created Israel? What did you create Israel for?"

Vyshinksy replied, "I can't say."

Chapter 18

When Laith was first afflicted by his encephalitis, Sarah had confided to a friend that she wanted to help mentally handicapped children by opening a school in Baghdad. She felt that if she could accomplish this, it would mean that Laith's life was not a loss. She had a favourite saying which she had learned from her mother: "No experience is a total loss." She hoped something positive could be done for others as a sort of tribute to Laith's life. However, she was at a loss as to how to go about it all. Her friend advised: "The way will open in God's own time. When Allah wills, it will come to pass."

These words resonated with Sarah and seemed to give her comfort. She was able to put this idea of hers into God's hands and she was more willing now to wait for a sign. She waited for almost ten years and then something happened.

"Mrs. Jamali, may I have a word with you?" It was a mother of a Down syndrome child who approached Sarah one day while Sarah was out for a walk.

"Certainly," Sarah stopped to chat with the woman.

"Why don't the women of your Society (The Women's Temperance and Social Welfare Society) start a school for retarded children?" The woman was a neighbour who was familiar with Sarah and her son Laith.

217

She knew Sarah to be a teacher and a member of the Women's Temperance group.

"Well, it has been on my mind for many years, in fact. I have wanted to start such a school but I have not ever found a building suitable to open a school. Believe me when I tell you—I, like you, see the need for such a school in Baghdad."

"I have a suitable house that you can have for a very reasonable rent," the woman offered. She was not about to give up easily.

"I will take your offer to the next meeting of our group. Thank you for your offer. I will do my best and will talk to you again very soon."

Sarah reported the woman's offer to the members of her Society. They discussed it eagerly and voted unanimously to start a class for mentally retarded children. The class soon became a school which they named, Ramzi School, after the first child to be registered.

They soon realized that they needed help to develop the school. A Swiss woman living in Baghdad gave them the names of Dr. Maria Egg and her twin sister, Madame Louise Rossier who were experts in the education of mentally retarded children. Sarah wrote to them and Madame Louise Rossier volunteered to come to Baghdad for two weeks to help the women of the Society get started.

The twin sisters were born in Budapest, Hungary, but later they moved to Zurich, Switzerland, and became Swiss citizens. One day a friend confided her troubles to them about her Down syndrome child. She could not find any place willing to take her child to teach her. The twins thought that every child had a right to an education, so they began to teach the child in Madame Louise Rossier's kitchen. Other parents soon heard of the progress they were making and came to seek help. This was the beginning of the first school for mentally retarded children in Zurich. The two sisters became world famous for the school and workshop they developed, and for the books they wrote describing and analyzing the education of children with mental handicaps.

Sarah remembered her friend's words, ". . . in God's own time. . ."

1952 Partition of Palestine Repercussions

As Fadhel had predicted, the vote for partition inevitably provoked resistance by the indigenous Arab Palestinians, both Christian and Muslim. The neighbouring Arab states came to their rescue and war began. On the southern front, the Egyptians were besieged in Falouga. Poorly led and with faulty arms and equipment, the Egyptian Army did not do well. For Jamal Abdul Nasser and his comrades, their defeat and humiliation as well as the betrayal by their leaders spawned the Egyptian Revolution (they later became known to the world as Free Officers).

Hostility between Iraq and Egypt was firing up. Fadhel was a [37]Minister Plenipotentiary and was dispatched to Cairo to meet with his friend, Egyptian Prime Minister, Naqrashi Pasha. One result of that meeting was the

---

[37]**Plenipotentiary** - a person, especially a diplomat, invested with the full power of independent action on behalf of their government, typically in a foreign country.

sending of three Fury fighter aircraft from Iraq to Egypt. Before arriving in Cairo, Jamali had stopped in Amman for an audience with King Abdullah. Jamali later reported how the Jordanian ruler opened up telling Jamali that although he (King Abdullah) was appointed by the Arab League as Commander in Chief, he had no knowledge of what was happening on the Egyptian front. He went on to say that Egypt had already confiscated a shipload of arms intended for the Jordan Army and that his army was not his own, since it was led by British officers. Fadhel remained in Egypt twenty-five days and then returned to Baghdad and to his position as Foreign Minister.

1953 Becoming Prime Minister

Syrian concerns over Iraq's desire to federate with them were eased in November, 1946 by two reassuring statements. One was Prime Minister Nuri es-Sa'id's declaration that "the Syrian people alone will determine the future of Syria." The other was a declaration by Fadhel Jamali in Cairo that the political committee of the Arab League had investigated the alleged "Greater Syria" controversy and found nothing in it to threaten the independence or the internal regime of any country.

In the ensuing years, Syria vacillated between Amman, Cairo, and Baghdad in her alignment and moved into dictatorship hoping to annex the Muslim areas of Lebanon. During this period, Jamali was Minister of Foreign Affairs without being a Member of Parliament, a condition legally possible for only six months. While he was in New York leading the delegation to the UN General Assembly, that six-month period expired, and he was appointed Permanent Representative of Iraq to the UN. This ended his close involvement with Iraqi-Syrian affairs for the moment. He hoped for a broader, Jordanian-Syrian-Iraqi federation. However, sensitivities and suspicions proved too strong. Fadhel was always true to his Arab Muslim heritage and he was always willing to speak on behalf of any country who wanted independence. He spoke on behalf of Morroco, Jordan, Syria and Palestine but there were always disagreeing factions and leaders who just couldn't agree on things. Like his colleague, and occasional adversary, Nuri al-Sa'id, he was very aware that Iraq was geographically the closest state to Soviet Russia. Due to fear of repeating what happened during the Cold War, he refused to trust in the effectiveness of the collective all-Arab security alliance favoured by President Abdul Nasser of Egypt. Therefore, he emphasized reliance on Britain and United States, launched a powerful anti-Communist propaganda campaign and fostered alliances with Turkey, Pakistan and Iran which became known as the Baghdad Pact. This alliance was a good idea as far as strengthening military forces but its main effect was dangerous as it only increased Nasser's hostility toward Iraqi leadership. Unfortunately, it drove Nasser's many supporters, including many Iraqis, closer to the Communist enemy. Sometimes Fadhel was very outspoken and there were times he made some enemies without any intention to do so.

ഇൻ

In 1953 King Faisal II of Iraq reached the age of eighteen and ascended to the throne. The King, although not considered to be overly handsome, was pleasant looking and had a winning smile. His dark curly hair was cut short and close to his head. He was always impeccably dressed. This was the young King that Laith and Usameh had played with as little boys when they were invited to the palace. When he was just a young child, his father, King Gāzl, had died and his mother, Queen Aliya died when he was only fifteen. The young king had been raised mainly by his aunts and his uncle, the Crown Prince Abdullah. His uncle reigned on behalf of the boy king up to this point. It would seem that the uncle still had a great influence over his nephew's life and his decision making.

That autumn the King chose Jamali as his first Prime Minister. Like Fadhel Jamali, the King had been Western educated and had democratic ideas that many younger generation Iraqis liked him for. During his first week, Fadhel was called to the residence of Crown Prince Abdullah. [38]Nuri Pasha was already there with the Prince. Nuri had received a letter from Dr. Ma'aruf ed-Dawalabi, a former Prime Minister of Syria, asking for Iraq's help to remove Syria's dictator, Col. Shishakly. To show his understanding and consideration to Dr. Dawalabi, Fadhel invited him to Baghdad, and special precautions were taken to keep the visit secret. Arrangements were made to loan Dr. Dawalabi a very secluded villa where his discussions with Iraqi leaders could take place in complete secrecy. This act of kindness toward Dr. Dawalabi would later cause Fadhel a personal problem.

---

[38] Nuri Pasha – was an officer in the Ottoman army. He was captured by the British and recruited to join the Arab revolt against the Ottomans (Usameh Jamali). Ottoman were primarily Turks but also included Arabs, Kurds, Greeks, Armenians and other ethnic minorities

There had been a couple of Israeli raids on Jordanian villages. One was the village of Qibiya and the other was the village of Nahaleen. Jamali had offered help and sent aid and donated money from Iraq to help with reconstruction.

April 1954 - Resignation

"Sarah, I'm home!" Fadhel called out as he entered the house after a day at the office.

"Good evening Sir," Um Sania greeted Fadhel. "Madam is in the garden, Sir. Shall I call her for you?"

"No, no, don't bother. I'll go through to the garden. Supper smells wonderful Um Sania!"

Fadhel found Sarah relaxing in the garden with her pen and pad on her knee. She was still writing her book about Laith. She had decided the title would be *The Story of Laith and His Life after Encephalitis.* She was deep in thought and Fadhel approached her quietly as to not disturb her in this pensive pose. He paused for a moment to just admire her and the thought struck him that her pose would make a perfect painting. She sat semi-reclined with her feet up on a chaise-lounge, garden chair with pillows behind her back. The day's light was waning but there was a lingering bit of sunlight that shone through the trees in streaks of light—like a spotlight— bathing her in an illumination in the centre of the garden with the beauty of the roses all around her in the background. The crown of her head seemed to have a golden glow and gentle wisps of hair, lightened in colour by the years of living in the sunny climate, curled softly from her classic chignon hairstyle. She wore a soft sage green printed dress that covered her legs as she sat with her knees bent, propping her writing pad. She had kicked off her shoes and her pink toes peeked out from under her dress. Even at 46 years old, barefoot and with slightly messy hair, she was a classic beauty in Fadhel's eyes. The moment broke as she turned to see him standing there.

"What are you doing creeping up on me like that?" she laughed as he came closer and gave her a peck on her cheek.

"I just stopped to admire the beauty in my garden and it isn't the flora that I refer to," he smiled at her. Um Sania stepped into the garden carrying a tray with two glasses of [39]Tamarind. She set the tray on a small bistro table between the garden chairs.

"Thank you Um Sania. You always know just what we like. Supper smells delicious. Is it close to serving time?" Sarah picked up her glass and took a sip.

"Yes Madam, it is almost ready but you have time to enjoy your drink," and she hurried off to tend to things bubbling on the stove.

The family was now living in a new home located on the Tigris River on the north side of Baghdad. The Jamali family had been renting their first home located on the south end of the city. The new house was jointly designed by well-known architect, Dr. Mohammed Makiya, Sarah, and Helen Jawdat, the US architect wife of an Iraqi friend of the family. Having Um Sania and her two

---

[39] Tamarind sherbet – a sweet, cordial, cold, refreshing, non-alcoholic drink made from fruits or flower petals.

224

granddaughters living with the family had been a little cramped even though there was a bit of space after Laith's bedroom became available. The main feature of the new home was the beautiful library on the ground floor. Fadhel had a considerable collection of books before he and Sarah were married but the couple's great literary interests had outgrown the library space in their first home.

[40]Sarah commissioned an artist friend, Beatrice Plain, to paint a large wall mural on the stairwell wall leading up to the first floor. Beatrice had been studying murals in ancient Ethiopian churches. Sarah chose to have Beatrice paint a portrait of Usameh. The eyes seemed to follow the beholder wherever he went.

Not long after they moved into the new house, Usameh moved out. During the summer of 1953, at age sixteen, he joined the Documentary Credit Department of the Rafidain Bank. Shortly thereafter, he was transferred to the bank's branch in Beirut, Lebanon. Work was mainly seasonal in the summer serving Iraqis who were vacationing in Lebanon. That winter Usameh registered at the American University of Beirut where his father had studied as a young man years before him. Now Sarah had two sons away from home to worry about. She still worried about Laith and missed him; although, from her visits and from reports, she felt he was doing well. Usameh was a fine young man and Sarah had faith in his abilities; however, mothers can't seem to help but worry about children when they leave home for whatever reasons. Sarah took comfort in knowing that she had

---

[40] As told to author, Jan Keating, by Abbas Jamali in email message.

instilled abhorrence for the use of alcohol and cigarettes in Usameh. Her definition of a cigarette was: [41]"A small fire at one end and a big fool at the other."

"How was your day today, Dear?" Sarah put her writing materials down and adjusted her pillows slightly.

"Well, it was interesting and inspiring until just after lunch when I got a visit from a messenger from Syria."

"Oh, that sounds ominous. Tell me more."

Fadhel took a seat in the chair beside Sarah and loosened his neck tie. "I was shocked to learn from this messenger that there has been a suggestion of a plot to assassinate Shishakly."

"What? Oh no! I know he's a ruthless dictator but that sounds frightening." Sarah sat up straight now and was slipping into her shoes as though she needed to be upright and more alert to hear more of this news. "What did you say to this man?"

"I was really quite angry and I made no pretense to hide my disgust for the whole idea. I mean, do these people not understand anything that I've been saying during meetings at the UN and every other public forum as well as any private discussions I've been part of?" Fadhel was now sipping his drink as if to calm the fire in his belly that had been churning all afternoon.

"I told him that as long as I had any say in the matter on behalf of my country, there had better not be

---

[41] As told to author, Jan Keating, by Usameh Jamali.

any further plotting. I told him to ask his contacts what gave them the idea that I would ever support such an evil solution. I have always promoted the idea that I am in favour of 'unity' and 'brotherhood'. I am a Muslim who believes in the sanctity of life granted by Allah. It is never our right to take a man's life. [42]We cannot have peace unless we learn to live together on the basis of brotherhood and Co-operation no matter how different our political creeds are."

"And what else?" Sarah was a little worried now.

"Not much other than I told him that the only way was to have Shishakly agree to leave the country peacefully." Fadhel stood up now and took Sarah's hand.

"This is worrisome. I don't know how you take the pressure some days," Sarah shook her head and stood up as Fadhel took her other hand to guide her to her feet.

"Let's not worry about it. I have stewed over it all afternoon and now I've shared it with you so it is time to go enjoy our meal. I'm getting very hungry!" Fadhel gave Sarah a hug.

౭౦ପ

In time, Shishakly was overthrown and was asked by Lebanese authorities to leave Beirut so he moved to Sa'udi Arabia. He was exiled peacefully just as Fadhel had insisted he should be. Unfortunately, simply having

---

[42] Experiences in Arab Affairs by Mohammed Fadhel Jamali, MA, PhD, LLD

this dictator removed was not enough to make way to the Syrian-Iraqi federation. Fadhel knew there was much more work to be done to make this happen. Fadhel met with Prince Abd al-llah and his Minister of Finance, Abdul Karim Al-'Uzri. After hours of discussion, a secret mission was devised. At midnight, the three men went to the home of the ex-Premier, Saleh Jabre and woke him to ask him to go to Beirut. They explained that his overt mission would be to hold discussions with Lebanese authorities regarding the Iraq pipeline branch from Mafraq in Jordan to Sidon but that his covert mission was to assist exiled Syrian leaders living in Baghdad. Jabre agreed to this. He was told that 100,000 Iraqi dinars (about US$400,000) would be sent to the Embassy in Beirut at his disposal.

In spite of the efforts to bring about the Syrian-Iraqi federation, there was still opposition from Riyadh and Cairo. In any case, pro-Baghdad elements in Syria continued to receive subsidies from Iraq. Nuri es-Sa'id also had doubts about the Syrian covert mission. Due to this, Fadhel knew he would not be able to get parliamentary support for even a modest amount of money required to fund the continued assistance to Syrian leaders, noble and as important as it was. He felt he had no other option than to resign.

He went to the Palace and expressed his desire to resign. He explained that before he resigned, there were two things he wanted to complete: The first was to ensure that the money already allocated to be spent be authorized; the second was to conclude Fadhel's negotiations with the American government on the Military Aid Agreement. King Faisal II and his uncle agreed with Fadhel and so he stayed in office until he had taken care of these two concerns. His resignation was officially carried out on April 19, 1954.

1954 Bad News and the Flood

On April 8, 1954, Sarah received the sad news from her sister, Lydia that their dear mother, Elizabeth (Libbie) Powell, had passed away. She had been living with Lydia and Ed Johnson in Prospect Park, Pennsylvania. The cause of death was stated as "chronic renal-cardiac disease and senility". She was eighty-five.

"I have deep despair about not being there with you and the family. I knew Mother was not doing too well, of course, but I had hoped to get there one more time to see her," Sarah began to choke up as she grabbed for a chair to sit at the desk to speak with Lydia. She felt guilty that she had not been there to help Lydia who had been the constant care provider for their mother.

"Don't feel bad, Sarah. We know you would have liked to see her before this happened but you know, quite honestly, she may not have even known you. She was getting very senile and confused. It was something I had hoped she would have been spared because she had so many other health issues, it seemed sad that she had to endure the loss of her memory on top of it all. As you know, Mother always prided herself on her mind."

"You have to be commended, Lydia, for all you've done for Mother. I know there's a reward in Heaven for you one day!" Sarah tried to lighten the moment.

"Well, truthfully, I feel I got my reward here on earth. I feel I'm the fortunate one who got to spend that extra time with our dear mother. I look at it as a privilege to have been able to comfort her in her old age after everything she did for all us children. We had many good moments together in spite of her difficulties. At least she came to be with us before she started losing her memory. She loved to look at family albums. Any time one of the grandchildren came to visit, all they needed to do was sit with her and look at photos. She could remember many things by looking at the photos. Memories from way back seemed clear; whereas, something she did or talked about five minutes earlier was gone. Anyway, we'll see to all the details. We'll see to it that she's put to rest beside Father. And we'll pray for a reunion with you one day again. Is there any hope of you coming soon?"

"Oh, I just can't say right now, Lydia. There has been so much rain and the rivers are beginning to flood. So, Fadhel is 'up to his knees'—pardon my pun! The government is working day and night to prepare for what is surely to come. I'm not even sure what will happen with our house at this point. So, I can't manage a big trip right now. Fadhel cannot possibly abandon his duties here now with the flooding and all his other concerns with the government. I feel I cannot leave him at the moment to travel far away. He needs me here. You are all always on my mind and I do hope to get away in the future but this just doesn't seem to be possible at this time. I don't mean to sound negative, we are both healthy and the situation will surely be resolved before much longer. But enough about us! How is Ed and what's new with the children?"

೮೦೦ಲ

In March of 1954, the Tigris and Euphrates Rivers had begun to reach dangerous levels and eventually began to overflow into the city of Baghdad. The flood caused great damage to agriculture, industry and transport. [43]This was the worst flood in Iraq's history up to that time and losses were estimated around $80 million. Approximately, 1,388,800 acres of cultivated land, as well as a great deal of uncultivated land was flooded. It was estimated that 40,000 people were displaced from their homes in Baghdad and approximately 150,000 from the whole of Iraq were affected.

The Government quickly set up committees to assess damages and planned to make immediate compensations to facilitate rapid restoration to agricultural and industrial production. Free food and clothing was immediately distributed and temporary accommodations were provided. Plans were implemented and new housing developments were soon underway. The Government conducted a vigorous campaign of preventative measures, including inoculations for typhoid fever. Flood victims would be compensated for their losses and a program to improve, rather than just restore, agricultural development was to be implemented. Plans included the introduction of new and better seeds, crop diversification and livestock improvement.

[43] Foreign Commerce Weekly, Vol. 51

Chapter 19

1957 Laith and Gogarburn Hospital

Sarah and Fadhel knew that Laith was not particularly happy in Garvald School any longer. It was never intended to accommodate adults. Laith was now 22 and he sometimes got annoyed with the noise and action of the young children at Garvald. Sarah had kept looking for a more suitable place for adults like Laith. Finally, in 1957, Laith was accepted into such a place—Gogarburn Hospital—which was a government facility with medical staff, a chapel, and many wards set on a wide acreage near Edinburgh.

ହ⊙ଔ

"Listen to this Fadhel. It's a letter from Pat," Sarah had just filled their cups with their morning tea. Their friend, Pat, was Dr. Pat Petrie. He was employed by the South East Regional Hospital Board of Scotland. He was Assistant Senior Administrative Medical Officer at the Royal Infirmary of Edinburgh and served on the Medical Personnel Committee. After his retirement in 1968, he was involved in the development of Post-graduate Medical Education. Prior to and during the Second World War, Dr. Petrie had been a medical missionary and personal physician to the Imam of Yemen (King and knowledgeable religious leader). Dr. Petrie had become Laith's guardian and Mrs. Petrie often visited Laith, took him sweets and gave him a ride around the grounds in her car.

"What does he have to say? Is everything alright with Laith?" Fadhel put down his newspaper and gave his attention to Sarah. "He says here," Sarah read out loud:

> "Dear Sarah and Dr. Jamali, I hope this letter finds you both well. I just wanted to inform you that you do not have to pay any fees to the hospital for Laith. It is Government policy to offer its services as an expression of international goodwill. I trust that this will give your hearts ease and Mrs. Petrie sends her regards as well. She was up to visit Laith yesterday and reported that he was in good health and he enjoyed his sweets and the car ride with her very much. Sincerely yours, Pat"

Sarah remembered her mother's advice and gave a prayer of thanks. She was thankful for the fact that God had provided these two kind people. It gave her great comfort knowing that Laith was getting visits from friends who could be her eyes and ears when she herself could not be there.

The year was by all reports a very pleasant experience for Laith in his new home. At Christmas there were special gifts of fruit or sweets or clothing brought to the patients by relatives or caretakers. In the summer, groups of patients were taken by their male nurses to summer resorts for a break of two weeks. Patients were provided with new shoes and items of clothing. An enjoyable program of activities was also provided. Laith loved the programs. Sarah felt that he was in good hands and his health continued to be good. Again, she had things to feel thankful for and she kept her word to her mother by giving her prayers of thanks daily. Who could imagine that her faith was about to be tested even more in the coming days ahead. . .

Shifting Sands & Health Issues

The day after Fadhel had submitted his resignation as Prime Minister, he was called to the Palace to meet the Crown Prince and Nuri Pasha. Nuri asked Fadhel to join the Government as Minister of Foreign Affairs.

"I am honoured and yet reluctant at this time. I must respectfully decline your offer," Fadhel spoke directly and honestly.

"I cannot believe you are saying this to me, Fadhel. I strongly urge you to join my Cabinet. You have the experience and you surprise and shock me with your reluctance. Did you not promise me you would work with me?" Nuri could not hide his feelings of being insulted in front of the Crown Prince. He had been so confident that Fadhel would accept this offer.

"I must remind you, Nuri, that my promise was 'conditional'. I told you it would depend on your reconciliation with Saleh Jabre. I made it clear that we needed your support with his work in Syria to support those leaders who had been exiled. Your obstruction on the issue of Syria in Parliament makes it impossible for me to accept your offer to join your Cabinet. I'm sorry," Fadhel kept his composure but was stating his feelings clearly so there would be no mistake on this.

As it turned out, there were other candidates with portfolios who agreed with Fadhel's stand. Therefore, Arshad al-Omari became Prime Minister for the second time and was asked to form a government. He, too, asked Fadhel to be his Foreign Minister. This time, Fadhel accepted on two conditions: first, that the policy of working toward a Syria-Iraqi federation should be continued; and, second, that the present Parliament would be dissolved and new elections held. These stipulations were accepted and a new government was formed.

ഇരു

Ring, ring, ring . . . Sarah hurried to answer the telephone. She had been working on her book about Laith and had been hoping that Um Sania would answer the phone.

"Hello," Sarah sat down at the desk in the hallway.

"May I please speak with Mrs. Jamali?" the voice on the other end inquired.

"Yes, this is she. How may I help you?"

"Mrs. Jamali, I'm very sorry to tell you but your husband collapsed at the office today and he has been sent by ambulance to the hospital. We thought we should inform you. Would you like us to send a car to take you to the hospital?" the woman sounded most concerned.

Sarah let out a gasp and tried to think clearly what she should do, before she responded: "No, thank you, I have a driver. Can you tell me anything more about his collapse? Is he conscious?"

"Yes, madam, he seemed very weak and rather faint but he was conscious when I saw them put him on the stretcher. I'm so sorry madam. I was just told I should inform you. I don't know much other than this."

"Of course, thank you for the call. I'll go straightway to the hospital. Good-bye."

Fadhel was eventually sent from Baghdad to the American University of Beirut Hospital in Lebanon. He was diagnosed with a duodenal ulcer. Sarah found that his room was too often crowded with Syrian leaders and Iraqi friends urging him to take action on the federation issues.

"Excuse me gentlemen, could I please have a private moment with my husband. I would like him to have his lunch and then he will be expected to have a quiet rest so could you all please come back later this afternoon or tomorrow sometime? Thank you," and she efficiently cleared the room. A nurse came in to give Fadhel some medication with his meal which consisted of a soft poached egg and some creamed soup and a soft custard for dessert.

"Honestly, Fadhel, do these men not have any understanding of your condition? You will never recover at this rate if they don't ease up on you. Can a man not even take a break from politics when he is ill?" Sarah was clearly frustrated and worried about her husband's health.

"I know. I have given it some thought and I've already called the Prime Minister and asked him to speak to Saleh Jabre. I've requested he be sent to give me some help. I am not up to long conversations yet and I realize it only too well. I wish I could say otherwise but I must be truthful."

237

"Well, I'm certainly relieved to hear this. I have had thoughts of taking you away from here to a secluded place where you might get some peace and quiet."

Following his release from the hospital, the couple did retreat to the Lebanese mountains to the Hotel Mont Vert in Broumanna, a well-known resort town. The hope was that he could rest and recuperate by reducing the flow of visitors but that was not to be the case. Pro-federation Syrians followed him there and continued to visit him to discuss the possible unity. These discussions were with the affirmation that King Faisal II would be the head of the federated state.

ഇ൭

Once more, Nuri was Prime Minister. He and Fadhel had managed to resolve their past differences with an understanding. Nuri had told Fadhel that he had serious doubts about a Syrian-Iraqi federation. He went on to warn Fadhel that Iraq may live to regret such a unification with Syria. He didn't trust that Iraq would be able to enjoy the fruits of its own oil production if Syria was involved. Although the two agreed to disagree, they were able to embrace and Fadhel continued to support Nuri in foreign affairs. He was eloquent in defending the right to freedom for Libya, Somalia, Ethiopia and North African Arab states—all of whom, to some degree, achieved that goal. But it remained a great disappointment that the UN never reached a satisfactory solution for the Palestine question.

Egypt, under the leadership of Major Salah Salem, Minister for the National Guidance met with the Syrian

Prime Minister and others, and their joint decision was to not join the Iraqi-Turkish Alliance. They announced their plan to form an Arab organization for mutual defense and economic cooperation which Jamali took as a thinly veiled attack on the Baghdad Pact. Arab policy remained divided.

From that point on, Egypt launched an intensive campaign (over their powerful national radio voice called, "Voice of the Arabs") against western influences and singled out Nuri es-Sa'id, Iraq's pro-western leader, in particular. This propaganda barrage against Baghdad continued until the 1958 Revolution.

Chapter 20

1958 Revolution

King Faisal II and his uncle, Crown Prince Abd al-llah, were summering on the King's yacht on the Bosphorus (the strait connecting the Sea of Marmara and the Black Sea) in the north of Istanbul. They arranged a meeting with Iraqi leaders and the Turkish President, Prime Minister Adnan Menderes and others, to consider the dangers of communist penetration in Syria.

Ali Jawdat al-Ayoubi was the Prime Minister of Iraq at this time. He questioned the Turks on their idea to contact the USA. He felt this would be a mistake but the Turks went ahead and did it anyway. Within a few days, Secretary of State, Loy Henderson, arrived in Istanbul to discuss the situation with the Turkish-Iraqi group. He informed them that America did not wish to intervene and would leave matters to the states in the area. He added that if there was trouble, the Sixth Fleet was, of course, bound to come to the aid of America's allies.

The Turks also did not wish to intervene in Syrian affairs, and they left it to Iraq, saying it was an inter-Arab matter. They did give assurances that if Iraq was involved and threatened, they would come to her aid. Although the Iraqi Prime Minister, Ali-Jawdat al-Ayoubi, spoke up saying he doubted there was anything to worry about as far as Communist penetration in Syria, the Syrians themselves were not convinced. Therefore, they turned to Egypt and a new United Arab Republic was formed with

Nasser, President of Egypt, as the head. This upset Jamali as he felt it was unnatural to unite Syria with Egypt before the Syrian-Iraqi federation had been achieved. This widened the rift between Jamali and Nasser.

ഇൻ

Fadhel had to leave the Syria-Iraqi federation on the back burner for the time being. He turned his attention to Jordan, suggesting that a federation be formed with Iraq. King Faisal II and his uncle agreed. The Constitution was revised accordingly. Nuri worked hard to get Kuwait to join but Sheikhdom was still under British protection. This meant that London controlled Kuwait's foreign affairs. In a meeting with the King and his uncle and British Minister for Foreign Affairs, Selwyn Lloyd, Jamali suggested that Kuwait be recognized as independent, ending British protection. Lloyd said it would be a cabinet decision. Later in June of 1961, recognition was finally accorded.

Meanwhile, in May of 1958, there were riots in Lebanon. There were communal disputes and tensions over the Baghdad Pact which had risen to dangerous levels. President Cham'oun (of Lebanon) was considered a friend of Iraq and the West and an attempt was made to amend the Constitution to allow him to serve another term. Those who opposed him were supported materially and with radio propaganda by Egypt and Syria. There was violence in the streets.

Ultimately, Lebanon took her case to the UN Security Council, in New York, accusing Egypt of interference in Lebanon's internal affairs. In the Security Council, Fadhel Jamali (at the insistence of King Faisal II) defended the

Lebanese position. In a speech he explained that 'Nasserism' meant not only domination of the Arab world by President Nasser but also the opening of its doors to communism. His arguments may have been correct but his tone was highly offensive which he later admitted cost him years in prison.

There was uncertainty about the Iraq Army. Jamali and Lebanese Foreign Minister, Charles Malik, met with Undersecretary of State, Christian Herter and another American Foreign Service Officer, Mr. Rockwell. They met for tea and when Jamali suggested that America provide air transport for Iraqi army units to intervene in Lebanon between the opposing groups and to subdue the riots, Rockwell asked, "Are you sure of your army." President Cham'oun of Lebanon also had doubts about the reliability of Iraq's army. Jamali replied that he had no information about the political currents among the Iraqi military leaders. This was a sad admission in light of the bloody revolution about to take place.

It would seem that even though Fadhel was not aware, there was a faction of military officials that were growing more discontent with Prime Minister, Nuri es-Sa'id's alliance with western powers in the region. [44]A growing number of educated elites in Iraq were becoming enamoured with the ideals espoused by Nasser's pan-Arab movement.

In mid-June, a few days before Fadhel was to return to Baghdad, an American friend, John C. Newington, gave a farewell luncheon for him at the Union League Club in New

---

[44] Wikipedia Free Encyclopedia – 14 July Revolution

York. Newington and other friends urged Fadhel to wait before returning to Baghdad because of the instability in the region. They expressed great concern and fear for him if he dared to return at this time.

"I appreciate your concern gentlemen but my wife, Sarah and my sons are there. I have responsibilities to the country. I love my country and I feel I must return."

Captured

On the evening of July 13, 1958, Fadhel left home to say goodbye to the Algerian delegation in Baghdad. As President of the Committee to Support Algerian Independence, he had been working with them to raise funds for the nationalist movement. He wanted to say his goodbye because the next day he was to head to Ankara first for the Baghdad Pact and then on to London with King Faisal II to discuss the independence of Kuwait. The young King was looking forward to meeting his young Turkish fiancée, Princess Fazilet, in Turkey on his way to Britain. The purpose of the meeting in London was to meet with other members of the Baghdad Pact. Jamali and his colleagues had previously met with Selwyn Lloyd, the British Foreign Secretary, to iron out some difficulties.

"Sarah, I forgot to mention earlier that I'm expecting Behcet Turkmen sometime this evening." Behcet Turkmen was the Turkish Ambassador and he had made arrangements for Fadhel to deliver a bag of coffee to Turkmen's family in Istanbul on his way to London.

"Alright, I'll put a tray of baking together so we can offer him tea, if he'll stay a while," Sarah went to the kitchen to prepare a snack.

When Turkmen arrived, he seemed disturbed. Fadhel introduced him to Sarah and invited him to come in and sit down. Turkmen smiled and greeted Sarah but his expression went from a quick smile and polite greeting to an intense worried look.

"Is there something bothering you, my friend?" Fadhel offered the tray of baking while Sarah poured them a cup of tea.

"I am very concerned about something I heard today. I don't know if you've heard any rumblings but I was told that there is a conspiracy in the Army. I thought I should warn you right away."

Fadhel felt a sudden jolt from this news. He thought about Rockwell's questioning him about the Army and about concerns that President Cham'oun (of Lebanon) had seemed to have as well. Now this news from Turkmen seemed to add more validity to the previous insinuations.

"Have you told Nuri and the Crown Prince?" Fadhel asked.

"Yes, but they did nothing! I can't believe it. I'm very worried."

That night, Fadhel went to the study to read the Quran; Sarah knelt by the bed and prayed for her husband and others. She prayed for her sons and asked for God's protection. Fadhel and Sarah went to bed with this disturbing news on their minds. Sarah held onto her husband as they lay nestled in their bed; neither seemed able to speak of the fears that were really on their minds.

July 14 Baghdad

"That's odd, why is your driver here this early? It's only six o'clock—he's an hour early." Sarah had been standing at the window and now headed to the door to see what the driver had to say. Fadhel quickly moved from the kitchen to join her at the doorway.

"Good morning," Sarah greeted the driver who was obviously distraught and nervous. He quickly removed his hat and got straight to the point of his early arrival.

"Sir, everything is upset; there is a revolution! I came early to warn you."

Fadhel thanked his driver and told him he could leave. He knew it would be too dangerous to get in the car as the vehicle would likely be followed. He went directly the telephone. He told Sarah to take Abbas and leave immediately.

"But Fadhel—where will we go? Where are you going? I want us to be together!" Sarah felt panic overcoming her whole body but she tried to remain somewhat calm. She didn't want to become hysterical for Abbas's sake, but nothing was making any sense.

"Sarah! Just go pack a small bag and get Abbas. I'll make arrangements and will explain to you but you must hurry. Take your passports in case you need them. I'm afraid this is very serious and they will be coming for me so we must move quickly."

Fadhel had called Rushdi Chelabi, Minister of Agriculture and Dr. Abdul Amir Allawi, Minister of Health. The two men came in a car immediately and picked Fadhel up. They escaped into the countryside to the Chelabi farm across the river northwest of Baghdad. They remained there for three nights.

Before Fadhel left the house, he instructed Sarah and Abbas to go to his brother Rassoul's home in Kadhmain. They spent three days there; however, Rassoul feared that the angry, murderous mob would soon come looking for them; he suspected it wouldn't take them long to think of searching his home. He warned them to call a taxi and try to find a place less obvious for their safety. Sarah and Abbas did take a taxi to the home of a Master sergeant in the US Air Force who was serving at the American Embassy. The sergeant recognized Sarah and said he would be willing to offer them shelter on the condition of secrecy. Sarah agreed and thanked him. She and Abbas sat in the taxi waiting for the sergeant and his wife to clear things with the Embassy officials. Sarah was thankful for one thing at that moment. She thought of Laith and knew he would be safe in Scotland. Usameh, who was still living in London, would be safe, at least for now, as well. He was still working at the bank there. She would try to phone him as soon as possible to let him know what was happening. He was expecting Fadhel in London and would be wondering if Fadhel did not arrive.

Abbas was now fifteen and he understood the seriousness of what his parents were facing. He felt it his duty to be a strong support for his mother at this time. He knew she would be counting on him. The only problem was he had no idea what they were going to be faced with and how he should be expected to react. But he knew one thing; he would stay by Sarah's side all the way through this. Luckily, Usameh received news of his mother and brother's safety through the Jesuit priests from his former high school, Baghdad College. Unfortunately, Usameh, also received the tragic news that his father had been shot to death by demonstrators who dragged his body through the streets of Baghdad.

When Sarah was able to get a call through to Usameh, he offered to rush to Baghdad to join his mother and Abbas but Sarah insisted that he remain at his job in London and stay where she felt he was safe. Having another member of the family in immediate danger was out of the question. He abided her wishes.

A few days later, the information about Fadhel was corrected. It was discovered that an innocent man who looked like him had been mistakenly killed by the mob and his body dragged through the streets. This brought on another shock and feelings of trauma; however, it was good news that Fadhel was still alive after all. Sarah made the call to Usameh to give him the tragic yet good news. There was still the great fear that if the mob got their hands on Fadhel, he would meet with the same end as the innocent man.

ℰℭ

The son of the Chalabi farm manager was an army officer and he took it upon himself to inform the army of Jamali's whereabouts. Fadhel had been hiding out at the farm water pump station by the river as the Chalabi women folk were in the farmhouse and he didn't wish to bring any danger to them. On the fourth day, he left his hiding place and fled to a far part of the fields. He was dressed like a Bedouin with a long nightshirt-like *dishdasha*, an *abba* (camel hair cloak), a *kaffiyah* (head cloth), a jug of water, a bag of bread and a cane. He made a tent for sleeping by throwing his abba over the thorn bushes. On July 17 at dawn, he heard a noise and saw soldiers rushing toward him with weapons.

"Don't shoot! I am ready!" He surrendered himself. As they grabbed him and smacked him, he cried out, "Let me alone! I'm your brother. I, too, am a nationalist!" His words fell on deaf ears and he was taken swiftly away.

Unfortunately, the corrected news did not spread as quickly as the mistaken news. The New York Times of July 16 reported the mistaken news. UN diplomats were shocked. On July 17 a meeting in his memory was held in the National Theatre in Washington where many spoke in his honour, and US Ambassador, Cabot Lodge, gave a eulogy and requested a minute of silence.

On July 18, following his arrest, Fadhel was detained in a room with 26 other prisoners. The prisoners were amazed to see him as they, too, had heard that he had been killed. The next day, the police guards pointed a pistol at his head and had the television take pictures. They said, "Here he is. He is alive; he was not killed. Why do you make propaganda against the revolution saying we killed Fadhel Jamali?"

The next day, Friday, July 19, authorities took the press corps to see Jamali. They reported that he was seen to be well groomed, dressed in shirt and trousers and wearing his usual spectacles.

Death and Destruction

Just as Jamali's driver had reported, the coup d'etat began early on Monday morning, July 14, 1958. The Twentieth Infantry Brigade of the Third Armoured Division took only a few hours to overthrow the monarchy and establish a military dictatorship with Army brigadier, Abd al-Karim Qasim, as the self-appointed new Prime Minister.

They struck at 5:00 a.m. and seized key bridges, crossroads and communication centres. By 8:00 a.m., the Regent's Palace was under fire. The Palace Guards had been captured in their barracks before they had any chance to defend the palace because they had been instructed not to defend the palace. King Faisal had come downstairs with his uncle, Prince Abd al-llah. The Prince attempted to draw his pistol as he faced the intruders but soldiers shot from the rear in a blaze of bullets that severely wounded the King and killed his uncle, the Prince, as well as killing three other officers. Prince Abd al-llah's wife, Princess Hyam; his mother, Queen Nafeesa; his sister, Princess Abadiya and several servants were all fired on as they attempted to make their way through the kitchen to escape. Princess Hyam and Princess Abadiya were shot in the legs and not fatally wounded. The King had been shot in the head and in the neck and he died in transport to hospital. Twenty lives were taken in that Palace skirmish. It was a bloody massacre.

In another incident, General Rafiq Aref issued ammunition to his troops and tried to resist. His troops turned on him and captured him. He was later tried. In a third incident, Major General Omar Ali, commander of the Fourth Division, ordered his men to attack the rebels. Instead, they seized him and took him into custody. He and Jamali ended up in the same prison cell and became good friends.

The following day, rebel soldiers found Nuri es-Sa'id trying to escape wearing women's clothing. He had made the mistake of wearing men's shoes which gave away his disguise. He tried to defend himself by shooting it out with an air force sergeant. He was shot and killed. His body was hung in a public place and later dismembered and dragged through the streets.

It is difficult to say if the Crown Prince had listened to the warning from Behcet Turkmen, the Turkish Ambassador, whether things would have turned out differently. If the Crown Prince had listened and warned the King, perhaps they could have tried to flee the country. However, the King's demise seemed inevitable due to his decision to allow the United Kingdom to retain a continued role in Iraqi affairs, through the Anglo-Iraqi Treaty (1948 not ratified) and later the Baghdad Pact (1955). Massive protests greeted news of each of these alliances, resulting in the deaths of a number of demonstrators and an increasing deterioration of loyalty to the Iraqi Crown. Because Fadhel was loyal to the Crown and had worked with Nuri es-Sa'id and the United Kingdom, he was automatically considered an enemy to the revolutionists.

As oil revenues increased during the 1950s, the king and his advisers chose to invest their wealth in development projects, which some claimed increasingly alienated the rapidly growing middle class and the peasantry.

The Iraqi Communist Party increased its influence. The gap widened between the wealthy and the poor intensifying opposition to King's government. Since the upper classes controlled the parliament, some opposition figures (who considered themselves "reformists") increasingly saw revolution as their sole hope for improvement. They would later come to regret their choice.

སྐ

The shock of all this took its toll on poor Sarah. She had been trying to be strong for Abbas. She wanted to keep her composure for the sake of all those around her; especially her hosts who were kind enough to give shelter and protection to her and Abbas. But holding all this inside, and the shock of hearing of all the murder happening in their midst, caused her to suffer from shingles and eventually she had a stroke at the age of fifty. Under the circumstances, it was understandable. The stroke caused her to be paralyzed on the left side, including her face. It is not clear whether she was hospitalized or remained under care in the shelter of the Embassy but she was reported as "missing" in a Philadelphia newspaper. The headline read, "Jamali Seen in Good Health; His Wife is Still Missing."

Her sister, Lydia Johnson, was interviewed and said that she had received a postcard from Sarah in which a vacation to Iran had been mentioned. Of course, due to the mail delivery and the time involved to send a postcard in those days, it was obvious that the postcard was sent long before the coup had occurred. It is possible that Sarah was missing at this time due to her stroke and recovery time. It would be assumed that her whereabouts was being kept secret during the stressful time that the coup was occurring.

252

The world was hearing the devastating news of the military coup. Ambassador Vreede of the Netherlands stated in a letter to his Foreign Ministry on July 24:

> "The military coup was a complete surprise . . . The coup was well organized and the preparations for it must have taken ample time. It is, therefore, incomprehensible that this conspiracy of a group mainly of field and general officers eluded the observation of Nuri and his very efficient secret police, as well as Western intelligence."

This, again, brings back thought of the questions brought forward earlier by Cham'oun, President of Lebanon, and Mr. Rockwell, American Foreign Service Officer to Jamali, "Are you sure of your Army?" Obviously, there were people in Washington who were knowledgeable enough to be disturbed, yet *Newsweek* wrote:

> Not only was the news momentous, the fact that it came as a surprise to (Allen) Dulles and his CIA represented a sorry failure for US intelligence.

Western capitals responded with preparations for any eventuality. The UN Security Council was convened. It was only American and British calls for restraint that prevented King Hussein from sending Jordan's Arab Army to avenge the death of his cousin, King Faisal II. British forces were put on alert and American Marines were landing in Lebanon at President Cham'oun's request.

Home Life and Prison Life

After a month, Sarah and Abbas returned to their home. Although matters were extremely tense, it was hoped that the revolutionists had taken all the prisoners they wanted and now Sarah and Abbas could resume a quiet life in their own home. While Sarah tried to make life at home as normal as possible, it was anything but normal for the household. Sarah was still struggling with her paralysis and, yet, she was determined to overcome:[45] Sarah was a fighter; she attacked the symptoms as if they were a mortal enemy. She maintained a disciplined regime of daily exercise. Within the year, one would be hard put to notice any difference.

Luckily, her faithful servant Um Sani was there to encourage Sarah to eat and not become too thin and run down. She needed to keep up strength and hope for the day that she would be allowed to visit Fadhel. For the first three months, he was being kept in solitary confinement in a cell near the toilets. A cruel communist Director of the prison brought people in to stare at the prisoners like animals in a zoo. He cut off cold water and the use of fans in the hot summer. He took the beds away from the inmates and made them sleep on the floor. Eventually, due to this man's being a drunkard and making accusations and insults toward the leader, he was ultimately fired. This brought some small relief to the prisoners. In his cell

---

[45] Email to the author from one of Sarah's sons (June 24, 2020)

254

alone at night, Fadhel thought about hanging. He thought to himself:

> "What if they hang me? It's like falling from an airplane, so why worry about it? If God has assigned me to die, I will die. Death comes anyway, but how we do not know. If God wants me to die by the gallows, I will die by the gallows."

Fadhel had a copy of the Quran with him. At first, this was the only book permitted. It was a great support. He read it faithfully and prayed throughout his days. One scripture was particularly comforting to him. It read:

> By eventide every man feels at a loss, except for those who believe, perform honourable deeds, encourage truth and recommend patience.

He began to have thoughts about his sons. Unfortunately, Usameh had been dismissed from his position at the bank in London, on August 15, right after the news of his father's arrest was made public. Although living in London and having nothing to do with the political unrest in his home country of Iraq, the Head Office of the Rafidain Bank did not see it that way. This bothered Fadhel, of course, but there was nothing to be done about it from his position in prison. The good news was, however, that Abbas would be allowed to continue his university studies in Beirut a year later. Fadhel also worried about young Abbas because he had less time to teach Abbas about religion than he had with Usameh. Usameh was now 22 but Abbas was still a teenager. As time went on, Fadhel decided to begin writing letters to Abbas about the Quran and to open discussions about religion and his faith in Allah. He instructed Abbas to not destroy his letters but to keep them.

Once Fadhel was moved out of solitary confinement, he was placed in a cell the size of a hotel bedroom with eleven other prisoners all of whom were sentenced to death. He was allowed half an hour of exercise a day. A former Foreign Minister, Burhan ed-Din Bashayan, was also assigned to the same cell and he told Jamali that they must help one another to strengthen their nerves and lift their spirits so as not to give in. They became good friends during this time.

Trial and Sentencing

A "Special High Military Court of Justice" was created to try the 108 persons accused after the Revolution (30 of who were military men). New laws were put into effect by the self-appointed military rebels: the "Law for the punishment of conspirators against the country's welfare" and the "Law for the corrupters of the Administration" were published. These laws were applied retroactive to prisoners of the Revolution. In addition, an article had been inserted in the Criminal Law by the Iraqi revolutionary government which stipulated that anyone who delivered a speech against an Arab head of state before an international organization should be sentenced to 20 years imprisonment, and that it be applied retroactively. This article was created solely for the purpose of sentencing Fadhel. He was the only person accused under this Article. It was payback from the insult to President Nasser, in his speech to defend Lebanon in New York in front of the United Nations. Clearly, these new laws were created and put into effect to punish people who had not committed any crime which previously existed on the books. The prisoners were being held while kangaroo court and laws were invented with which to lay charges against them.

The trials started in mid-August. The sessions were open to the public as well as transmitted on radio and television. On November 10, 1958, nearly four months after their arrest, General Rafiq Aret, General Ghazi Daghestani and Dr. Jamali stood handcuffed and were sentenced to death by hanging by the five-man Military Tribunal. Jamali was also sentenced to 55 years in prison and fined 100,000 Iraqi dinars (about 300,000 US dollars).

Thunderous applause broke out as each sentence was pronounced. Reporters in the press box stood and cheered, "The court's just decision!" It took about 105 minutes to read the indictments. The charges against Jamali were that he had conspired to bring about a coup in Syria with imperialist backing, had insulted President Nasser (in front of the UN), had rigged elections and squandered public funds. He denied all charges and pled for mercy. Three days later, his friend, Burhan ed-Din Bashayan, received the same sentence—death by hanging.

Sarah felt a sudden heat flush to her face as she sat straight-backed and emotionless. Her hands clasped gently in her lap, were a deliberate attempt on her part to resist clenching them into fists. She sat looking stoic yet calm while the sentence was read. Although every nerve in her body was taut and perspiration trickled down her spine, she was determined to hold her composure through this and not give reporters and cameramen the satisfaction of seeing her break down. She held her head high as she left the courtroom, making her way through the mobs yelling, "Hang them! Hang them all!"

She remained completely silent and composed while being driven by her chauffeur. She held herself in check while she unlocked her front door for fear a neighbour or passerby might see her and be in judgment against Fadhel. Once inside, she stopped to face Um Sania who came rushing to the door and now stood perfectly still with a questioning stare on her face, too afraid to ask the question out loud about the verdict. Sarah paused and looked at Um Sania. She could no longer hold her true feelings in check. She did not break down. It was not her nature to give in to hysterics; but she was deflated and so weary from it all. With slumped shoulders, she shook her head and looked down. At this moment she had no words and no words were necessary. Um Sania stepped forward and took Sarah by the hand.

"Come madam, I've made you a cup of chai tea."

Chapter 21

Family Visits

After the death sentence, Sarah was finally permitted to visit Fadhel. She was allowed to see him in the jailer's office once a month. Unfortunately, Usameh, who was back to his studies at the Columbia University in New York, read the news of his father's death sentence in the New York Times. He was shocked to see his father's picture on the front page of the Times.

Abbas accompanied Sarah on visiting days and he also rode his bike to the prison to deliver meals once a week that were prepared for Dr. Jamali by Um Sania. She prepared all his favourite dishes which gave her a great feeling of being able to contribute something and it was most appreciated by Fadhel. Sarah tried her best to share family news and make their visits as pleasant as possible. Fadhel was always happy to see her and Abbas and if he felt down, he tried hard not to show it. He considered time with his wife and son to be a blessing and he wanted them to see him in his best spirit possible.

"Abbas sometimes reads your letters out loud to me," Sarah sat across the table from Fadhel. Abbas smiled and nodded in agreement with this. Sarah and Fadhel were not allowed to embrace but she could hold his hand. He was in handcuffs which seemed to make him feel awkward about holding hands; he preferred to keep his hands hidden under the table.

"Yes, indeed, and I certainly enjoy receiving your letters as well, my son." Abbas smiled again while his father went on explaining to Sarah, "We are writing about the Holy Quran. I was pleased when you told me, Abbas, that you are reading and that you find it soothing. I, also, am 'soothed' as I read the scriptures every day. The Quran is light, guidance, counsel, mercy and a cure for inner troubles."

"Yes Father, that is very true. Thank you for all the effort you are putting into your letters to help me. I do appreciate it very much."

"Fadhel, you know that Abbas received a letter of acceptance from the AUB (American University of Beirut); I believe we mentioned it last time we visited you."

"Yes, of course I remember."

"Well, I regret having to tell you this but since then, we received a second letter stating that he will not be permitted to leave the country," Sarah lowered her voice and covered her mouth with her hand slightly so as to not draw unfavourable attention to her conversation.

"Well, we'll see about that," Fadhel squirmed in his seat and brought his handcuffed hands to the surface of the table in a clenched grip, then swung them back under the table. His jaw clenched making the veins in his neck stand out hard and rigid; Sarah could see he was upset.

"Father, please don't make a fuss about this to anyone if it means putting yourself in further danger," Abbas tried to calm his father.

"Leave it to me. I will think it over."

Fadhel later sent a telegram to revolutionary Prime Minister, Abd al-Karim Qasim, saying, "If I am a criminal, does that make my son criminal also? What did he do?" So Abbas was finally given his permit which allowed him to leave the country and attend university the next year.

Confinement and Writing

Sarah needed something to occupy her days during the confinement after Fadhel's arrest. Sadly, the work at Ramzi School had come to a halt during the Revolution. Sarah had not been able to give the support that she would have liked during the upheaval. It was far too dangerous for her to be out in public and after suffering her stroke, her own health had to take precedence. Sadly, there was no choice but to close the Ramzi School.

She was still working on her book, *The Story of Laith and His Life after Encephalitis.* She thought perhaps this was a good time to go back to her interest in writing about the folktales of Iraq. The story about Laith was still an ongoing work in progress and she worked at it as life unfolded. Due to her confinement and not being able to travel to see Laith, she turned her thoughts toward another project concerning the folktales. It had been about twenty years since she had first become interested in these wonderful stories. It had always been her desire to get the stories written before they became extinct. The tales were told by one generation to another but society was changing and people who knew the stories were becoming less available or less inclined to keep up the tradition. Sarah had always felt these wonderful stories were an important part of the historical culture of Iraq and she feared they would become extinct and fade away without proper recognition.

[46]In 1952, Sarah contacted the Archives Department of the Library of Congress in Washington, DC explaining about these historical stories and requested to borrow their recording equipment. She was first put in contact with the department through Ralph Solecki, a Smithsonian researcher, who had taken part in an early 1950s University of Michigan anthropological expedition to Northern Iraq. He had used the recording equipment for a similar project and had suggested Sarah might do the same.

The equipment loan was approved by the Archive's Head at the time, Duncan Emrich, who wrote: "This seems to be an excellent opportunity to cooperate with a university expedition as well as to obtain unusual material from a country which is not as yet represented in the Archive." Therefore, an Eicor tape recorder, two microphones, a generator and battery, valued in total at $400 were sent to Sarah. Ten tapes and two empty spools were sent to her as a starter, all of which she received in August 1953. So, Bahiya and Sarah worked together to make recordings. Bahiya had an artful talent for using different voice tones as she depicted different characters in her stories. Often, she would tell a story to illustrate a point that had come up in conversation. She had a great memory and one story would often lead her to remember another and another. A year later, Sarah submitted two tapes to the Archive, the recordings that came to comprise the Sarah P. Jamali Collection.

---

[46] **See Library of Congress -** "The Gal Who Will Use the Recording Machine:" Insights into the Sarah P. Jamali Collection

Shortly after receiving the recording equipment, it was arranged that it would live permanently at the University of Baghdad, after Sarah was done using it. Funding in the amount of $400 from the Rockefeller Foundation made this donation possible; this was a gift to the University of Baghdad from the Foundation, which reimbursed the Archive for the equipment. Emrich was very supportive of this donation, believing the University in Iraq should have the capabilities to record culture.

Sarah was able to retrieve the recorder and begin her project with Bahiya. They spent many happy times together once again. It was a productive and very healing time for Sarah but, of course, there would be no complete solace or healing as long as Fadhel was locked away in prison. But, at the very least, it provided a good distraction from depressing thoughts during the day. In the evenings she tried to listen to their favourite classical music but it often brought tears and feelings of deep emotional sorrow so it was better to read or write to avoid melancholy.

Bahiya had lived her whole life in the holy city of Kadhimain, famed for the mosque with its two golden domes and four golden minarets. Many Muslim pilgrims would trek to Kadhimain to visit the tombs of the two Imams (religious leaders) who are enshrined in the mosque, so it is not surprising that some of the stories told came from other lands such as Iran. Bahiya had remained a close family member to Sarah, Fadhel and the boys even after her husband (Fadhel's father, Abbas) had passed away. It seemed only fitting that Sarah should include Bahiya as she began the project of translating the tapes into English. Sarah invited Bahiya to come for lunch. It had been a long time since their last visit due to the disruption of their lives by the Iraqi Revolution.

ഇൗ

"It is so wonderful to see you again," Sarah greeted Bahiya and gave her a hug. "Let's go out into the courtyard. It is such a lovely day and Um Sania has set a lunch out for us there," Sarah led the way through the house to the back yard. It was a beautiful day and the flowers and greenery were looking very beautiful. Um Sania had set the table with all the best dishes and created a beautiful centre piece by floating red, yellow and pink hibiscus blossoms in a shallow clear glass bowl of water.

Bahiya followed, her dark robes flowing gracefully as she walked. She was a traditional Arab woman who always dressed appropriately in an abaya (robe covering the body from neck to ankle) with a niqāb head covering. With a round face, somewhat broad nose, full lips, dark piercing eyes and black eyebrows, her expression often gave the appearance of a thoughtful and solemn personality. However, at family gatherings, she was never without a twinkle in her eye and a smile at the corners of her mouth. She would be the life of the party and would have everyone laughing as she enacted her folktales with great animation.

"Oh how lovely," Bahiya smiled as she took a seat at the table. "I have wanted to come see you for a time now but was not sure if you felt up to visitors."

"Yes, I'm very up to visitors. This house is far too large and empty these days. I'm very lonely for Fadhel and I miss the boys and I especially worry about Laith all the time. I write postcards to him and I receive little gifts from him and some reports about his progress—or, shall I say, lack thereof. I suppose I'll never get over missing being able to see him."

"Well, that is to be expected. After all, he was like your shadow every moment of the day for many years. You will be able to visit him soon, I hope. Things need to settle down and I know you have many worries on your mind these days. I hope there is something I might be able to do to make you a little bit happy."

"Just seeing you always makes me happy. That is exactly why I wanted to speak to you today, Bahiya. You know that years ago I was trying very hard to record your folktales. . ."

"Yes, I remember our many happy days working together on the recordings. But at that time we had to do things in secret because I feared that other family members would not approve of this project," Bahiya placed her napkin on her lap and Um Sania brought a platter of hummus, naan bread, olives, bright red-coloured pickled turnips, sulta (salad) and fresh fruit for the women to share.

"Thank you Um Sania. Bahiya, the apricots were picked just this morning from our tree over there. The dates are also from our palm tree. Abbas planted these trees and they are thriving well. I hope you'll enjoy tasting the fruit from them," Sarah went on to continue with the topic of conversation, "That's correct—I realize you were a little uncomfortable about family's opinions about us doing the recordings at the time. It was likely that some people thought that folktales are just superstitions and, therefore, out of place in a progressive, modern society. But, as you know, things are more liberal now in that regard. Now, if you are still willing to spend time with me, we can freely acknowledge that you are the narrator of the stories. I want to sit down with you and listen to the tapes we recorded and translate the stories into English. I want to write the stories into a book! What do you think? Are you still up for this?" Sarah plucked a grape from the fruit platter and popped it into her mouth.

"Of course, my dear—it would be my pleasure to spend more of my days in your company! You know, I'm an old woman now and I get lonely too. We shall have a laugh and enjoy one another's company."

"Alright, then, it is settled. If you will be willing to come here, I will provide meals together and I can also have my chauffeur pick you up and bring you here. You won't have to be here every time as I can work on my own a lot but I thought it would be a nice chance for us to be together as we are both lonely these days. Would that work for you?"

"Most definitely—you have made this old lady feel wanted and useful. How could I refuse?"

"Stop saying you are old! You still have a lot to offer and you have a lot of life left to live. This is exciting and for the first time since this awful coup, I'm feeling as though I have something to look forward to. Thank you so much, my dear. Now, please enjoy your lunch and we'll talk about the stories after we eat. Enjoy this lovely meal prepared by my Guardian Angel. You must tell me about the news of your daughters. I hope they are well . . ."

266

Sarah continued her visits to Fadhel. He was very pleased to learn of her book project about the folktales. He thought it was a blessing that Sarah was enjoying the companionship of his stepmother, Bahiya. He knew of her ability to make people laugh and he knew Sarah could use a bit of laughter in her life. He was happy to see that she looked healthy. He had worried about her but now that she was sitting in front of him, he could smile. As she sat chattering away about Um Sania's granddaughters, Bahiya, and her writing, he noticed some of that girlish freshness to her that he had fallen in love with so very long ago. Her eyes sparkled as she laughed and chatted. A petal pink colour had returned to her cheeks. He noticed how lovely her teeth were, her hair, her fingernails, her fragrance, and just the sound of her voice—it all seemed so near and yet so far. When would he ever be able to hold her in his arms and kiss her in the way he wanted to in this moment? Although he held a smile on his lips, his heart was aching.

"Fadhel—are you listening to me?"

"I'm sorry, Dear— my mind sometimes wanders a little. I don't mean to be rude. I was just admiring your beauty and I guess my thoughts went off to things from the past. I was daydreaming for a moment about us. I yearn for the music, the moonlight and the sweet intoxicating perfume of the jasmine flowers at night with you."

"Oh, I know Darling—I, too am yearning. I can't enjoy the music without you. But let's cheer up now. What I was just telling you was that I spoke with Ahmed

Saleh al-Abdi (Military Governor of Iraq). He has granted permission for me to bring you books! I've brought a few today. I know you love reading the Quran, but these will help to fill times when you are bored, I hope," she reached into her tote bag that had been searched before she was allowed to bring the books to Fadhel.

"Thank you Sarah. These books will be a wonderful diversion from my surroundings. Perhaps I may share these with my good friend, Burhan ed-Din Bashayan."

"Yes, of course. If either of you has any special requests, just write to me and I'll do my best to bring them to you. As you know, we have a wonderful library in our home—thanks to you!"

It may not seem so momentous, but this act of kindness was not easily carried out. Just as Sarah had walked the streets of many cities and written many letters in her search to find a suitable place for Laith, she was now doing everything possible to help her husband. Little gifts and acts of kindness were not always easily achieved. People in positions of authority were not always easily reached and requests for something as simple as being allowed to have reading material were seldom granted. In spite of this, Sarah was determined. Accompanied by Sadiqa, a cousin of Fadhel's, she went to see Prime Minister Qasim. They were driven there by Allawi, son of a dear family friend, Najat Ossairan Allawi. These friends gave her some moral support that day as she met with Qasim and told him: "I want Fadhel's life from you." He was polite and listened to her but of course, he made no promises at that point.

Sarah paused for a moment and studied her husband's face. "Fadhel, why does your face seem to be swollen? I'm just noticing it now. On one side, especially—but both cheeks seem to look puffy."

"Oh, it's nothing. I think it is from grinding my teeth during my sleep. I have sometimes bitten my cheek. It is not painful. It will go away. Don't worry, it's nothing."

The truth was, Fadhel had been interrogated several times. When he was first arrested, he had been beaten when he was brought before the Minister of Defense. Luckily, Sarah had never seen him after that as he was placed into solitary confinement and for the first few months he had been denied all visitors. Several times recently, he had been interrogated and his face had been slapped repeatedly. However, in spite of this, he felt that his treatment was the best treatment possible and the least cruel compared to what some others had to endure. But Fadhel did not want Sarah to know about the slaps or the brutality to any of the other prisoners—it would only keep her awake at nights.

One military revolutionist, Abdul Salaam Aref, wanted all the prisoners arrested with Jamali to be killed. Surprisingly, Abdul Karim Qasim said, "If any one touches these men, I will kill him." He gave orders that the men should be well treated. It was he who permitted food to be brought in from the homes of the prisoners and later he also allowed books to be brought to prisoners.

Chapter 22

Prayers and Interventions

Sarah knelt beside her bed one evening. She didn't ask God to get Fadhel out of prison but she prayed, "Dear God, do your best!" One day when she was going to the prison for a visit, she prayed, asking the question: "Dear God, what shall I say?" and the words came to her mind: "They won't hang you; you're too precious." When she arrived at the prison that day, a kind commander of the prison allowed them to meet in his office, rather than the cell. As a way of caution, she and Fadhel nearly always spoke in Arabic so the guards would understand their conversations and see that they were not guilty of anything untoward in their chats. But before she left that day, in one quick moment, she turned to her husband and said quietly in English, "They won't hang you; you're too precious." Her visit and these words were a comfort to both of them and each slept better that night for the first time since their separation.

Sarah and Fadhel had been married for nearly 27 years by this time and had a very touching relationship built on love, certainly—but even more solidifying was their deep respect for one another in their different religions. This is not to say that there were no quarrels or strong disagreements in the earlier years. Like any couple, they struggled to find mutual ground. Sarah is quoted as saying:

[47]"It was not always like this! At first we ran on separate tracks. [48]Moral Re-Armament made it possible to bridge our language gap—our 'communication' gap. Earlier, he had his religious ideas and I had mine. Moral Re-Armament gave us a new common language."

ഇരു

Sarah wasn't the only person praying for Fadhel. Friends around the world prayed for his safety. Among the many who intervened on his behalf were Dag Hammarskjold (a Swedish economist and diplomat who served as the second Secretary-General of the United Nations), Pope John XXIII, the President of the Federal German Republic, the President of Pakistan, the President of Tunisia, and the Masjumi Party (the largest political group in Indonesia).

In 1958, just before the revolution, Fadhel had given a 'fiery speech' at a Security Council meeting defending Tunisia against the French bombing of the Tunisian village of Sakiet Sidi Youssef. He had been a staunch supporter to the independence of North Africa and because of his continued support, the Tunisian President,

---

[47] Sarah and Fadhel Jamali. Interview notes, Zurich, 4 September, 1985 (Source: Iraqi Statesman by Harry J. Almond)

[48] Moral Re-Armament (MRA) – Also called Buchmanism or Oxford Group, a modern, nondenominational revivalist movement founded by American churchman Frank N.D. Buchman (1878-1961). It sought to deepen the spiritual life of individuals and encouraged participants to continue as members of their own churches.

Bourguiba sent his special representative, Habib Chatti, to Baghdad to intercede on Fadhel's behalf.

Surprisingly, even Gamal Abdul Nasser, of Egypt, was active in seeking commutation of the death sentence for Jamali and others. One report stated: He (Nasser) has advised the Iraqi government through their Ambassador in Cairo, "Follow my example. Sentence these people to death but do not execute them."

1960 Ramadan & Reprieve

In the streets of Baghdad, Muslims were being called to prayer by the muezzins as their sing-song, haunting, melodious calls echoed loudly from the summits of the tall minarets. This was normal to hear five times a day throughout the year but it was the month of Ramadan so Muslims were being reminded of this special religious time. Although Sarah was not Muslim and was not required to take part in Ramadan, she did follow the fasting and her own regime for prayer from her home. She was giving prayers of thanks for her improved health after the stroke, the fact that her husband was still alive, her renewed time with Bahiya and the folktales project, her home, her sons, the support of good friends and so many other blessings. Of course, she prayed more often for Fadhel than for anything. She prayed that he would stay healthy, sane and that his life would ultimately be spared. She prayed this so often that sometimes the prayers almost played automatically in her mind throughout the day.

Um Sania would follow tradition during Ramadan with the foods she prepared for Fadhel. She was proud to deliver him his meal which he would be taking after a day of fasting. He would typically be fasting all day so Um Sania would prepare an [49]iftar meal of hearty stew with rice and flat bread which she would deliver to the prison at the end of the day.

During this time, King Mohammed V of Morocco was visiting other countries. Fadhel had been a guest of the King's in the past and they were always on very good terms. When the King was invited to include Iraq in his visit to other countries, he replied that he could not come to Baghdad while Jamali was under a death sentence. Fadhel had defended the King and his country in the UN against the French colonialism and the King took this opportunity to defend his good friend. Baghdad countered, 'Come to Baghdad and we will consider his case.' Could this indicate a glimmer of hope?

ℰↄ☙

"Um Sania, Abbas, Bahiya, girls—come listen to the radio with me!" Sarah called to the family. It was the last day of the fasting for Ramadan and Sarah had gathered the family together for the feast day. Um Sania's granddaughters and Bahiya's daughters as well as Fadhel's brother, Abdul Rasoul, and his family were all included to help the family celebrate. Sarah had received word that there would be a special announcement made

---

[49] Followers of Islam believe that fasting teaches patience, modesty, and spirituality. Meals are served before sunrise, called suhoor, and after sunset, called iftar, and eaten with family or with the local community.

on the radio. They all gathered in the living room and listened as the announcement was broadcast that Jamali's death sentence had been reduced to 10 years in prison. Shouts of glee and tears of joy were immediate as everyone hugged and jumped for joy.

The official announcement was made on March 27, 1960. The death sentences of General Daghestani, General Omar Ali and Ahmed Mukhtar Baban were also commuted in the same decree, issued by Abdul Karim Qasim. For over a year and a half, Fadhel never knew when he heard footsteps in the corridor in the early morning whether it was guards bringing him his breakfast or the hanging squad coming for him.

Of course 10 years was still a very long time to be imprisoned but Fadhel's life had been spared—Sarah's prayers had been answered. Usameh was in Libya, employed by the National Bank, when his good friend, Dr. Ali Attiga, came across from his residence to inform Usameh that his father was released. He quickly called his mother to hear more details from her about the good news.

Freedom

Once the death sentence had been lifted, Fadhel could receive visits from other family members. In a letter to Abbas dated, March 24, 1961, he wrote: "My health is all right, praise to Allah. Your mother visited me with several relatives and friends to visit every day of the blessed Feast." (the time at the end of Ramadan). Sarah was devoted to Fadhel and to her sons. She had spent every ounce of her inner strength to do what was best for Laith and now she was devoting her energy to her husband. There were times in prison when his health had suffered and this worried her. She knew that her constant visits and the support of others would bring Fadhel good cheer and lift his spirits. Um Sania continued to provide healthy and delicious meals to contribute to his good health.

Each week while in prison, Fadhel wrote letters to Abbas without fail. However, there were times when Abbas and Usameh did not manage to respond with a weekly letter. This would cause some aggravation for their father:

Baghdad, May 5, 1961

[50]"Dear Abbas,

After sending you my good greetings, I pray for your safety, success and guidance.

I have received no letter from you this week as yet, and it seems that your letters come every other week which means that you do not write weekly as we had agreed. As for Usameh, this is the third week in which I have received no letter. I hope that this is not due to an accident or disease. I believe that duty requires you to write regularly so as not to cause anxiety and disturbance to your parents.

In my last letter I wrote to you about the six duties in the Islamic religion: prayer, fasting, zakat, pilgrimage, jihad, and commanding good

---

[50] Excerpt from, *Letters on Isalm, Written by a Father in Prison to His Son,* by Mohammad Fadhel Jamali

deeds and forbidding evil doing. In that letter I referred briefly to prayer, fasting and zakat. . . "

Usameh was now 25 and Abbas was 18 and both young men were in university. They were busy with their studies, no doubt, but it would also stand to reason that they were young and active socially as well as scholastically. Abbas was enjoying his life away from home and he became involved in drama and swimming. He took part in several plays at the university and he once won second place in a swimming championship of the University. He achieved his Life-Saving qualifications as well. All those times spent with his mother and brothers, swimming in the Tigris River had given him a good start in his love of the water.

In Fadhel's letters to Abbas, he made it clear on more than one occasion:

[51]". . . that the purpose in my writing is to acquaint you with my point of view and it is not my purpose to enter into a debate with you. Still, I am ready to answer your constructive remarks within the limits of my knowledge and ability. I am not one of the scholars of religion; I am only a beginner in the pursuit of knowledge. However, relatively long experience in life, old and new, eastern and western, encourages me to meet with the rising youth, like you, on condition that they are seekers of truth—truth in the largest sense."

---

[51] Excerpt from *Letters on Isalm, Written by a Father in Prison to His Son,* by Mohammad Fadhel Jamali

Abbas did as his father bade; he kept the letters from Fadhel and eventually in 1965, Fadhel had the letters published into a book entitled, *Letters on Islam Written by a Father in Prison to His Son*. Although the letters were primarily for the purpose of guiding Abbas in religion and philosophical ideals promoted by his father, there was one letter to Usameh also published in the book. When questioned about this one letter, Usameh responded: [52]"Regarding the sole letter addressed to me, it was in response to my raising the issue of 'preordination'. If your life and actions are preordained, what meaning is there for a day of reckoning and judgment?"

Baghdad, January 12, 1960

"Dear Usameh,

After greeting you, I pray Allah for your complete health and success.

I was greatly delighted to receive your letter and especially to know that you are indulging in your studies and that some serious problems engage your thoughts. You have asked me about an abstruse, philosophical, religious question, and the person questioned does not know more than the questioner. I, like you, think about and investigate this subject as a beginning student and no more.

I herewith summarize my views for you with complete brevity. . . "

---

[52] Email message from Usameh to author, Jan Keating – May 20, 2020

The letters, usually lengthy and well written, were the organized thoughts and philosophies of Fadhel's. The personal greetings were usually short and the lectures were written from his heart for the intention of giving moral and religious guidance to his son who he worried about. He felt the need to write to Abbas in the absence of his ability to be there in person to have deep discussions with the young man. Usameh, on the other hand, had the benefit of his father for more of his formative years than did Abbas. The need to teach Usameh was not as pressing; thus, fewer letters to Usameh.

ಬಿೂ

Abbas had been home from university in July of 1961 and visited Fadhel at the prison. Sarah accompanied Abbas. She knew that seeing Abbas would be emotional for Fadhel.

"When I look at you now, I see a man rather than the boy I last saw," Fadhel embraced his son with a firm handshake and a kiss on both cheeks. He was permitted to embrace a family member now during visits. He no longer was required to wear the handcuffs during a personal visit. His sentence had been shortened even more by degrees as each feast or official holiday came around. By the beginning of July, 1961, his sentence had been reduced to six months in prison.

"Well, soon you'll be home, Father, and you will not have to miss so many changes in my handsome looks!" Abbas chuckled. He was so happy to see his father again but he was afraid to make the moment too sentimental for fear of tearing up in front of Fadhel. He wanted to keep the visit uplifting for everyone's sake.

"Yes, it will be such a wonderful day for us all to be reunited at home. I dream of it and pray for it." Fadhel looked at Sarah and she nodded. She had also kept this same prayer every day and every night. She knew God was with them and she remembered the message that came to her through prayer, "They won't hang you; you're too precious."

ဆဣ

On the night of July 13, 1961, Prime Minister Qasim ordered seven political prisoners, including Fadhel, to be brought to his office. The men learned that their records had been called for and that they should be ready the next evening to go to the Ministry of Defense. The next evening, on July 14, they were transported there. Later, they were met by Prime Minister Qasim. The first thing he said to the men was:

> "You are people who have served the country and we never forget your good work; but the people wanted to kill you, and I protected you. After you are served coffee, all your death and prison sentences are wiped out."

Qasim seemed to want to relieve himself from any ill will or responsibility for the death sentences. He put the blame on all this on the 'people' of Iraq. Did he have a guilty conscience for all the murders during the uprising that maybe left him with no stomach for the deaths of these men? Perhaps, but also very possible was the fact that there had been so much outside support from people in high places for these men's lives to be spared. With the pressure of high ranking foreign dignitaries, Qasim could see that there would very likely be consequences dealt if he were to sanction and carry out death penalties.

Qasim continued to expound to the men about his achievements for an hour and half. He talked about the irrigation canals that he had opened, construction projects, development plans, etc. At the end of his talk, he asked the men if there was anything that anyone needed. Fadhel told him that he had no special needs but that he wanted to thank the Leader for giving him the opportunity to study the Quran. Qasim responded, "Yes, I recite verses from the Quran too." He then told the men that those of them who had cars could leave in their own cars, and for those who did not have a car, the Army would transport them home. Fadhel accepted the offer and was driven straight home.

The house looked more beautiful to Fadhel than he had remembered it. He paused on the street and took in the welcoming warmth of the radiant glow of lights from within. Knowing that Sarah was inside brought tears to his eyes. He took out his handkerchief and wiped his eyes and removed his hat before opening the door. He stepped into the warmth and the light; he could smell the aroma of rich dark coffee and the sound of friendly chatter and laughter.

"He's here! Fadhel is home!" someone called from the living room. There was a rush of people all smiling and grabbing him to hug and kiss him. Women kissed him even though it was forbidden to do so. Then, as he stood there trying to get his bearings, the crowd parted and there stood Sarah. Fadhel opened his arms and she rushed to his embrace. "Welcome home Dear."

Chapter 23

The morning after Fadhel's 'welcome home' party, Sarah awoke before Fadhel. She lay very still with her face close to his. It was the first time in three and a half years since she had lain beside her husband. She studied his face while he slept so peacefully. It was the face of a 58 year-old man. She didn't often think of either of them as being in their fifties. She felt as though it was only a very short time ago that they had married and started their family. However, at this moment, she admitted to herself that the last few years had taken its toll on both of them with her stroke and his ulcers. The events of the recent years had beaten them down but not defeated them. Fadhel attributed his survival to his faith in Allah, a clear conscience, loyal friends and the comfort and strength he found in reading the scriptures of the Quran. Sarah had also depended on her faith in God and by keeping herself busy with writing, daily exercise and spending time with family. But at the core of it all, was their devotion to one another and their deep unwavering love.

Now as she lay thinking and watching Fadhel breath in and out in peaceful and much needed sleep, she noticed his hair was quite 'salt and pepper' grey and almost pure white at his temples. There were little creases at the corners of his eyes. She thought she probably didn't notice this before because she had not seen him with his glasses off for over three years. Thin lines were forming from the corners of his mouth to the base of his chin. She thought how people refer to lines in aging faces as "laugh lines" but sadly there had not been many things for years now for either of them to laugh about.

He was thin but not skeletal. This was mostly due to his ulcers which sometimes caused him grief and made digesting certain foods difficult. He also suffered from dental discomfort. He had not been able to get the proper care for his teeth while in prison. But, all in all, she thought him to still be a very striking and handsome man. Tears welled up in the corners of her eyes and fell onto her pillow as she lay there thinking how blessed she was to have him beside her again. These were not tears of sorrow but tears of joy and thankfulness to God. In her deepest and darkest moment, she had opened her thoughts to Him in prayer and He had sent the words she needed to hear, *"They won't hang you; you're too precious."* She knew she and Fadhel were not alone. They were in God's hands. God was listening and He was watching over them. She didn't want to move for fear of waking him before she had finished absorbing this precious moment.

She let her thoughts go back in time to her days in Weyburn as a child and a young girl, growing up on the prairie. They were times of blissful days with no worries or fears. She was thankful for the parents she had been blessed with and how they had given her the freedom to run, play, learn and explore the joys of being a child. And, she couldn't help but think that she had been blessed to grow up on the prairies where life was, for the most part, very simple—at least from a child's perspective. There was something about the harshness of the elements of prairie life that she believed built character in people. She had so many happy memories of her brothers and her sister. She remembered family gatherings and times spent with friends, making snow men, laying in a snow bank and making snow angels, having snow ball fights or sledding in winter, climbing trees to steal crabapples, picnics in summer, swimming and enjoying the regattas at Carlyle Lake, school plays, glee club choir in high school, dates with boys and the whole gamut of her youth.

For just a fleeting moment, she recalled her mother's objections and warnings against marrying Fadhel. She was thankful that her parents had not lived to learn about the Revolution and all that had happened to Fadhel. They would have been so upset and worried and it would have been very painful for Sarah to know that her aged parents would be fretting. She wondered what her life would have been like if she had given in to her mother's wishes. Would life have been easier? Perhaps but, no—she wiped her tears and swallowed the lump in her throat—she had no regrets whatsoever. Fadhel was the right man for her over thirty years ago when she first fell in love with him and he was still the right man for her after twenty-eight years of marriage.

Her thoughts moved on to their beautiful sons. Oh how she thanked God in this moment for giving her three beautiful sons. She loved each one and in her heart she believed that there was much to be thankful for in regard to Laith in spite of the encephalitis. She hoped now that Fadhel was home, they might begin to plan for a visit to Scotland to see him. This was a day to absorb God's blessings on their family.

ℰꙅ

Fadhel and Sarah soon closed their doors to visitors other than a few close friends and family members. One ex-minister, named Abdul Karim Kenna, who had been released from prison along with Fadhel had so many visitors and did so much celebrating upon his return home that Qasim had given a stiff warning that he would take them back to prison if it continued. He said they were drawing too much public attention and he felt it undermined him and his authority. Fadhel was also warned that he must never enter politics again or he would most surely go back to prison. He knew this to be serious and to not be taken lightly.

Having these warnings made it possible to excuse themselves from obligatory feelings of the necessity to entertain guests. Also, Fadhel's health had declined while in prison and he needed quiet time to rest and recuperate. He was content for now to be close to Sarah. They spent days puttering in their garden, admiring the different bird species, reading or writing and listening to classical music. Um Sania pampered Fadhel at every opportunity to feed him or serve him some refreshment. She made it her mission, along with Sarah's help and encouragement, to feed Fadhel foods gentle on his stomach and yet full of nourishment to strengthen his body.

ಬೊೆೋ

Ring, ring, ring . . . Fadhel answered the telephone in his study. "Hello."

"Fadhel, is that you?"

"Yes, who is calling, please?"

286

"Frank Buchman, here, Fadhel. I hope you are well and I'm sure you are enjoying life with Sarah and your family. I'm so happy for you to be home again."

"Frank—how wonderful it is to hear your voice! I have some days that are not so good and, yet, I hate to complain as it is so good to be home again. I hope you are well."

"Yes, thank you. My dear friend, I am calling to invite you to join me. You should come right away to the MRA (Moral Re-Armament) Assembly in Switzerland! You could surely use the uplifting benefits."

"Oh, that is a very wonderful idea. I thank you for the invitation; however, I am not permitted to travel. I am restricted to staying close to home."

Shortly after this conversation, Fadhel was dining with Jamil al-Urfali, who had been Minister of Justice in the Jamali government. Fadhel told his friend that he feared his health was deteriorating. Urfali mentioned that his niece was married to the Military Governor General of Iraq and that they were coming to his house for lunch. He offered to speak to the Governor on Jamali's behalf. Soon afterwards, he called and told Fadhel: "Make a good petition to Qasim and ask for permission to leave for medical treatment." Fadhel followed this advice and, within a fortnight, he was called and told that his passport was ready.

୫ୠ

"It seems we've only been home together for a few months now and already I am helping you pack a suitcase

287

once again. It seems no matter what we do, we are always being separated. When you were in politics, you were gone so much." Sarah was folding shirts and picking out ties to help Fadhel with his packing.

"I know but you realize this is for the best, I'm sure. If I don't get out of here quickly, I may box myself in. Once the Communists realize that I have a legal passport to exit the country, I have no doubt that they will try to block me somehow."

"I know you are right. I've just been enjoying our time here together so much. I've missed you for so long."

"I understand but this is not a normal life, Sarah. I am still like a prisoner in my own home. I cannot live every day wondering who is coming for me next. We've no chance of a normal existence here and this has been fine for the past ten months but I want more for us in the future. This is not true freedom, living in fear of another possible imprisonment."

"Yes, I'm totally in agreement with you on that. I know we have some wonderful allies and good friends and family connections here but I also feel the hatred and feel the suspicious eyes on me when I go out anywhere. I think it is very lucky that you were able to get the early KLM flight to Zurich."

"Yes, and it is true about our good fortune in having close friends. I am totally lifted by the kindness of our dear friends who have helped finance my trip. I told them all that I would only accept on the condition that they consider it a loan. I intend to pay them all back even though they have insisted that the money is a gift."

"I wish we could leave together."

"I know you do but it has to be this way to prevent drawing attention to my exiting the country. The less anyone knows about our business right now, the better. It will appear more normal if you are still here. You are free to move about without any restrictions. I want you to make arrangements to have someone from our family move into our house. Once you have that accomplished, you will fly to Zurich to join me."

"Yes, alright, Dear, I will. I wonder if I should call your brother to see if he wants to move into our house."

"Yes, call him first. Give him and his family first opportunity but, also, there is Bahiya. I know her daughters are married now. Perhaps in her old age, she would like to live here with one of them."

"That is also a good suggestion. I would like someone who would be willing to keep Um Sania employed. She is getting up in years and I feel her tasks should ease up. I would make a suggestion to whomever we get to move in that they consider another servant to do all the cleaning. Um Sania could handle just the cooking and that would give her more hours in her day to relax," Sarah put a clean pair of pajamas on top of the clothes so they would be the first thing he would take out once he got to his destination. Everything was clean, pressed and packed. She closed the suitcase and Fadhel took her in his arms and kissed her. It was May 8, 1961; he would be leaving early the next morning.

ॐ

On his arrival at the Kloten airport, Fadhel went straight to the Hotel Royale, across the River Limmat from Hauptbahnhof. The first thing he did was telephone Mrs. Rudolf Huber. She and her husband, who was the Director of the Oerlikon Machine Co., had met Fadhel and Sarah in 1956 at a Moral Re-Armament Assembly in Caux. They had become friends over a great conversation that Mrs. Huber recalled about the status of women in Islam. She had been most impressed with Fadhel's attitude toward the importance of women being treated equal in society. This was refreshing and something she had not heard many men address and she had not expected to meet a Muslim man who thought so liberally in that time. She admired the relationship of great respect and love she could see between Sarah and Fadhel.

Mrs. Huber had followed the news about Fadhel's imprisonment. She was very happy to hear from him and once she realized he was in Zurich in a hotel, she hurried down to meet him and to take him to her home. Not only did she welcome him into her home, she also saw to it that he got medical and dental attention immediately. He received all treatment for free as the doctors all knew about the history of his plight and were happy to help him. It was uplifting to receive such care and compassion from complete strangers. The world was not all evil!

Fadhel explained to Mrs. Huber his plan to have Sarah join him as soon as she could settle things with their house in Baghdad. In the meantime, Fadhel worked on following doctors' orders, taking his medications, getting work done on his teeth and keeping up with his regime of prayer each day. He frequently used the Huber family living room for his Muslim prayers and to receive guests in his usual manner. He was fortunate to know many people in Zurich. A lifetime in travel through his teaching and political careers had afforded him an opportunity to travel and make friends in many places.

Fadhel, being a man who was constantly learning, decided to learn German. He would read children's fairy tale books while sitting in doctors' waiting rooms. The Huber boys were amused by this and they dubbed him, "Herr Was Heisst?" (Mr. What is it called?), because he was so determined to learn German that he was always asking them what this or that meant.

Eventually, after a stay of twenty-four days, Sarah joined him. Fadhel's brother, Abdul Rasoul, had accepted the offer of the house in Baghdad. He moved into the house and rented his house out to someone else. Fadhel would not consider the thought of selling the house and it was left to Usameh and Abbas (and remains owned by the brothers to this day). Although Fadhel would never return to his home in Baghdad, it was always in his heart and as his son Usameh said: [53]"My father never countenanced a finality with respect to returning to Baghdad whether in flesh or in spirit."

Fadhel had tried to find a suitable hotel for the two of them but had not succeeded. Sarah had spoken to a Swiss friend who had advised her on the education of mentally handicapped people. This friend found them a place in the Righiblick, a modest alcohol-free hotel to which they continued to return to each summer for many years to follow.

---

[53] As told to the author by Usameh Jamali – Email message (June 2, 2020)

Chapter 24

1962 Tunisia

It would seem that for as much as some people hated Fadhel, there were just as many, if not more, that loved and respected him. President Habib Bourguiba, of Tunisia, had heard that Fadhel had been invited by King Hassan of Morocco and King Hussein of Jordan to move to their countries. When Bourguiba heard that his friend, Jamali, was in Zurich, he sent the Tunisian Ambassador in Bern to enquire after him and to invite him to move to Tunisia. After discussing this offer with Sarah, the couple decided to accept and to make Tunis their new home. Fadhel told Bourguiba, "I don't want to sit idle as your guest. I am a hard-working man. Do you have a job for me?"

Although Fadhel never asked about a salary, he did receive a modest one and the use of a car and a driver as Lecturer on Educational Philosophy at the University of Tunis. Although the retirement age there was 60, Fadhel actually started his teaching career in Tunis at that age.

Tunisia is situated on the Mediterranean coast of North Africa, midway between the Atlantic Ocean and the Nile Delta. It is bordered by Algeria on the west and southwest and Libya on the east. [54]While most modern day

---

[54] Demographics of Tunisia - Wikipedia

Tunisians identify as Arabs, Tunisian ancestry is mainly derived from native Berber groups, with substantial Phoenician/Punic, Arab and Western European input. Tunisians are also descended, to a much lesser extent, from other African, Middle Eastern and/or European peoples.

As they approached their landing, Sarah looked out the window of the airplane and was struck by the contrast of the shimmering white plaster buildings against the cerulean and azure blue waters of the Mediterranean Sea. There were endless miles of soft, white, sandy beaches, palm trees, Cypress trees, cacti, cork oak trees, and pine trees. They were picked up at the airport and driven by their personal driver in the car provided to Fadhel by President Bourguiba. They spent the first while in a hotel but eventually were able to rent a house with a view of the Sea.

Tunis is the capital city of Tunisia. It is located along Lake Tunis just inland from the Mediterranean Sea's Gulf of Tunis. Sarah loved that everywhere she looked she saw blue skies and blue waters. Much of the general sights of the city were familiar to her. There were paved streets with automobiles sharply contrasted by carts drawn by donkeys. There were narrow ancient streets where open markets were noisy with music, bartering venders and shoppers. There were enticing smells of food cooking next to disgusting smells of camels and goats. But it was all very invigorating and it represented a life of freedom for the couple. They were anxious to begin this new chapter in their lives together.

Their home, located in La Marsa, was owned by an Italian doctor who only used the house in summers. Since Fadhel and Sarah planned to travel to Scotland to see

Laith during summers, this arrangement worked very well for the first while. The house was somewhat small and typical in design with square-block architecture, white-washed, clay exterior, rounded domes, arched doorways, and a central patio. It was situated on a hill with a view of the sea which could be enjoyed from sitting in the front yard or through the large picture window of the living room. The layout of the house was typical of many homes with every room opening onto a central courtyard patio. Once again, the Jamali's had a fountain in their courtyard. This offered the couple a private sanctuary where they enjoyed the beauty of a small flower garden, some fruit trees and bird watching.

Fadhel had a wide range of interests and collections. In time he had all of these things shipped to their new home in Tunis. He had a large assembly of pocket knives and between homes in Baghdad, Tunis and Zurich, he managed to acquire nearly two hundred canes during his travels. Of course the couple also had a large collection of musical recordings which included works of Mozart, Bach, Schubert, Brahms and Beethoven, great church and choir works and many Arabic recordings.

Fadhel began lecturing at the university soon after they were settled into their new home. Sarah was not permitted to teach as her degree in teaching was from the United States rather than from France and was, therefore, not accepted. Although she found this to be disappointing, she again made the statement that she had said many times in the past but now she had added a tag to her phrase, [55]"No experience is a total loss—short of hanging!"

Fadhel wasted no time before he began exploring and socializing with friends and dignitaries. [56]He soon began a ritual of walking one day in the forest and one day on the beach. His driver would drive him to his spot where he would begin his walk. He had at least two regular groups on two specific days of the week which would join him in the walk as well as have tea with interesting discussions.

Sarah hired a woman to assist her with household duties. This woman did not live with the Jamali couple as Um Sania had in the past, but instead came to the house every morning and left every afternoon. Having a servant was very much a constant in Sarah's life since her childhood days in Weyburn and through her married life. Although they were not wealthy people, having servants was quite affordable. Sarah was always appreciative and treated people in her employ with great affection and respect.

Shortly after the move to Tunisia, they received word that Bahiya had passed away. Sarah was so glad that they had spent some wonderful days together and that the book they had worked on was nearly ready for publication. The book entitled, *Folktales from the City of the Golden Domes*, would eventually be published in 1965. Although

---

[55] Quote of Sarah's after Fadhel's imprisonment and death sentence as told to the author, Jan Keating, by Sarah's son, Usameh Jamali.

[56] Fatima Jamali, Sarah's granddaughter (the first grandchild) shared with author, Jan Keating, in email message, dated June 29, 2020.

the book contained only a portion of the recordings she had translated, it was a fine tribute to Bahiya. She would have been most pleased.

In the same time that Fadhel was making new friends and connecting with old friends, Sarah was making her way in social circles as well. [57]She joined the American Women's Club, the Elizabethan Club and the International Women's Society to meet other women. She was pleased to reacquaint herself with some old friends from Baghdad as well. Farhan Shubeilat and his wife, Farida Qutub, were special friends from Baghdad who had been married in the Jamali home on the Tigris years earlier. Fadhel had given the bride away during the wedding ceremony and Fadhel and Sarah were happy to have played matchmakers in bringing this couple together. Farhan became the Jordanian Ambassador in Tunisia and their grandson would later marry Sarah's granddaughter, Fatima. Fatima was the first grandchild born to Abbas and his wife, Dr. Layla Jamali.

As usual, the Jamali home was a favourite place for friends and family to gather. It was common for students of Fadhel's from the university to pop around to have long intellectual chats with their favourite professor. He would delight in sharing his knowledge and wisdom with them. [58]They wanted to hear from him about the history of the region, the Arab-Israeli situation and the formation of the United Nations and his role as signatory on behalf of Iraq. One man who came to visit, and later went on to become an Orthodox priest, made an audio

---

[57] Fatima Jamali – in notes to author, Jan Keating

[58] Abbas Jamali – in notes to author, Jan Keating, dated July 25, 2020

recording of an interview with Fadhel. When the man returned to the US, he sent the recording to Abbas as a gift for Fadhel's retirement.

1962 Laith – Gogarburn Hospital, Edinburgh

Now that Fadhel had his teaching position as Professor of Education at the University of Tunis, the family benefited from the academic summer vacation periods. This allowed Sarah and Fadhel to travel to Edinburgh, Scotland to visit Laith. As soon as they arrived in Edinburgh, they called the Hospital to let the staff know they would be coming to visit him in the afternoon. When they arrived, he was waiting eagerly to meet them. There he stood, smiling from ear to ear—a rather toothless young man of 27 years. Teeth or no teeth, he was a very welcome sight, indeed! Sarah's heart was overjoyed to see her son once more. She was thankful that Laith had been spared all the horrors of the Revolution in Baghdad and had remained safe and happy in Scotland.

They enjoyed taking Laith to the little shop on the hospital grounds where he could buy a bag of his favourite Liquorice-allsorts. They had a wonderful outdoor picnic one day but they kept apart from others because Laith made it clear that he wanted his family to himself.

On one occasion, Sarah noticed that Laith walked very slowly when it was time to return to his ward. He had been transferred to a new ward and seemed very unhappy about this change. Sarah decided to ask why he had been transferred as he had been very happy in his other ward. The answer was that there was a new psychologist who was 'upgrading' the wards by using a mental test.

298

Apparently, Laith had not passed the mental test. Due to his speech problems, he had not been able to answer the mental test questions. It had been decided that he was profoundly mentally retarded and was, therefore, assigned to the lowest ward. Sarah spoke to her old friend, Dr. Petrie, about the matter and he saw to it that Laith was returned to his old ward where he was once again comfortable and happy. These were the kind of things that kept Sarah awake at nights, worrying and fretting about Laith. It was so disheartening for her after all these years that, with all the information she had given about her son, people still neglected to understand him. His needs were not always being met fully because people neglected to read the information that was available to them. It was upsetting to Sarah that something like this new person's attempt at upgrading could have such an adverse affect on her son and go unnoticed until she herself made the discovery. How many other things like this had happened in her absence, she wondered.

∞∞

"Laith, tomorrow we won't be coming to see you. We have to go home for a while now," Sarah and Fadhel would always try to be honest and to prepare Laith for their parting. He seemed to understand and he would go to the lounge area in his ward and wave good-bye to them through the window. Sarah's eyes would moisten with tears. Every parting was gut-wrenching for her. It was a sorrow that she would never be able to overcome.

Of course her life with her husband and their other two sons was bound to go on. That was the way of life—

299

forever moving forward. Abbas and Usameh were moving on as well in life. Abbas was married to Layla who was a doctor and they had three daughters: Fatima, Asma, Souad and one son, Fadhel, named after his grandfather. Usameh married Maysoon, an architect, in 1979, and they had two daughters, Seereen and Sema. Sarah moved on in sync with life as it unfolded but there was always that deep sorrow and longing for Laith.

Jean Bruce

Although Sarah regretted that she could not be by Laith's side on a more frequent basis, she and the family did make trips to visit him every summer. The good thing was that there was a group of very kind Scottish women who kept visiting Laith for more than forty years. Some of these women were friends of Sarah's, like Mrs. MacPhail and Mrs. Petrie but some women were hardly known to Sarah and yet they continued this humanitarian service. These volunteers were there to check on Laith and be Sarah's eyes and ears when it was impossible for her to be there. They provided companionship for Laith which was so appreciated. One gentleman, by the name of Mr. Melville, was taking Laith out for regular visits along with his daughter who was also a resident. However, at a meeting of The Scottish Society for Mentally Handicapped Children, Mr. Melville explained that he would no longer be able to take Laith on outings as his daughter was becoming quite violent with jealousy.

Jean Bruce, a new member of the committee, volunteered to become a visitor to Laith in place of Mr. Melville. For their first introduction, Mr. Melville met with Laith and Jean and her husband, Donald Bruce.

300

"Laith, I want you to meet Jean and Donald Bruce. They would like to be your friends," Mr. Melville smiled and Laith got up from his chair and shook hands with Jean and Donald. Mr. Melville had told the Bruces that Laith loved a car ride. So, they offered to take him out for tea. Jean reported later, "We took to each other very quickly because we discovered that he likes classical music, especially Mozart, and poetry recitations such as nursery rhymes and poems by Robert Louis Stevenson. He knows *My Shaddow* by heart."

One day Jean went to pay Laith a visit and was alarmed to learn that he had been taken to the Royal Infirmary of Edinburgh.

"And who went with him?" Jean asked.

"No one," was the response she got.

"But why wasn't I notified? The head nurse has my name and address and telephone number to use in an emergency." The response she got was a mere shrug of the shoulders.

With that, Jean hurried off to the Royal Infirmary. She found Laith in one of the men's wards and walked hurriedly toward him calling, "Laith, Laith, it's alright!"

Laith smiled and stretched out his arms to her. The situation was not a happy one. The staff didn't know anything about Laith's speech problems and he could not initiate the speech to tell them. He was confused and frightened and would not let anyone examine him. But thankfully, in Jean's presence he calmed down and allowed an examination to take place. Jean explained to the staff that Laith's comprehension of spoken speech was perfectly normal, and that he could answer 'Yes; or

301

'No' if asked a direct question. Once this was cleared up, the hospital staff got along well with Laith and by the time he was ready to leave, they all loved him.

One old gentleman in the bed beside Laith had overheard Jean's explanation to the staff about Laith and got tears in his eyes when he overheard Laith reciting 'Mary Had a Little Lamb'. He said to Jean, "And I thought him demented."

This is just one example of how a small oversight or careless action can cause devastation for someone mentally handicapped like Laith. If Jean had not happened along that day and had not been able to be at Laith's side, he would have suffered more than he already had to that point. Jean was right to question the staff and to point out her frustration with their recklessness in not following through with their own protocol. Someone should have called her as the contact person in such cases. Just as Sarah had often had to intercede, Jean had also done so; and, sadly, it was not the only time.

Taking a moment in the day to pay attention to detail and protocol, could be a huge benefit to the patient and to the people trying to help in the case of medical staff. Once Laith was spoken to and given chance to take in what was happening, he could respond better and cooperate. People like Jean and so many others who volunteer their time and patience to extend a little human kindness to people like Laith are so important. They help provide something that regular caregivers may not always have the extra time to give. However, there is no excuse for what happened that day. These are the things that cut into the hearts of family members who cannot be there every moment to protect their loved one.

Chapter 25

1967 New Hope and New Beginnings

Sarah was determined not to sit idle once she was settled in Tunis. Fadhel was busy with his teaching position at the university and because Sarah was not allowed to teach in Tunisia, she decided she would put her full efforts into initiating a school for mentally handicapped children and adults. She made enquiries everywhere she went asking people, "Do you know of any Tunisian who is interested in the education of mentally handicapped children?" Over and over she got the same response, "It is up to the government," and the government said, "Our priority is the education of normal children." It all seemed so familiar to Sarah from past experience with struggles in Baghdad but she knew she would need to have patience and perseverance.

One day, a friend called saying, "I couldn't sleep last night, Sarah. I was thinking about a child whom I love dearly."

"Oh, I'm sorry to hear. What is the problem?" Sarah was always willing to help a friend in need.

"This little girl is mentally retarded. Her mother has been consulting with doctors here and in France to see if her daughter is capable of some education."

"I see—I can relate to her concerns."

"I know you can. Do you mind if I bring the child around to meet you? You are a teacher and you have had so much personal experience with Laith and other children. If you would be willing, maybe we can help this child and her mother. The mother knows the value of education and she is eager for someone to start a school for mentally retarded children here in Tunis."

"Of course! I would be more than happy to meet them both. Please come with them and we'll have tea. I'll do whatever I can to assess the child. I'm not a doctor but, as you say, I do have a lot of experience and this is my passion to help other children. You know that I, too, want such a school here for children like Laith—so, by all means—please come as soon as you can make arrangements with the mother. I'll be waiting to hear from you soon."

In the meantime, Sarah had heard from a friend, Madame Biérent, wife of a French doctor and the mother of a mentally retarded daughter. Madame Biérent was active in the French Parents' Association for mentally retarded children. She was planning a trip to Tunis so Sarah asked her if she would be willing to meet with a group of parents to discuss the work she was doing in France and to see if she could help to arouse enthusiasm in Tunis for a school.

Sarah received a call from another mother of a four-year old, Down syndrome boy. She offered a large room in her home to be used as a meeting place for their first meeting. Things seemed to be moving in a positive direction. Sarah took this as a sign from God and it gave her courage to call on a neighbour whom she knew had a teenaged, Down syndrome, boy. She wasn't sure how receptive the parents would be to her invitation to attend her first meeting. However, she was welcomed into their home and greeted warmly.

"I just wanted you to know that I have a son like yours. His name is Laith and, although he is not Down syndrome, he suffered severe brain injury from a disease. I, like you, kept my son at home for years and because there was no school for him in Baghdad, I had to search elsewhere. He has been living in a school in Scotland for some years now. I have a friend who has started a successful school for children like ours in France. She is coming to speak to a group of us parents about the possibility of starting a school here in Tunis. I was hoping you might be interested in attending our meeting." Sarah smiled and shook their hands as they welcomed her into their home.

"It is so wonderful to meet you, Mrs. Jamali. Please, step inside. Do you have time to join us for a cup of tea?" The wife smiled and beckoned Sarah to step inside.

"Thank you. That would be lovely. I would love a cup of tea."

"We knew you folks are new to the neighbourhood and we wanted to call on you but we were just shy to bother you too soon. Please have a seat." The woman called her servant and directed her to make a pot of tea. They all sat down in the living room.

The husband began the conversation, "When our son was very young, we took him to see a doctor in France. We had heard there were good doctors and new schools for children like him."

"Yes," his wife piped up in agreement. "But much to our surprise, the doctor we saw advised against us

305

putting our son in any school there." She poured tea and passed Sarah a plate of biscuits and jam.

"I see, that's interesting—did he tell you why he was advising against leaving your son in a school there?" Sarah spread a little jam on her biscuit and sipped her tea waiting for a response.

The husband once again picked up the story, "Yes, he told us that a son like ours needs the love and protection of a family. He pressed my hand and said to me in such an earnest tone, 'Never give up hope!' and here we are now talking to you 17 years later. Perhaps you are the answer to our prayers for our son." The husband pulled out his handkerchief and wiped his eyes. His wife jumped up to pour him more tea. Sarah could see she was trying to give comfort to her husband without embarrassing him in front of Sarah. The man cleared his throat and thanked his wife for the tea. The parents continued their friendly conversation about the details of the upcoming meeting and Sarah was glad she had taken the opportunity to approach them. They were eager to attend.

About fifty people attended the first meeting and listened to Madame Biérent's speech. After her speech, it was decided to hold another meeting to form an association of friends and parents of mentally retarded children. From the second meeting a group of ten interested people decided to form a play group for mentally handicapped children. A year later, in 1967, the group applied to the Ministry of Interior for permission to form an association. Permission was granted and L'Union Tunisienne d'Aide aux Insuffisants Mentaux (UTAIM) was founded.

For the next thirty years, Sarah and the members of the association worked together to expand. There was such a need in so many communities for schools for mentally handicapped children and young adults. Eventually, there were scores of remedial schools and workshops operating throughout Tunisia.

Sarah was thrilled to see her efforts rewarded as the years progressed. President, Zine El Abidine Ben Ali, was supportive and encouraging to any organizations working for humanitarian services in Tunisia. He went as far as to appoint a very active Minister of Social Affairs, Chadli Nafati, who took interest in these humanitarian organizations.

Sarah's experiences, as a teacher and parent who had seen many schools through her days of searching things out for Laith's sake, served an invaluable asset to the association. Through her and the other parents, they managed to incorporate values that gave a new spirit to their schools. Instead of indifference, backbiting, or criticism, there was love, sympathy and interest in the lives of fellow teachers, staff, pupils, parents and volunteers. Their work was based on love, honesty and unselfishness. These principals helped them to work together efficiently and the results were noticed by all who visited their schools.

Local women volunteered to collect clothing and gifts to give to the children for every religious festival and end of term parties. Head Mistresses and teachers worked to plan activities, monthly birthday parties, and weekly picnics. Senior girls were taught how to set and clear the tables for lunch, and how to wash and put away the dishes. Senior boys were introduced to practical jobs in the school. They would go to the cook and get a list of supplies she needed and then they would go to the storeroom where, under supervision, they would measure out and count the required supplies. The students were being taught useful tasks which gave them a feeling of pride about themselves as they learned to contribute to the successful operation of their own home. They learned the skills of how to get along with others in a cooperative manner.

One day, Sarah invited a friend who had been asking questions about the schools to visit the school. Before they entered the school, the woman spoke to Sarah about her concerns about the visit.

"Please excuse me if I choke up and have to leave the classroom. I'm deeply affected by the sight of mentally handicapped children."

This comment bothered Sarah, of course, but she understood that many people were just like her friend and it was the fear of something unknown or different to them. Perhaps people like her had seen things in the past that had been traumatizing. But Sarah was happy when the visit was over and the friend's face was radiant as she exclaimed, "Oh but this is different. These children are happy! They have a future!"

This comment meant a lot to Sarah. This was what she wanted people to see. She wanted people to see that children and adults like Laith could learn things. They just needed time and patience and proper training for their individual levels. Sarah was encouraged every day by the progress of any one of these students. She knew how love and kindness and encouraging words could help to build the confidence and the desire for these students to achieve. If society could see the progress being made and give it recognition, then she felt this to be the reward for her efforts. Visitors were always welcome and they helped to spread the word about positive results being achieved.

Although Sarah would never expect any formal reward for her accomplishments in her work to help mentally handicapped people, it is important to recognize that her work was given recognition in 1996 by Minister of Social Affairs, Chadli Nafati, when he presented her with an award for the work she was doing in Tunis. She graciously accepted this award saying: "I accept this award in the name of all those whose initiative and hard work has developed an important service for people with mental handicaps."

She was 88 but it was difficult to consider her as frail at that age. She was still very active, socially, physically and mentally. She still walked a lot with Fadhel who continued with his walks along the beaches and in the forest. They both had good appetites and each of them had many interests. It seemed that as long as Sarah felt there was still work to be done for the cause for the mentally handicapped children, she had the vitality to rise to the occasion.

June 1970 - A Visitor from America

Sarah and Fadhel were pleasantly surprised to learn that Sarah's great nephew, Robert Jerome (from Whittier, California) was going to be coming to Tunisia to study Arabic and French at the university. Robert was the grandson of Sarah's brother Oliver Powell. Oliver's daughter, Ellen, was Robert's mother. He was born in Minneapolis but his parents moved to California when he was three. Robert remembers letters arriving from Iraq from Sarah and Fadhel with exotic stamps. Sarah was a favourite aunt of his mother's and he stated: "I think my mother admired Sarah's independence of spirit, and as evidence of her devotion, my older sister's middle name is Sarah."

Robert also remembered when he was only ten years old, seeing his mother in tears when she received the devastating news that Fadhel had been stoned to death during the 1958 coup. Of course, this was the mistaken identity and the family was relieved to learn that Fadhel was, indeed, very much alive. He recalled one interesting visit to Sarah and Fadhel's home in June of 1970:

> [59]"I had just graduated from Pomona College in 1970, and had escaped the draft with a high lottery number. I had no idea what I wanted to do with my life, but the idea of a mini-foreign adventure sounded grand. Two years in the Peace

---

[59] Email letter from Robert Jerome to author, Jan Keating (June 29, 2020)

Corps seemed like too much of a commitment; so, I came up with the idea to go to Tunisia to study French and Arabic. I got to spend a great deal of time with Sarah and Fadhel and greatly enjoyed the stimulating and challenging talks. They were an important influence on my life, challenging me to both articulate—and live—my beliefs.

I often took the bus from downtown to their place, and went on several hillside walks with Fadhel, where he chatted about all manner of things, especially, America's disproportionate interest in Israel, which of course, I could not defend. One time I went and noticed several limos in front of their house. Entering the back kitchen door, I found Sarah and asked her what was going on. She said it was Fadhel's birthday, and several ambassadors had come to wish him well. I was clad in student 'grubbies' (torn jeans, ratty tee-shirt), and Sarah said I should go in and say hello. I said, 'I can't go looking like this,' and she replied, 'Rise above it!' I will never forget those words!"

This tells us that even though Fadhel was warned to never go into politics ever again, he still had a very political mind and his opinions were freely shared with young university students as well as scholars and ambassadors who enjoyed his company. He was free to speak his mind and share his ideals. However, he was not aspiring to any political position ever again.

It also speaks to Sarah's congenial disposition in life. She thought nothing of her young nephew's casual appearance. To her, he was someone she loved and was very proud to introduce him to people. She wanted him to go see his Uncle Fadhel on his birthday and meet the ambassadors. It mattered not to her that he was wearing torn jeans and a ratty tee-shirt. To her, the ambassadors were just friends—regular people who likely had grandkids at home that dressed just like Robert! Robert did see his uncle on his birthday and was greeted by the ambassadors with kindness. It was memorable for him and he was glad he didn't have to miss out on the experience. Sarah would not allow that to happen.

While Robert was in Tunisia, he enjoyed doing some sightseeing with friends and his second-cousin, Ed Miller. Ed was the son of Dr. Fred Miller and Miriam Powell (Miriam, Sarah's aunt, was sister to Sarah's father, Harvey O. Powell). [60]Ed and his wife, Ruby, and their two children, Jane and Neal, were the first US cousins to visit the Jamali family while they were living in Baghdad and they visited again in Tunisia. Having family visits meant a great deal to Sarah. She had made a life with Fadhel and his family and she knew she was loved by them and she felt the same for each of them; however, it was very special to have the opportunity to welcome members of her own family to their home. Fadhel was a gracious host and was happy to meet members of Sarah's extended family.

Sarah and Fadhel were sorry to see Robert leave. He headed back to the US and settled in Washington, DC. He finished his doctorate, wrote two books and several

---

[60] As told to author, Jan Keating, by Abbas Jamali (Sarah's son) – Email message, July 13, 2020

articles and eventually worked at the University of Maryland.

Chapter 26

Sarah learned of a new residential home for mentally handicapped people, called Howden Hall Road, located in south Edinburgh. The facility was a home for only six elderly residents. Sarah wanted Laith to have the opportunity to live in a place that would be more suitable for him in his later years. This place sounded more like a home atmosphere than the hospital ward where he was currently living. She contacted Jean Bruce to help Laith make a trial basis transition to the new home. She asked Jean to go see the home and report back to her. Jean was concerned about this as Laith had been a resident at Gogarburn Hospital for so long but he loved Howden Hall Road and made the move successfully. He was now 57 years old.

Sarah was delighted with Howden Hall Road when she and Fadhel visited Laith for the first time in his new home. Abbas and his famiy were also with Sarah and Fadhel at this time. As usual, Laith was happy to see them all and gave them a warm welcome with hugs and kisses. Sarah asked him if he would show her his room. He seemed happy to do this. Sarah noticed that the room was furnished with cupboards, tables, and chairs. In Laith's cupboard, she saw that his suits and sweaters were lined up neatly on clothes hangers. Other clothes were folded neatly and placed on shelves. What a contrast to Gogarburn where there was no private space for patients in the crowded dormitory! At first, Laith would hide his favourite possessions under his pillow, but now, he was beginning to understand that he could keep his things safe in his cupboard.

He had a good friend, George, who was his roommate. George had difficulty walking and used a wheelchair. Laith would happily wheel George around to activities. They shared a common interest in cars. There was a resident dog, named Collie (named after his breed), who also became one of Laith's special friends. Sarah found it most amusing that Laith was encouraged to dust and tidy his part of the bedroom; although, he still needed to be reminded to do this. He also helped to clear the dining room tables. Sarah was pleased to see him doing these little tasks. She was impressed with the idea that members of the home are like a family and families have little tasks that they share and take responsibility for doing. She saw that Laith could carry out these tasks and it made her very proud of him. It also reaffirmed to her that she had done the right thing by Laith to place him in the care of others who could teach him these things. She knew it unlikely that she would have expected him to execute such tasks. Seeing him becoming more independent and capable, was a great thrill to her.

"Good morning, Mrs. Jamali. Hello Mr. Melville," Susan Hart was addressing visitors that morning as she made her rounds. She was the woman who managed Howden Hall Road and she was a very pleasant woman.

"The residents may be a little tired today because they were out dancing last night until midnight," Susan explained.

316

Sarah, Fadhel and the other parents all looked at one another in wide-eyed amazement. Apparently, one of the oldest residents had an 80th birthday and relatives from Edinburgh had arranged a birthday party for him in a private room in a hotel. All the residents had been included in this birthday celebration. Susan showed the parents pictures of them dancing. Although they didn't partner dance, they were dancing and having a great time.

Sarah recalled how Laith would sit alone in a corner of the lounge in Gogarburn and she noticed that now, he was happy to intermix with the other residents in the living room. She found him to be more willing to be social. However, there were times when he still enjoyed his own company. He could still pass time contentedly knitting, singing along to recorded nursery rhymes, watching TV, particularly programs about animals or cars, and looking at picture books.

For the past twenty years, Laith had not had a tooth in his head, but Susan Hart arranged for him to be fitted with dentures. They were a great success. This improved his facial appearance as it was more filled out.

Laith was in a habit of twisting buttons off his clothing. One day, he tore a button from his jacket. Susan gave him a needle and thread and said, "Sew it back on." That was the end of that bad habit. Sarah was impressed with this and thought how wonderful it was that someone could get him to do this. It would never have entered her mind to expect him to sew his button back on. Laith was capable of much more than some people would give him credit. Susan Hart was just the right person to push Laith to his fullest abilities. Sarah recognized this and felt that

317

Laith was in the best place he could possibly be, even if she couldn't see him as often as she would like.

Susan and her husband, Ian, eventually got a mini-bus and took the residents on many outings. There was a social centre for handicapped people not far from Howden Hall Road. Ian would drive Laith and the other residents to the centre where they would enjoy a cup of coffee together. They also went sightseeing and picnicking in the beautiful countryside.

Improvements in Laith

Another year, Abbas and his wife and young daughters accompanied Sarah and Fadhel on a visit to Laith. Sarah asked Abbas's wife, Dr. Layla Jamali, if she would speak to Susan Hart about Laith because Sarah wanted to spend her time with Laith as their time together was so important to both of them. Dr. Jamali was happy to ask questions on Sarah's behalf.

"Does Laith have epileptic seizures anymore?" Dr. Jamali asked Susan.

"No. He has been here for a year without a single seizure, but every day at 5 p.m., I give him a little medication to prevent a seizure."

"I see. I'm happy to hear this. We are also wondering—does he wet the bed at night?"

"No!" exclaimed Susan, "I didn't know he had a problem."

This was very good news for Sarah and the family. Ian Hart reported that they continued to work with Laith on his speech and that he could put a few words together such as, "Ian bus Club" which communicated that Laith wanted to go on the mini-bus with Ian to the Club where they would play bingo and have coffee. So, although it was not normal speech, it did show that Laith could put a thought together well enough and with a phrase, he could manage to communicate. The staff also tried to incorporate Laith's love for poetry and rhyme into catch phrases. For instance: 'a shave a day keeps the beard away' which mimics, 'an apple a day keeps the doctor away.' Things like this would help Laith to catch on to communicating some simple things. However, it was always a work in progress but at least he was in a place where the staff wanted to work with him. Having only six residents to deal with was probably a contributor. It was much easier to get to know the individuals in depth and to try to find innovative ways to help them with their specific needs.

Susan Hart was a nurse trained by the Catholic sisters who worked at Gogarburn Hospital. When she was given the choice of continuing at Gogarburn or running a residential home, she decided that she could probably do more to help patients in the residential home atmosphere. Laith was a prime example of someone who benefited from her decision. People who had known him when he lived in Gogarburn and saw him later when living at Howden Hall Road were amazed at how much better he looked physically and mentally.

The ultimate goal of the home was to ensure that the residents had a comfortable, enjoyable, happy life within their own individual needs, abilities and wishes. For Laith this was certainly the case and Sarah's heart was finally at peace for her beloved son. To see him in a place where he was treated with such respect and caring, to see him making even the smallest improvements, and to know that he had friends and a life worth living gave her such relief. She thanked God every night for the home, the caregivers and the volunteers who cared about her son.

Chapter 27

Sarah and Fadhel had moved from the first house to a second-story apartment, located close to several of their friends, in the suburb of El Mersa, meaning, the harbor. This area was a popular escape from the city and although it could hardly be described as a diplomatic enclave, it did house the residence of the French ambassador. The villa was built on a slope and was owned by a Tunisian naval engineer and his family who lived on the ground floor where there was a garden. The back porch of the Powell's apartment had a panoramic view of plains with farms as well as a view of the Gulf of Tunis. There was a large library and living room with ample space to entertain their grandchildren.

They had lived a very balanced and organized life in Tunisia with Fadhel's teaching career at the university and Sarah's involvement with her mission to organize schools for the mentally handicapped. Although they were not considered wealthy, they were comfortable and had no worries financially. They had enjoyed a very active social life with many friends from far and wide and attended events and concerts which Fadhel especially enjoyed. He had written his biography and Sarah did all the typing. She had written and published one book and the book about Laith was still her ongoing project. Fadhel was finally obliged to retire as an active Professor but the university authorities arranged for him to continue as a

Research Fellow and he was invited to lecture all over the country and to participate in graduate students' examination committees.

Each summer the couple had traveled to Scotland to see Laith. They were usually accompanied by Usameh and Abbas and their families. They also enjoyed many yearly vacations to visit friends and former students in London, to go for medical check-ups in Zurich and attend Moral Re-armament summer reunion in Caux.

Unfortunately, Fadhel's health was declining and on May 24, 1997, he succumbed to a peaceful death from pneumonia. He was 94. His life had been very rich and full. He had accomplished many things and he lived and died truly devoted to his faith, his wife and family, his country and many friends. He had written several books on Islam and educational issues. He had suffered the years in prison but he had so many more wonderful years before and after that time that he could leave this earth feeling blessed. He would always be remembered and loved; the circle had been broken for the family but the imprint he left on their lives would live on and sustain them. He is buried in a cemetery that he often walked by on his way to meet his friends and had pointed out that he wanted to be buried there. His wishes were honoured.

Perhaps his life is best summed up in his own words, as follows:

[61]"I have come from a very narrow community to a broad, universal view of life and faith, and now

---

[61] Interview taped by H.J. Almond, author of Iraqi Statesman, Zurich, August 31, 1988

I stand for world peace—for all humanity, not for one section against the other. I signed the UN Charter, and I am a believer and live by those principles. I do not believe in confrontation, I do not believe in wars. I do not believe in dialectical materialism. I do believe in harmonizing and integrating opposites.

I had an early sense of destiny that involved bridge-building; first of all among the Iraqis, then among the Arab people, then in the Muslim world, then in international affairs—East and West—even between capitalism and communism."

ℰℛ

For the next three years, after Fadhel's death, Sarah moved to the home of her youngest son, Abbas, and his wife Dr. Layla Jamali and their four children (Fatima, Asma, Souad and Fadhel) in Amman, the capital city of Jordan. Everyone knew that Sarah would find it very difficult living alone without her beloved husband, Fadhel. They had been married for 64 years and their love and devotion for one another had stood the test of time. In the recent years since Fadhel's retirement, they had grown even closer to one another. In the earlier years, there had been many business and career obligations that had required them to be apart but after retirement, they enjoyed a peaceful closeness that now left a huge void in Sarah's life. She was thankful for her family's support and moving in with Abbas and his family lifted her spirits.

At this time, Abbas was Professor of Plant Biology at the Jordan University of Science and Technology (JUST), located near Irbid (a northern city of Jordan). Layla was working at the hospital across the street from their home. Their two eldest daughters, Fatima and Asma, were studying molecular biology at JUST where their father taught. Souad was about 17 and Fadhel was about 15. While Layla worked, Sarah was kept company and cared for by the family's faithful domestic helper, Chandra, who was from Sri Lanka.

Sarah was now 89 and beginning to suffer the inevitable affects of her age. Her muscles had become weak and she required the use of a wheelchair. She had developed diverticulocis which required her to eat only soft foods. Her diet usually consisted of avocados, potato puree and banana milkshakes. She also had high blood pressure but this was kept under control very well with the specialized care given to her by Layla who was a very talented cardiologist. Sarah and Layla were very close and Sarah loved Layla as a daughter. With Abbas working in Irbid at this time, most of the care and attention to Sarah was given by Layla and Chandra.

ℰᗞᑫ

"Would you like a milkshake, Bibi?" Fatima poked her head into Sarah's room one afternoon. Sarah was affectionately known to her grandchildren as [62] 'Bibi' or 'Bibi Sarah'.

---

[62] Bibi – in Arabic means, "grandmother" or a term of endearment and great respect to a mature woman.

"What kind of milkshake do you have?" Sarah looked up from her magazine. She spent much of her time reading and would always be looking for a new book to read.

"Banana, of course—it's your favourite. I made some for both of us." Fatima handed Sarah the milkshake and sat on the bed beside Sarah's wheelchair.

"What are you reading Bibi?"

"I found this article in the National Geographic that I thought you and Asma might like to read. It's called,[63] 'Mapping the Brain'. It says there are different areas in the brain with specific functions, those for speech being areas for speaking words, for generating words, for seeing words, and for hearing words. I found it most exciting to read this because it now seems that Laith can hear and speak words but he cannot see them. I'll put a bookmarker in it here and you can look at it later. I have a pile of articles that I've clipped out of the newspaper over on my night table. Perhaps I'll share this article with the family tonight at mealtime. I know your father will likely have a story to tell us all about his favourite character, Dennis the Menace! He loves that cartoon character. I don't know if it is because it reminds him of him when he was a boy—or, maybe he sees his own son, Fadhel in the character. It is most charming and certainly makes us all have a good laugh at any rate."

"Yes for sure. Thank you, Bibi. You really love the National Geographic, don't you?"

"Yes, I do. I've had a subscription to it for many years. Not only are the articles well written, fascinating and educational

---

[63] Mapping the Brain – article in National Geographic Magazine of June, 1995, pp 18 and 19, referenced by Sarah in her book, *The Story of Laith and his life after encephalitis* pp 80

but I love the beautiful photographs. They are so colourful and professionally portrayed. I also like the International Herald Tribune. There's always something of great interest and something new to learn. You know, we're never too old to stop learning new things. Although my body may be withering away, my mind is still working well enough," Sarah chuckled.

"I agree that your mind is very sharp. I have found an interesting article myself which I plan to share with everyone tonight. I will only tell you that it is about genetics and stem cell research. I am finding the topic has opened my mind to a whole new possibility for my career choice."

"I will look forward to hearing more about this new interest tonight. I am so pleased to see you seeking more knowledge about the world we live in and the human aspect concerning genetics. You will never regret learning new things, even if your career path goes in a different direction. No knowledge ever really goes to waste if we seek to improve our lives through it. I always say, no experience is a total loss— short of hanging!" They both giggled at this.

"You are so wise, Bibi Sarah! I have heard you say that phrase before and I think you have lived long enough to know what you are talking about. What age do you hope to live to?"

"That's a curious question, Fatima. I suppose I would like to live into my nineties, like Fadhel did. As long as my mind is good and my eyesight allows me to read, I feel I can go on. I want to see you children succeed in life too, God willing."

"I think you shall make it easily to your nineties! You are almost there now!" Fatima and Sarah both had a laugh.

There were many happy moments during this time with her family. The children always brought laughter and life into the home. She loved watching Abbas and Layla interacting with the children. It brought back memories of earlier days with Fadhel and their sons. She remembered when their house was noisy, busy and vibrant. She thought about many good meals around the table served to them by Um Sania, the antics of the boys as they were growing up, picnics, rowing on the Tigris with Fadhel and those sweet late moonlit evenings on the rooftop listening to classical music. She was thankful for all the happy memories—even though remembering often brought tears to her eyes.

And then there was Laith . . . oh, how she longed to see him just one more time. But she supposed that was not to be. Travel now was out of the question for her. He was in her heart and on her mind every night when she said her prayers. She thought how maybe it was for the best that when she saw him the last time, she didn't realize it was to be the very 'last time'.

This led to the thought about other partings in her life. Her parents never had managed to come to Iraq for a family visit. This may have been a personal choice on their part or, more likely—it may have been too taxing for them as their health declined in their later years. Although Libbie and Harvey had not been in favour of Sarah marrying Fadhel and moving to Baghdad, they had come to terms with it to some degree and they did not dislike Fadhel. Over time, they had come to realize that he was a good husband and father.

Sarah's trips to Canada and the United States were infrequent as well. She looked back on this as a bitter-sweet time. She was so full of love for Fadhel in her youth that she felt she had no choice but to follow her heart and be with him wherever he lived. But she now thought that she probably hadn't realized how difficult it would be in her future to see her parents and her siblings. She had pictured in her mind, more trips would be possible. But, as life had unfolded, with Laith's illness, Fadhel's duties and obligations, and the coup . . . well—it just hadn't gone quite the way she had envisioned it those many years ago.

1999 Laith

In 1999, Laith and his good friend, George, moved on together to Guthrie Court Nursing Home. Laith was now 64. Their photos were moved and placed on the walls of their bedroom and their toy cars were parked on all their shelves. There were new caregivers and new fellow residents to become acquainted with but they both seemed to adjust well to this new phase of their lives. Jean and Peter Bruce continued their friendship with Laith and his brothers, Usameh and Abbas, and their families continued to visit once a year.

Abbas's daughter, Fatima, recalled: [64]"My parents made it an annual habit to visit him (Laith). I saw him last time around September of 2001. He seemed happy, singing as usual and enjoying the outing and reading books. I personally found visiting him painful; although, I always forced a smile on my face. I thought he was the best looking among his brothers and he seemed very kind. But that was the tragedy my grandparents and their sons had to go through—we don't choose our challenges in life. Bibi Sarah made the best of it, certainly, and turned it into a positive energy towards the societies she lived in."

---

[64] Letter to the author, Jan Keating from Fatima Jamali, April 2020

Dr. Monica Spooner

Dr. Monica Spooner and her husband, Professor Roger Spooner, had met Sarah and Fadhel through the Moral Re-Armament organization some years earlier. They had become very close friends and Dr. Spooner took an interest in Laith. She, along with her husband and their daughter, Jo, had made a trip to visit the school in La Marsa, Tunisia. They met with Jouda Gritli, the director, and she showed them a little alcove that had been dedicated to creating a museum in honour of Sarah and all her contributions to helping to start schools and provide education for mentally handicapped people. They made a video tape of their visit to the school. Dr. Spooner was delighted that some of the staff still remembered Sarah very vividly. She recorded friendly messages from the staff to Sarah. She also videotaped their visit with Laith and his dear friend, Jean Bruce.

A few months after this trip, Dr. Spooner and her husband visited Sarah at Abbas's home. They showed the video to Sarah and her family. After it was over, Sarah smiled and commented, "And I thought I would never see my son again."

In addition to the video, [65]Dr. Spooner had brought a pre-print copy of Sarah's book about Laith. The book had a yellow cover and it also had a big bush

---

[65] Explanation by Abbas Jamali (Sarah's youngest son) to author, Jan Keating in email letter, dated July 25, 2020.

(something from an old Islamic medicinal plant) and Sarah wasn't happy with either the colour or having a bush on the cover eclipsing the title; so, for the final version of the book (published after Sarah's death), the bush was much reduced in size and the book's cover was changed to light blue which Sarah said was Laith's favourite colour.

This visit to Laith and the Jamali family by Dr. Spooner and her family meant so much to Sarah. It was not the last time that Dr. Spooner would extend her kindness through her friendship with Sarah.

February 2000 - A Final Party

"It's Bibi Sarah's birthday this week. I think we should have a little party for her, don't you?" Layla asked the children and Abbas one morning. It was the weekend so Abbas and the two older girls, Fatima and Asma, were home from Irbid.

"I'm sure she would be pleased if you did that for her. She loves any social event. If she has chance to chat with friends, it always lifts her spirits." Abbas smiled at Layla as he cut his hard-boiled egg open for breakfast.

"I love that idea! Should we surprise her?" piped up Souad.

"I don't think a surprise is a great idea in case it gets her blood pressure up." Layla was always looking out for Sarah's health.

"Oh yes, I think you are right. I would like to get her a birthday gift." Souad loved her grandmother very much as did the whole family.

330

"That's very thoughtful," Abbas patted Souad on the shoulder.

"What will you buy her?" young Fadhel reached for the orange juice. He was a handsome young boy about aged 15. He had been named after his beloved grandfather. This was most pleasing to Sarah, of course, and Fadhel Sr. had been very honoured by this grandchild being named after him. Fadhel took a big sip of his juice.

"I want to buy Bibi Sarah a new book!" Souad proudly answered her brother's question.

"What can I buy her?" Fadhel looked suddenly worried.

"Why don't you buy her a book too—you know how fast she reads and we can go shopping together."

"OK, but books are expensive and I don't have that much money." Fadhel was still not convinced.

"We can look at the book store as they always have books on sale. We'll have lots to pick from, you'll see." Souad wiped her mouth with her napkin and asked to be excused. She was anxious to get started with the shopping. She loved to shop!

"Will we invite friends to Bibi Sarah's party?" Fadhel asked as he rose from the table to join his sister.

"Let me think about that. I can call some of her close friends to see if anyone could come. I think it would be lovely for her to see her friends." Layla started clearing the table while Abbas sipped on his coffee.

"We can help you with details, Mother," Fatima volunteered on behalf of herself and Asma.

331

"I'd like to go shopping too," Asma motioned to Souad to wait for her. "I think I will find Bibi Sarah a new nightgown."

"Well, I might as well go along too, because maybe I can get her some bubble bath or a pair of slippers." Fatima smiled and finished her cup of breakfast tea.

"I think that would be very nice for her. You are all in the spirit to make a great party!" Abbas got up and gave Layla a kiss on the cheek and took the newspaper to his den.

Everyone scurried off to begin their day. Layla went to check on Sarah and to help her get ready for the day. She always liked to check her blood pressure and pulse and would help her to dress. Sarah could do some things but Layla liked to be handy to assist her where needed. On weekends, Layla took charge of such things and Chandra concentrated on household tasks.

ഇൻ⊗

Layla did make some calls. She kept the guest list small as she felt that if there were too many friends at the birthday party, it might overwhelm Sarah. Two special friends and their families happily accepted the invitation.

Farida Shubeilat (from Nablus in Palestine) and her daughter, Luma, attended the party. Farida and her late husband, Farhan (from Tafilah, Jordan), as previously mentioned, were married in Fadhel and Sarah's home in Baghdad over sixty-five years earlier.

332

The second close friend, Widad Haddad from north Lebanon, was accompanied by her son, Dr. Fadi Haddad (a well-known Urologist) and his wife, Vera. Widad's late husband, Ralph Haddad, an electrical engineer from Salt (a town near Amman in Jordan), had been a friend of Fadhel's from their days as students at Columbia University. Like the Shubeilats, Widad and Ralph had also met through Sarah and Fadhel. These two couples were of the many successful matches Sarah and Fadhel had arranged. Farida, Farhan and Widad had all been recruited by Fadhel to teach in Iraq. Like Sarah, both her friends, Farida and Widad were now widows.

The final, but not least important, guest at the party was Chandra. She was treated as a member of the family. She had helped Layla with all the food preparations for the party. The children had picked some flowers for the table as well as hung up some colourful paper streamers and balloons to make the atmosphere very festive.

Sarah looked radiant for a woman who was turning 92. Her eyes twinkled and she smiled sweetly at everyone that day. Her soft, lustrous hair was now completely silver-white and still neatly done in her signature chignon hairstyle. Her face and hands were somewhat wrinkled and her body, although not heavy, had now rounded out a little due to her more sedentary lifestyle. She wore a rich burgundy coloured, long-sleeved, velvet dress which was a lovely contrast to her silvery-white hair. Similar to her mother's body in old age, Sarah's ankles were now a little thicker. Again, this change was due to her not being able to walk as much as before.

"Abbas, I have something I'd like to speak to you about." Farida gently touched Abbas's arm and spoke quietly to him while the others were chatting and not taking notice of Farida and Abbas's conversation.

"Certainly, Aunt Farida," Abbas always referred to Farida as 'auntie' as a token of his great admiration and respect for his mother's friend.

"I know your mother's book about Laith is not yet published but I have a copy of her type-written manuscript and I will leave it with you today so you can read it. I don't know if you know it or not but she wrote this book especially for you."

"No, I have not yet read the story and I would love to read it. I had no idea that she wrote it for me. Did she explain why?"

[66]"Yes, she told me that she wrote it for you so you would know what happened since you were not born when Usameh and Laith were sick with measles and encephalitis." Abbas later recalled that he did read the book and found it most fascinating.

Sarah's heart was filled with love and appreciation for the effort her family had gone to on her account. Everyone sang Happy Birthday to her and they all ate soft cake which had been prepared especially for Sarah's benefit. Although Sarah was always content and patient, the day with all her family and good friends had left her exhausted. Her granddaughter, Fatima, tucked her into bed that night and recalls the event as follows: "I helped

---

[66] Abbas Jamali – in notes to author, Jan Keating (July 25, 2020).

her go to bed and to tuck her in. For the first time that night, she told me, 'I've had enough.' It felt a bit strange coming from her. I tried asking her what was wrong but she just repeated the same sentence. I felt sad for her but, little did I know, it was the last thing I would hear her say."

She woke up the next morning (March 3, 2000) and spoke to Abbas, who was watching television in the den across the hall from her bedroom. Then, she returned to her room and passed away quietly alone in her bed. She left the world just as you would expect—with quiet grace, making no fuss for anyone in the process.

Fatima went on to describe what followed saying: [67]"It was the second hardest, and most painful, day of my life after my grandfather's death. My sister, Souad, and I washed her with scented water with the help of an expert who kept a cover on her body all the time while performing the Islamic rituals. She was given an Islamic burial after performing the prayer in the mosque. She left this world in dignity just like she was in her life. May God bless her soul and reward her in heaven for her virtue and patience and giving spirit."

Perhaps Sarah's deepest feelings that she leaves us with are expressed in her own words as follows:

> [68]"Throughout the universe there runs a stream of good that brings growth and renewal to God's creation. Many, many people contribute to this

---

[67] Letter to the author, Jan Keating, from Fatima Jamali (April 2020)

[68] Iraqi Statesman by Harry J. Almond, pp. 163 as quoted from Sarah P. Jamali in "How it Began". Unpublished article pp 3.

stream of good—even, I believe, the mentally retarded.

One day, my daughter-in-law said to me, 'What a pity your eldest son is handicapped. He might have been a great engineer.'

In reply, I said, 'Yes, he might have been a great engineer, but how many people would he have been able to help? With his broken life he has helped hundreds, even thousands of others and made his little contribution to the stream of good.'

My husband says that I have not told you about the years of work I put into helping the mentally retarded and now, as a weak old woman, I am still keeping on. I do not think it necessary to say that I worked hard in the company of many, many others. I cannot count the effort of the past when there is so much to be done to meet the needs of today.

On the whole, I am truly grateful that I have seen the happy transformation of some of those living on the dark side of life. It is more than enough to know that God sustains us and that His blessings are amazing results from the sincere work we offer in His service. I feel deep regret for the mentally handicapped we were not able to help."

And so, the prairie girl from Weyburn, Saskatchewan, who lived in Baghdad (and Tunisia) had been steadfast in her love of her husband through many challenges and sacrifices. She left her home and country to follow her heart and was true to her decision to do so to the end. Although she left her family and home, her fond memories remained intact within her heart. She embraced her new home, family and country with an open heart and the love just continued to blossom for the life she and her husband created together. She left a legacy of love, respect and hope for the mentally handicapped in memory of her beloved son, Laith. She had taken the advice of her mother who had said, "Don't let it make you bitter. Find some way to turn it into good."

In her words, her sincere desire for Laith's troubles in his life was: [69]"to hasten help to other children, so his life would have achieved something, whether he knew it or not, even if his own part was to stay on the sidelines and live out his tragedy."

Sarah's unselfish and determined efforts were certainly instrumental in changing attitudes and helping mentally handicapped children and adults. Her mission was accomplished and, although she never wanted any praise for her personal work in this field, it is only fitting that we recognize the work she and others who helped along the way put forth. They saw need for change and moved mountains to make it happen.

ॐ

[70]Thanks to the determination and efforts made by Sarah and her team, awareness was recognized. The right of all

---

[69] *The Story of Laith* by Sarah Powell Jamali, pp 9

[70] Iraq Childhood Development and Disability Survey –University of Manchester Research

https://www.research.manchester.ac.uk/portal/files/36763409/FULL_TEXT.PDF

children to education, including disabled children, has been enshrined in the 2005 Iraq Constitution (see Article 32 and Article 34):

> **Article 32:** The State cares for the handicapped special-need people and ensures their rehabilitation for their reintegration into society. This shall be regulated by law.
>
> **Article 34:** First: Education is a fundamental factor in the progress of society and is a right guaranteed by the State. Primary education is mandatory and the state guarantees to combat illiteracy. Second: Free education at all stages is a right for all Iraqis. Third: The State encourages scientific research for peaceful purposes that serve humanity. And it supports excellence, creativity, invention and the different aspects of ingenuity. Fourth: Private and public education is guaranteed. This shall be regulated by law.

Laith passed away on October 26, 2008, at age 73 in Edinburgh. The cause of death was sudden cardiac arrest. Family friend, Dr. Monica Spooner took great care of his burial in an Islamic cemetery and stood in for his family as no one was with him at the time of his death. Usameh and Abbas were both in attendance at Laith's funeral. As I thought about Laith's death, I was thankful that Sarah was spared this one thing after all she had endured in her lifetime. She went to her end knowing that he was happy and properly cared for in his last home in Scotland. Dr. Spooner remains living in Edinburgh, Scotland. Her friendship to Sarah and the Jamali family has been, and still is, steadfast and appreciated. She wrote the Foreword in Sarah's book, *The Story of Laith and His Life after Encephalitis*.

According to Dr. Spooner, Sarah worked on editing and perfecting her book about Laith up to just weeks before her death. Her mind was sharp and clear to the end. Her book was published after her death, in 2000, by her beloved son, Dr. Abbas Jamali. My intent is to donate a copy of this book to the Weyburn Public Library. It was thanks to my finding Dr. Spooner online that I was able to receive two copies of the book as a gift from her. My cousin, Stewart McKendrick, who lives in Glasgow, was most helpful in facilitating my eventual receipt of the books. Through my contact with Monica, she informed me that she was still in contact with Sarah's sons, Usameh and Abbas. She said they would be interested to learn about my interest in their mother's life and asked if I wanted to be put in touch with them. Of course I was very interested in this and made contact with them right away. Abbas's daughter, Fatima, coordinated a video chat that included Usameh, Abbas, Fatima, Asma, my husband (Jim) and me. We have remained in contact throughout the writing of the book to the present. It has been a joyful experience for me.

Usameh, age 85, is retired and living in Kuwait with his wife, Maysoon. He specialized in energy economics after his banking career. He served for 36 years with the Organization of Arab Petroleum Exporting Countries (OAPEC), based in Kuwait. Since 2010, he has been with the Australian College of Kuwait (ACK) as an advisor and he lectured at one of the Bruno Leoni Institute's conferences.

Usameh and Maysoon have two daughters, Seereen and Sema. Seereen is a senior, deep-water engineer with Shell and is in her fifth year working in Sakhalin (Russian Far East, Northern Pacific Ocean). Sema works for the Scottish government and lives in Edinburgh, with her two sons, Faris (age 4) and Jad (age 2.5).

Professor Abbas Jamali, the third and youngest of Sarah's sons, age 77, retired from his position as C/O at the Jordan University of Science and Technology (JUST) Agriculture, and living with his wife, Dr. Layla Jamali, in Jordan. They have three daughters: Fatima, Asma, and Souad as well as one son, Fadhel.

Fatima, the first grandchild to Sarah and Fadhel, achieved her MSc and PhD, and works as Head of Neuroscience Research in the Cell Therapy Centre, University of Jordan, in Amman. She is mother to Jana, age 14 and Laith 12 (named in honour of his uncle, Laith Jamali).

Asma achieved her Masters degree in Diagnostic Molecular Biology and Human Genetics. She resides in Toronto (in the suburb of Mississauga), Ontario, Canada. She is the mother of three children: Sarah, age 16 (the first grandchild named after Sarah Powell Jamali), Mahmoud, age 13 and Alya, age 5.

Souad worked for the United Nations and currently resides in Dubai, United Arab Emirates. She has two sons, Hussein, age 9 and Mohammed, age 7.

Abbas's son, Fadhel, did his BSc in political science and computer science. He took different entrepreneurial jobs as well as sales positions in Nissan and Ford car companies. He presently resides in Alexandria, Virginia, United States.

References and Sources

Iraqi Statesman: A portrait of Mohammed Fadhel Jamali by Harry J. Almond

The Story of Laith and His Life after Encephalitis by Sarah Powell Jamali

Folktales from the City of the Golden Domes by Sarah Powell Jamali

Letters on Islam: Written by a Father in Prison to His Son by Mohammed Fadhel Jamali

How the Scots Invented Canada by Ken McGoogan – article on *Nellie McClung: The Right to Vote*

Hey, Seeds! Published by The Soo Line Historical Society written and edited by The Weyburn Writer's Association – article on Sarah (Powell) Jamali taken from the Weyburn Review in part (submitted by the late Allen Moffet of Weyburn), pp 48.

In His Hands - Published by The Weyburn New Horizons Book Committee (1967)

Experiences in Arab Affairs, 1943 – 1958 by Mohammed Fadhel Jamali, MA, PhD, LLD, Former Prime Minister of Iraq

Minnesota Historical Society – Biographical Notes on Powell family history

Jeannine Kater – present owner of the historical home of the Powell family in Weyburn – provided source materials and detailed information about the house.

Ancestry.com – Powell family history, photographs and Census Canada records provided by Mary Elizabeth "Betsy" (Powell) Polglase, Sarah's niece.

Harvey O. Powell and his sisters, Amy (left) and Birdie (centre) 1888, River Falls, Wisconsin

Harvey O. Powell, River
Falls, Wisconsin

Harvey O. Powell, General Manager, Weyburn Security
Bank

Elizabeth "Libbie" Fayerweather (nee: Knox) Powell – November 11, 1893 (Wedding photo)

"Libbie" Powell 1895

Libbie Powell – about 1918, Weyburn

A "Suffragette", Temperance Union member and strong Presbyterian

1911 - Lydia (6) and Sarah (3) in front of their first home in Weyburn (20 Second Street, South). Sarah liked dressing like her big sister.

Sarah Hayden Powell age 3 or 4

Lydia Powell and little sister, Sarah

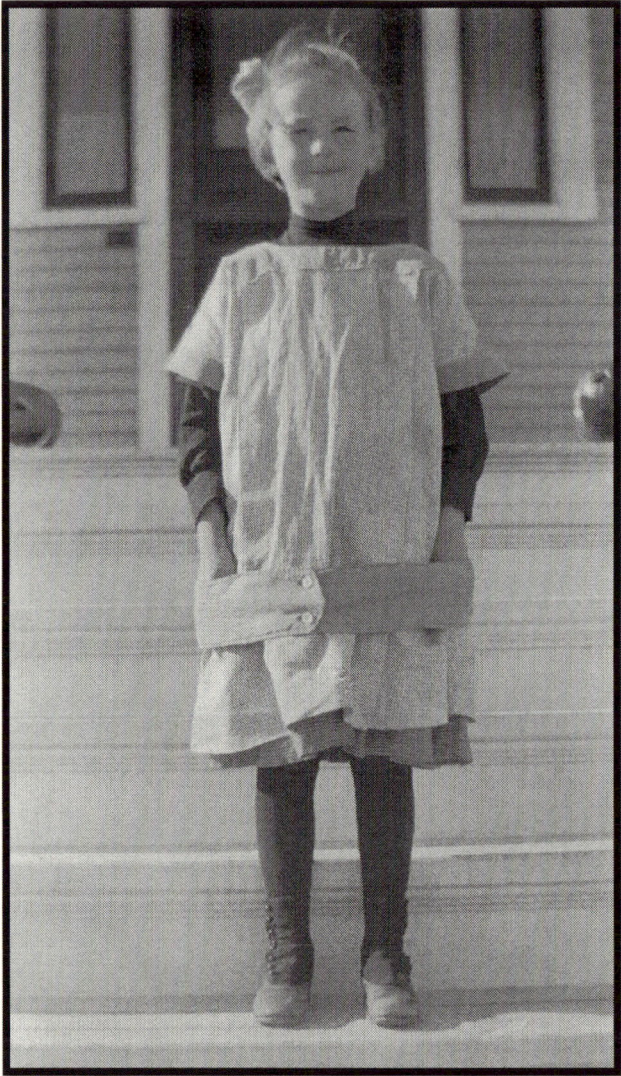

Sarah (age 4 or 5) on front step of Powell house

**Souris School 1912 – Front Row Left to Right:
Lyman Powell, Louis Powell, Unknown frowning girl,**

Lydia Powell

Oliver Stanley Powell 1908 sitting in veranda of the
house on Second Ave. south in Weyburn with baby
sister, Sarah, in the pram in background.

Sarah (about age 7) possibly heading to Sunday School on Easter Sunday sporting her Easter hat

Powell children left to right: Louis, Sarah, Lydia, Lyman and Oliver (Knox absent in this photo) taken across the street from their house seen in background.

Louis Harvey Powell, Weyburn Collegiate Institute photo

356

Harvey with his trusted hunting dog, "Mutt".

The family would have goose (slung over his shoulder; one in front and one at his back) for Thanksgiving supper.

Lyman with Mutt. (Moffet house in background)

Oliver Stanley Powell (USA navy)

Lydia (left) and Sarah. Sarah was happy to finally get eyeglasses like her big sister (photo taken in front of the Powell home)

Lydia Powell 1920

Sarah Powell - age 18, 1926 (Weyburn

GEORGE FREDERICK POULSEN Architecture
Chicago, Ill. . Marinette, Wis., High School
Architectural Society (1) (2) (3)—Cyma—Class
President (2)—Class President (3)—1917 Gopher
Staff.

KNOX ARCHIBALD POWELL . Engineering
Weyburn, Sask., Can., Weyburn Collegiate Institute
Cosmopolitan Club (2) (3).

OLIVER S. POWELL . . . Academic
Weyburn, Sask., Canada

KATHERINE PRICE . . . Nursing
Minneapolis . Tracy, Minnesota, High School

EVERETT WILLIAM PRICHARD Agriculture
Randolph, Wisconsin . Randolph High School
Y. M. C. A.—Agricultural Club.

CHARLES E. PROSHEK . . Medicine
New Prague . . New Prague High School
Alpha Kappa Kappa—University Orchestra—
Class President (1).

H. FRANK PROSHEK . . Architecture
New Prague . . New Prague High School
Cyma—Y. M. C. A.—Associate Member Archi-
tectural Society—Komensky Club (1).

EARL DE WITT PRUDDEN . Academic
St. Paul . . Mechanic Arts High School
Sophomore Vaudeville (2)—Daily Reporter (2)—
Minnehaha Staff (2) (3).

536

Knox A. Powell and younger brother, Oliver S. Powell from page in yearbook (University of Minnesota, 1915)

362

Sarah Hayden Powel

Mohammed Fadhel Jamali and Sarah H. Powell
Wedding photo 1933, Baghdad

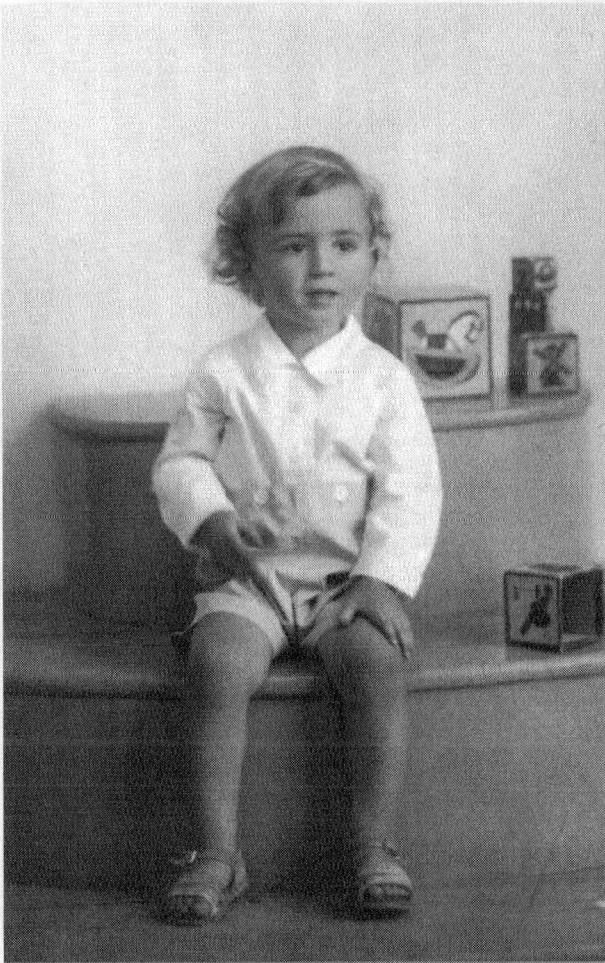

1937 Laith Jamali, age 23 months

1937 Usameh Jamali, age 8 months

1937 Fadhel (holding Laith) Sarah (holding Usameh) on first-floor landing of their home on the Tigris River in Baghdad

Usameh (3) and Laith (4) – before measles and encephalistis

1939 Sarah's visit to USA and Canada - Powell siblings (left to right): Oliver, Knox, Lydia, Sarah, Louis and Lyman

Photo taken at the home of Oliver and Ada Powell. Ada organized a family gathering at their home in Hennepin County, Minnesota in honour of Sarah and her two sons, Laith and Usameh (Abbas was not yet born).

1939 Powell grandchidren of Harvey and Libbie Powell taken at the family gathering arranged by Ada Powell

Left to Right: Arlene Powell (Lyman Powell's daughter), Usameh Jamali (Sarah's son), Ellen Powell (Oliver Powell's daughter), Mary Elizabeth "Betsy" Powell (Louis Powell's daughter), Robert "Bob" Powell (standing in back; Oliver Powell's son), Louis Jr. (Louis Powell's son)., Harvey Johnson (Lydia's son) on knee of Richard "Dick" Powell (Oliver Powell's son) , and Laith Jamali (Sarah's son)

1939 Home of, Harvey and Libbie Powell in Regina, Saskatchewan

Left to Right: Laith, Sarah, Usameh, Ruth Leroux (Sarah's childhood friend), Harvey Johnson (Lydia's son), Harvey O. Powell, and Lydia Johnson (nee: Powell)

**1939 Left to Right: Usameh Jamali (age 3),
Harvey Johnson, Laith Jamali (age 4)**

Powell Family 1939 Minnesota

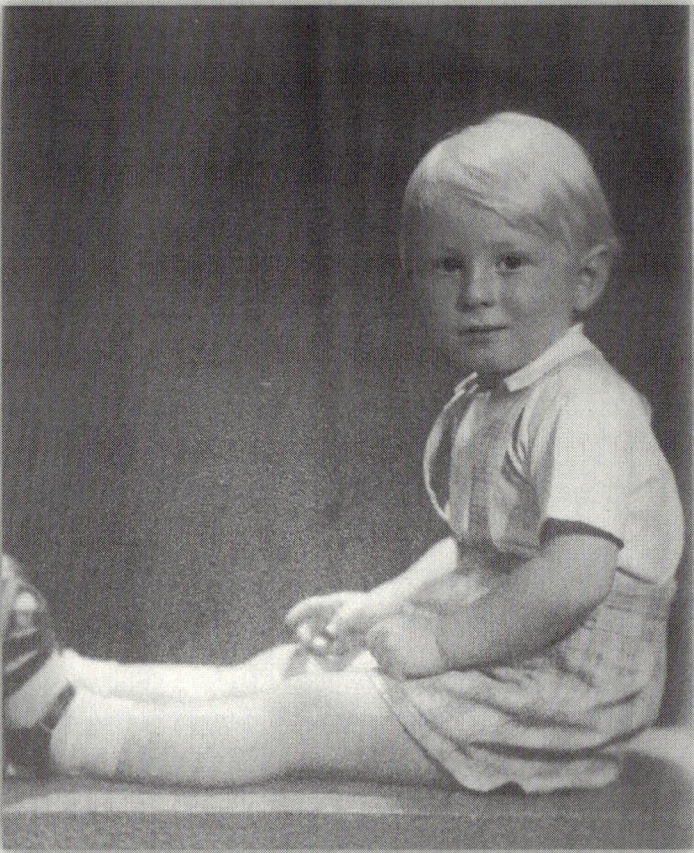

Abbas Jamali (Lion #3)

Abbas (on rooftop of the house on the Tigris river, Baghdad)

Abbas Jamali, Boy Scout

Sarah (about 40) without make-up and neatly coifed in her classic "chignon" hair style

Dr. Fadhel Jamali standing in witness box in court

Angry mob in the streets of Baghdad during the coup of 1958

Jamali Seen in Good Health; His Wife Is Still Missing

PHILADELPHIA, Pa. —(AP) —The fate of a former Minneapolis woman, who is the wife of Iraq's ousted foreign minister, Saturday was still unknown.

A sister, Mrs. Lydia Johnson, of suburban Prospect Park, said she last heard **Mrs. Jamali** from her sister Monday. A card bearing a postmark she could not read arrived then.

It told of a vacation in Iran, Iraq's neighbor.

Mrs. Johnson therefore assumed that the card was mailed before the revolutionary coup in Baghdad. There was no way of knowing whether her sister had returned to Baghdad before the upheaval.

Mrs. Johnson' sister is the former Sara Hayden Powell, a 1928 graduate of the University of Minnesota, now married to Mohammed Fadhil Jamali. Jamali first was reported slain in the overthrow of the Iraqi govern-

ment earlier this week. Later reports said he was in prison awaiting trial.

(In Baghdad, government authorities took newsmen to see Jamali. He appeared in good shape and was well groomed.

(Government forces had found Jamali hiding out in a chicken farm belonging to his relatives outside Baghdad.)

The Jamalis have three sons: Abbas, 15, who was with his mother on holiday; Usameli, 22, and Laith, 23.

Possible that this gap in the unknown whereabouts of Sarah was when she and Abbas left her house to go to the home of a sergeant in the US Air Force who was serving at the American Embassy. She went there for safety during the initial upheaval of the coup in 1958.

Sarah with Laith when he was at Garvald in Scotland

Usameh Jamali

Abbas Jamali

Sarah and Fadhel in Tunis, 1976 - together, "free" and enjoying life after imprisonment

The Powell House, Weyburn, Saskatchewan

The historical house where the story all began (photo
compliments of Jeaninne Kater, present owner)

Canadian artist and author, Jan Keating (shown painting a mural for Calvary Baptist Church) grew up in Weyburn, Saskatchewan. She currently resides with her husband, Jim, at their waterfront home at Kenosee Lake, Saskatchewan. They have two daughters: Tara (Dave Jaap), Weyburn and Trenna (Alden Adair), Toronto. Jan enjoys summers at the lake golfing, boating, fishing, painting, writing and spending time with family and friends and her winters in California, relaxing in the sun with more golfing, painting and socializing with many friends.

Her first book, *A Normal Boy: Living in an Asylum* is a compelling novel inspired by a true story and may be found on Amazon.ca (in Canada) or Amazon.com (in USA) as well as many other countries. To see Jan's art, Google her web site at: Art by Jan Keating https://jankeating.com/home.html

Manufactured by Amazon.ca
Bolton, ON